The Nyāya-sūtra

Selections with Early Commentaries

The Nyāya-sūtra

Selections with Early Commentaries

Translated with Introduction
and Explanatory Notes by
Matthew Dasti and Stephen Phillips

Hackett Publishing Company, Inc.
Indianapolis/Cambridge

Printed in the United States of America

22 21 20 19 2 3 4 5 6 7

For further information, please address
Hackett Publishing Company, Inc.
P.O. Box 44937
Indianapolis, Indiana 46244-0937

www.hackettpublishing.com

Cover design by Brian Rak
Composition by Graphic World

Library of Congress Cataloging-in-Publication Data

Names: Gautama (Authority on Nyāyaśāstra), author. | Dasti, Matthew R. | Phillips, Stephen H., 1950–
Title: The Nyaya-sutra : selections with early commentaries / Translated with Introduction and Explanatory Notes by Matthew Dasti and Stephen Phillips.
Description: Indianapolis : Hackett Publishing Company, Inc., 2017. | Includes bibliographical references and index. | Includes translations from Sanskrit.
Identifiers: LCCN 2017007005 | ISBN 9781624666162 (pbk.) | ISBN 9781624666179 (cloth)
Subjects: LCSH: Nyaya—Early works to 1800.
Classification: LCC B132.N8 G36513 2017 | DDC 181/.43—dc23
LC record available at https://lccn.loc.gov/2017007005

The paper used in this publication meets the minimum requirements of American National Standard for Information Sciences—Permanence of Paper for Printed Library Materials, ANSI Z39.48–1984.

Contents

Acknowledgments

The final form of this volume would have been very different without the gracious assistance of several colleagues. Edwin Bryant read the entire text in its penultimate form and also piloted several chapters with his students at Rutgers University. He provided us with several useful suggestions. Malcolm Keating and Agnieszka Rostalska made helpful comments on early portions of the manuscript. Malcolm also piloted two manuscript chapters with his students at Yale-NUS College and provided valuable feedback. Special thanks also to Brian Rak and his team at Hackett for their willingness to take on this project and carry it to completion.

Matthew would like to thank his family, Nandanie, Ana, and Leela, for constant support and love, as well as the faculty of the Philosophy Department at Bridgewater State University for fostering an environment of exceptional collegiality. He dedicates this volume to those teachers and friends with whom he has stood shoulder-to-shoulder in pursuit of the truth, engaged in *vāda* of the most important kind: *taṃ śiṣya-guru-sabrahmacāri-viśiṣṭa-śreyo-'rthibhir anasūyibhir abhyupeyāt* (*Nyāya-sūtra* 4.2.48).

Stephen would like to thank his wife Hope along with his teachers, in particular N. S. Ramanuja Tatacharya. He is also grateful to Malcolm Keating and Kisor Chakrabarti for providing early input on a draft of the first chapter of the *Nyāya-sūtra* commenced before this collaboration. The Research Institute of the University of Texas at Austin provided a semester free of teaching. Special thanks go to Stephen's colleagues in the Philosophy Department and the University's College of Liberal Arts for now decades of support and encouragement. He dedicates this volume to Arindam Chakrabarti, his longtime friend.

for compositional defects. These sorts of passages are less relevant for an introductory volume than those laying out the primary views of the school. Even regarding core positions and arguments, we find far too much in the original sources to capture in a single accessible text. Thus the goal of this volume is to provide a representative sample of the major views and arguments of the early school. We have also included introductions and explanatory notes at the beginning of chapters and interspersed throughout, providing context, continuity, and, as needed, explanation. Our own writing is set in italics to distinguish it from the translations of sūtras and traditional Sanskrit commentaries. At times, our remarks will preface a passage to prepare the reader. At other times, we have placed remarks after a passage in the interest of continuity and flow of the readings. In order to maintain a clear focus on the sūtras throughout the volume, all translations of the sūtras are in boldface font. Footnotes serve the sole function of providing references. At the end of each chapter, we also provide study questions and a list of suggested readings. Our selections of works of scholarship on Nyāya have been made on the basis of accessibility as well as other criteria of excellence.

When attempting a translation of this sort, a scholar has three competing voices in his or her ear, each demanding adherence to a different set of norms that determine a job well done. There is the philologist, who demands strict fidelity and historical accuracy while rendering the source language into the target language; the philosopher, who demands that one translate with an eye to perennial philosophical problems while using logical and technical terminology that allows for conceptual precision; and, finally, the teacher, who demands that, above all, the text be accessible to readers. All too often this last voice is neglected, and here we have taken pains to provide the clarity required by the novice. We have thus minimized, for example, the use of parentheses for restored material in Sanskrit dropped by ellipsis. We treat understood or elided ideas as being on the surface of the text. In our view, overuse of parentheses inhibits readability, and we avoid it. Ultimately, we intend to do justice to all three voices, providing a text that is as readable as possible, while centered on the philosophical richness of early Nyāya and faithful to the linguistic and historical context of the sūtras and the commentators.

Nyāya within Indian Philosophy

With a copious literature stretching for practically two thousand years, Nyāya is a leading school of classical Indian philosophy. Broadly within the "Hindu umbrella" of communities that saw themselves as inheritors of an ancient Vedic civilization and cultural traditions, Nyāya is one out of about fourteen or fifteen distinct philosophic schools and traditions to be counted as Vedic—as opposed to Buddhist, Jaina, and other schools that reject Vedic cultural practices but are nevertheless important players on the classical philosophic scene. Among these traditions and schools, Nyāya is celebrated in late classical doxographies as well as by modern scholars as pioneering developments in epistemology, metaphysics, and logic in particular for all the philosophies and world views of India. The word *nyāya* means "right reasoning" and is often translated with the shorthand "logic." The term, however, does not do justice to the breadth of Nyāya contributions to classical Indian philosophy.

A whole set of interlocking views and arguments arrived at by critical reasoning are presented in the *Nyāya-sūtra* itself, which is the oldest Nyāya text. It is attributed to Gautama, who was also referred to by an epithet suggesting being lost in thought, "gazing at his feet" (Akṣapāda). Gautama's 528 sūtras range over the whole world of philosophy, with an emphasis on epistemology and philosophic method, logic, and critical reasoning.

Nyāya's development as a school of philosophy occurs primarily through commentaries on the sūtras in the early period, which extends to the time of Udayana. With Udayana, however, Nyāya begins a new phase, crystalized in the work of Gaṅgeśa Upādhyāya (c. 1325), whose *Wish-Fulfilling Jewel of Reflection on the Truth* (*Tattva-cintā-maṇi*) comes to displace the *Nyāya-sūtra* and its commentaries as the focal point in subsequent traditions. Works in New or *Navya* Nyāya proliferate in the fourteenth and later centuries, indeed into the modern period, comprising hundreds of texts and contributing to one of the longest-running and richest traditions of philosophy in all history, including China and the West.

Nyāya's philosophical project is centered on the notion of *pramāṇa,* "knowledge source." These sources are processes such as perception and inference by which an individual gains knowledge, that is, belief that is true by virtue of having been generated in the right way. Nyāya is devoted to identification and extensive analysis of the knowledge sources. In this context, the school develops innovations in epistemology, logical theory, theory of cognition, and the nature of rationality. *Pramāṇas* are the sources of an individual's justified beliefs, and also the final court of appeals within philosophical dispute. They are also, when self-consciously employed, methods of inquiry.

Also prized as an adjudicator of disputes is "suppositional reasoning," *tarka,* which is a lot like the Socratic method or *elenchus,* whereby an opponent's views are found to be fallacious. But such reasoning cannot make us know something on its own. It has to be founded on the delivery of a *pramāṇa,* a knowledge source. Nyāya thus returns again and again to knowledge sources and to "suppositional reasoning" to buttress its philosophical holdings. To use an example from the tradition, Nyāya argues that it is right to hold that there is an *ātman* (deep self), despite Buddhist arguments to the contrary. Why? One reason is that there are properly formed inferences that establish such a self. As inference is a legitimate knowledge source, its results are binding, so long as it is well formed. But Buddhists put forth counterinferences in support of a "stream theory" of the person, and Nyāya philosophers resort to *tarka* to attack the Buddhist theory. Much of Indian philosophical dispute may be framed as careful, critical examination of the legitimacy of inferences put forth in support of disputed claims, and both logic—the study of legitimate inferential patterns—and philosophical argument more generally, are firmly entrenched within Nyāya's *pramāṇa* and *tarka* methodology.

Why should an individual care about truth and "getting things right" in the first place? A standard theme in Nyāya is that proper understanding of the inventory of reality is a precondition to act effectively; success in action is predicated upon cognitive success. This is underscored in the opening lines of Vātsyāyana's commentary:

> When an object is comprehended through a knowledge source (*pramāṇa*), it becomes possible to engage in successful goal-directed activity. Thus, a knowledge source is useful (*arthavat*). Without a knowledge source, there would be no effective cognition of an object. Without such cognition, there would be no successful action. (*Commentary* 1.1.1)

Throughout the *Commentary*, Vātsyāyana returns to this tie between cognitive success and success in action:

> All sciences, all goal-directed actions, and indeed the conventions of all living beings, depend on the findings of knowledge sources. (*Commentary* 4.2.29)

> Why would one investigate something that is not properly known? Because she thinks, "I will avoid, pursue, or remain indifferent towards an object that is known as it is." And thus the point of knowing something as it is, is to determine whether to avoid, pursue, or be indifferent to it. This is the purpose of systematic investigation. (*Commentary* 1.1.32)

Indeed, the famous four goals of classical Hindu culture rest on cognitive success, according to Vātsyāyana:

> Motivation to seek righteousness (*dharma*), wealth, pleasure, and liberation proceeds through comprehension of knowledge sources and their objects. (*Commentary* 2.1.20)

The self-conception of Nyāya as a system, from Vātsyāyana onward, is that it provides tools for rigorous, self-conscious reasoning, akin to what we call critical thinking, which is one key component to living well. Vātsyāyana equates *nyāya* with *ānvīkṣikī*, "critical reasoning," one of four "sciences" or intellectual disciplines mentioned in ancient texts on medicine and statecraft. In these sources, *ānvīkṣikī* is focused on settling disputes over political, ethical, and religious issues. In the *Mahābhārata*, the "Great Indian Epic," *ānvīkṣikī* is associated with the ability to solve difficult theoretical problems as well as practical ones. The notion of critical reasoning shines throughout the writings of the Nyāya school, focused as it is on rational deliberation on fundamental questions that are disputed or doubtful. Vātsyāyana calls attention to the fact that *ānvīkṣikī* starts from the findings of common experience and authoritative testimony and reflects on them through systematic inquiry. Importantly, Vātsyāyana summarizes the entire Nyāya philosophical method as "investigation of a subject by means of knowledge sources" (*Commentary* 1.1.1). Uddyotakara adds, "The best reasoning occurs when the knowledge sources are employed collectively in the establishment of something . . . as this demonstrates the truth of one's position" (*Gloss* 1.1.1).

Nyāya's influence on Indian philosophy was extensive. Its methods of analysis and resolution of controversy influenced much of classical literary criticism as well as jurisprudence. Its knowledge-source epistemology set a standard for almost all the schools, not only Hindu but also Buddhist and Jaina, which borrowed from as well as criticized Nyāya. Nyāya also became arguably the leading voice of Indian philosophical realism, adopting the realist categorical metaphysics of its sister school, Vaiśeṣika, and defending a robust realism through debate with Buddhist anti-realists and flux theorists. It is no overstatement to claim that some of the most profound debates in classical India were between Buddhists and Naiyāyikas (Nyāya philosophers) over the nature of the external world, the nature of cognition, and the reality of traditionally held objects such as mountains, trees, and bodies, a personal self, and a creator God. But among Nyāya's opponents were also fellow "Hindus" in the Mīmāṃsā and Sāṃkhya schools, and others, as we shall see.

Chapter 1 of our volume presents Nyāya's view of the knowledge sources and the school's understanding of how they generate knowledge. Chapter 2 lays out Nyāya's philosophical methodology and how its theory of default trust in cognition is used to respond to skeptical challenges. Chapter 3 continues with the theme of skepticism and methodology, focusing on Nyāya's defense of realism, broadly construed, in the face of anti-realist and skeptical attacks. Chapter 4 centers on Nyāya's defense of an enduring self, a psychological "substance" that bears psychological qualities such as desire and knowledge. Chapter 5 studies the structural features of the world according to the school, with a special focus on substance and causation. Chapter 6 presents Nyāya's natural theology and the argument that certain features of the world would not be possible without a creator God. Chapter 7 focuses upon philosophy of language and, in this context, Nyāya's account of universals. Chapter 8 takes up value theory and ethics, including Nyāya's endorsement of the soteriological values associated with yoga traditions in classical India. Chapter 9 is an exposition of the school's debate theory, including identification of common fallacies and proper procedure in expressing an "inference for others," a formal proof with steps or "components." Appendix A provides an overview of the entire *Nyāya-sūtra*, to help readers achieve a synoptic understanding of the work as a whole. Appendix B lists all of the sūtras that we have translated by chapter.

More broadly still, our chapters are organized in the following way:

Epistemology: Chapters 1–2

Metaphysics: Chapters 3–6

Philosophy of language: Chapter 7

Ethics and value theory: Chapter 8

Logic, rhetoric, and debate theory: Chapter 9

Finally, let us note that our layout is a little different from the organization of the *Nyāya-sūtra* itself, which is set by its first sūtra and a concern for a supreme personal good called *apavarga*, "supreme felicity." We focus on that idea in our Chapter 8 on value. But let us take a quick look at the first sūtra to see Gautama's own delineation of principal topics:

1.1.1. Knowledge sources, objects of knowledge, doubt, motive, example, accepted position, inferential components, suppositional reasoning, certainty, debate for the truth, disputation, destructive debate, pseudo-provers, equivocation, misleading objections, and clinchers: from knowledge of these, there is attainment of the supreme good.

Note that the list begins with "knowledge sources" and ends with items important to debate theory. We, too, begin our study by taking up ideas about knowledge sources and end it with consideration of debate. However, our order of topics amounts to a reorganization that is hopefully more friendly to modern students and instructors.

Suggested Readings

Sibajiban Bhattacharyya, *Development of Nyāya Philosophy and Its Social Context*. Vol. 3, part 2 of *History of Science, Philosophy, and Culture in Indian Civilization*, General editor D. P. Chattopadhyaya. New Delhi: Centre for Studies in Civilizations, 2010.

Surendranath Dasgupta, *A History of Indian Philosophy*. Vol. 1. Cambridge: Cambridge University Press, 1963.

Jonardon Ganeri, *Philosophy in Classical India: The Proper Work of Reason*. London; New York: Routledge, 2001.

N. S. Junankar, *Gautama: The Nyāya Philosophy*. Delhi: Motilal Banarsidass, 1978.

Daya Krishna, *The Nyāyasūtras: A New Commentary on an Old Text*. Delhi: Sri Satguru Publications, 2004.

B. K. Matilal, *Nyāya-Vaiśeṣika. A History of Indian Literature*. Vol. 6, Fasc. 2. Edited by Jan Gonda. Weisbaden: Otto Harrassowitz, 1977.

Roy W. Perrett, *An Introduction to Indian Philosophy*. Cambridge: Cambridge University Press, 2016.

Karl H. Potter, ed., *Encyclopedia of Indian Philosophies*. Vol. 2. *Nyāya-Vaiśeṣika*. Delhi: Motilal Banarsidass, 1977.

R. S. Sharma, *India's Ancient Past*. New Delhi: Oxford University Press, 2015.

S. C. Vidyabhusana, *The Nyāya Sūtras of Gotama*. Originally published 1913. (Accessed February 21, 2016.) https://archive.org/details/TheNyayaSutrasOfGotama.

Chapter 1

Knowledge Sources

Epistemology, the theory of knowledge, is launched from the recognition that cognition is not always veridical or true. We sometimes have false beliefs or doubtful apprehensions. One of the most important concerns in epistemology is the search for factors that indicate that a belief is true, that what we take to be truth-revealing cognition is indeed knowledge. Minimally, we hope to understand what criteria ensure that a belief is held reasonably or properly. In the broadest sense, we are looking for factors that contribute to positive epistemic status. Having identified these factors, we can put ourselves in a better position to gain knowledge and avoid error.

The Sanskritic philosophical lexicon has a number of words that are commonly translated "knowledge," although often what is meant is not standing knowledge, such as knowledge of a phone number, but rather occurrent knowledge, such as coming to know something in one's immediate environment perceptually. Nyāya subscribes to the thesis that standing or non-occurrent knowledge, which is dispositional, depends upon occurrent knowledge, such as seeing and reading a phone number for the first time, making it possible to remember it later. Translators (including the two of us) have sometimes used the general English term "cognition" instead of "knowledge," because it is more amenable to a focus on occurrent awareness, and because sometimes the corresponding Sanskrit words (such as jñāna*) do not entail truth of belief. For the sake of readability, however, in this translation we shall normally use "knowledge," while occasionally employing "cognition" and phrases such as "a bit of knowledge" when context demands.*

We should also be aware that Nyāya epistemology is quite distinct from a significant, internalist *strain in Western epistemology.* Internalism *is the view that the things that contribute centrally to knowledge or justified belief are accessible to the knower or believer. In short, what distinguishes knowledge or justified belief from error or fancy is that someone has good reasons for her belief, reasons that she could articulate if called upon. These are "internal" to her in that these things could be discovered by her own reflection. In Western epistemology, internalism is typically wed to the idea that epistemic responsibility and fulfillment of epistemic obligations (e.g., "Don't believe beyond the available evidence") are central to knowledge and justification. Modern views that make epistemic dutifulness central to belief and justification are sometimes collected under the banner of* deontology. *One reason for the primacy of internalism and deontology in modern Western epistemology is a recurring concern with cases of massive illusion or mistake. The most famous of these is Descartes' "evil demon." What if we were completely tricked by a powerful demon, and under illusion regarding almost everything in our lives? Similarly, some ask, "What if you were a just brain in a vat, made to have your experiences by scientists turning nobs?" Such thought experiments have led some modern philosophers to accept that one could still be a reasonable, thoughtful person despite such massive cognitive failure. Given internalist and deontological principles, a person may be epistemically praiseworthy despite the falsity of her beliefs about almost everything.*

Nyāya takes a radically different approach. It denies that knowledge requires such inner access and responsibility. Nor does the school see knowledge as "justified" true belief, if we take justification to require a person consciously to entertain a good reason for what she believes. Rather, Nyāya focuses on the processes that consistently generate true belief or veridical cognition, processes called pramāṇa, *"knowledge sources." Nyāya would sympathize with what is currently called* reliabilism*: knowledge takes place when cognition is formed in the right way, by the right sort of mechanism. Often this means that processes that are inaccessible to* *the knower or believer, such as proper neuro-perceptual functioning, are more important to knowledge than fulfilling epistemic obligations. Knowledge depends on various sorts of processes operating properly, and a large part of epistemological refinement consists in understanding and availing ourselves of such processes.*

Despite such thoroughgoing externalism, *there are some internalist features of Nyāya's approach. Inference, for example, which is one of four knowledge sources recognized in Nyāya, often requires careful, self-conscious attention to good reasons and avoidance of sloppy thinking, at least in a philosophical context or in a debate. But even inference can also work automatically in a non-self-conscious way, our Nyāya philosophers contend. The other knowledge sources also work automatically, and often perception or reliable testimony serve just fine in the production of knowledge, without a need to "think through it" and consciously justify a belief.*

As a rule, Nyāya has an "innocent until legitimate doubt" view toward cognition and belief. Self-conscious reasoning becomes central only when there is reason for doubt, which leads to cognitive review and resolution. When doubt arises, we must sift through the available information and weigh the evidence at hand to come up with a reasoned conclusion. Here again is the internalist strain in Nyāya epistemology. Nyāya has a two-tiered approach to knowledge and justification, since once a proposition has been brought into reasonable doubt, we step back from our default trust and justification becomes a matter of self-conscious investigation "by means of the knowledge sources and tarka *(suppositional reasoning)." Since all the major claims of philosophy are considered to face challenges, inference and suppositional reasoning typically come to the forefront when articulating and defending philosophical views.*

While it is not an official knowledge source, tarka *captures much of what has developed as philosophic method in the West, in that it involves tracing out what are taken to be undesirable entailments of an opponent's view in order to refute it. Such is the standard form of* tarka *as classically conceived and employed by Nyāya philosophers as well as Buddhists and others on the classical scene. But there are various forms and practices within the "philosophical method" or* nyāya *in the word's technical sense, which, in sum, involves investigation by means of the recognized knowledge sources supplemented by* tarka. *We will take up* tarka *and cognitive review at length in Chapter 2, "Doubt and Philosophical Method." Now, our commentators introduce the sutras on knowledge sources.*

Introductory remarks preceding *Nyāya-sūtra* 1.1.1

Vātsyāyana [1.1–2.1]: When an object is comprehended through a knowledge source (*pramāṇa*), it becomes possible to engage in successful goal-directed activity. Thus, a knowledge source is useful (*arthavat*). Without a knowledge source, there would be no effective cognition of an object. Without such cognition, there would be no successful action. When someone grasps something by means of a knowledge source, the person may desire to obtain or to avoid it. *Goal-directed activity* is the effort of someone who acts because of such desire or aversion. For goal-directed activity, *success* is a relationship with its result: achieving or avoiding the *object*, which may be happiness or unhappiness respectively, or some means to achieve either. The purposes served by the knowledge sources are innumerable, since the living beings who employ knowledge sources are themselves innumerable.

When knowledge sources are connected to an object, so too are the knower, known, and knowledge. Why is this? Because in the absence of any of these, it would be impossible to have knowledge of an object. Of these, the person who acts possessed of desire or aversion is the *knower*. That by which something is known is the *knowledge source*. That which is known is the *object of knowledge*. And veridical cognition produced in the right way is *knowledge*. Truth is fully grasped when these four are in place.

What then is truth? It is the notion of existence applied to something that exists and that of non-existence with respect to something that doesn't exist. Grasping what is as what is, there is truth, the "as it is," the "uncontroverted." Likewise, grasping what is not as being what is not, there is truth, the "as it is," the "uncontroverted."

How could something non-existent be cognized through a knowledge source? At the time something existent is cognized, there is non-cognition of something non-existent. Just like the light of a lamp: when something visible is seen through the light of a lamp, something that is not seen in the light is understood to be absent. One thinks, "If it were there, it would have been seen. But it was not seen, so it is not there." Thus, when something existent is known through a knowledge source, something not grasped may be known to be non-existent.

*Vātsyāyana inaugurates his commentary by noting a close tie between knowledge sources and successful action. He notes that in veridical cognition, four factors all come together: the knower, the thing known, the means of knowing, and the knowledge itself. For knowledge to occur, these four must be properly related to each other. Centrally important here is the notion of "usefulness" (*arthavat*). The term* arthavat *has a semantic range that includes "effective," "accurate," "successful," "significant," and "fitting." To say that a knowledge source is useful means that it serves our purposes because it functions properly in revealing objects. Immediately below, Vācaspatimiśra takes* arthavat *to mean that a knowledge source is inerrant or factive, being tied to its object by definition.*

Vācaspatimiśra [4.18–21]: In Vātsyāyana's opening passage, the phrase "useful" (*arthavat*) employs the possessive affix (*vat*) indicating constant connection, and this means non-deviation. The import is that a knowledge source does not deviate from its object. A knowledge source's non-deviation amounts to the fact that there will never be disagreement anywhere, anytime, in any condition, between the nature of the object and what we are taught by the knowledge source.

The notion that knowledge sources are inerrant would seem to contradict our basic experience that we sometimes misperceive or make bad inferences. But the commentators frame such error as our mistaking "imitators" for real knowledge sources. The Sanskrit term for this is pramāṇa-ābhāsa, *"semblance of a knowledge source," or "knowledge-source imitator." Internal to the concept of knowledge sources is that they produce veridical cognition. Mistaken imitators are not, therefore, genuine* pramāṇas. *The following remarks by Uddyotakara and Vācaspati make this point clear.*

Uddyotakara [2.21–3.4]: A *pramāṇa* provides definitive ascertainment of an object. There is also a counterfeit which, owing to similarity with the real thing, is spoken of figuratively as *pramāṇa*. What similarity is there between this imitator and a genuine knowledge source? It is ascertainment through universals. Both the real thing and the counterfeit present universals. But acting on the basis of a genuine source leads to success, while acting on the basis of the counterfeit leads to failure. A genuine source is thus defined by Vātsyāyana as useful, since it is through a genuine source that an object is ascertained.

Vācaspatimiśra [9.3–10]: It is wrong to think that a knowledge source may be either factive or errant. The idea of an errant knowledge source is a contradiction. Therefore, Uddyotakara explains, "a knowledge source is that which provides definitive ascertainment of an object." . . . Yet, the counterfeit is mistakenly taken to be the real thing. Without similarity to knowledge sources, there would be no such mistakes. Uddyotakara asks, "What is the similarity?" His answer is that they both present universals. . . . The erroneous cognition of a piece of silver provides a distinct presentation of something that possesses whitish color. The subsequent veridical cognition that it is a shell does too. The idea is that there are two kinds of cognition in relation to a single object. One cognition projects silver where it is lacking, while the other serves as a corrective, presenting the object as it is. They relate to each other as defeated and defeater. The impetus to act follows from both, but the true knowledge source alone leads to success in action, while the non-knowledge source does not, as it deviates from the object.

Vācaspatimiśra's argument employs a stock example of perceptual illusion in Indian thought, seeing a shell and mistaking it for a piece of silver. Both shell and silver are grasped as possessing a certain reflective illumination, here "whitish *color," and in the erroneous case the reflective illumination of the shell is taken to be the shine of silver. When Uddyotakara and Vācaspatimiśra say that both "present one with universals," this means that both erroneous, pseudo-*pramāṇas *and accurate, true* pramāṇas *present to awareness common properties thought of as universals. But only in the legitimate case is the universal presented as located where it actually is. The Nyāya view is that memory formed by previous experience of silver makes possible the false projection onto the shell, given common properties—universals—such as whiteness.*

The next section of sūtras are Nyāya-sūtra *1.1.3–8, which define each of the knowledge sources. Here commentators are concerned to explain how it is that each distinct knowledge source is a unique process that generates knowledge. Causation is central in this account. Knowledge is caused in the right sort of way, as opposed to error, which involves misfires or deviant causal chains. The commentators further reflect on the way that knowledge sources may intersect and converge on their objects. And they usually try to explain etymologically why Gautama uses the particular word he does for each source. The etymology given serves as a working definition that gets refined in later sūtras.*

1.1.3: The knowledge sources are perception, inference, analogy, and testimony.

Vātsyāyana [8.17–9.5]: To follow the etymology of the word, **perception** (*pratyakṣa*) is the functioning of each *sense faculty* (*akṣa*) upon its *own proper* (*praty*) object. . . .

To follow the etymology of the word, **inference** (*anumāna*) is the *source* (*māna*) that works *after* (*anu-*). Inference normally occurs after perception, giving knowledge about something that possesses an inferential mark by means of knowing the mark.

To follow the etymology of the word, **analogy** (*upamāna*) is the *source* (*māna*) that shows *proximity* (*upa-*), nearness, as in "A buffalo is like a cow." Proximity should be understood here as a connection with universals, shared properties.

To follow the etymology of the word, **testimony** (*śabda*) is that by which something is asserted, *is heard* (*śabdayate*)—so it is spoken of, that is, made known.

That the **knowledge sources, *pramāṇa*,** are causes of veridical cognition can be understood from etymology: *pramīyate 'nena*, "It is known by means of this." For the word *pramāṇa* designates something that is an instrumental cause. The names of some of the particular instances—**inference**, for example—is explicated too just in this way, as an instrumental cause for inferential knowledge.

Although the dominant understanding of pramāṇa *in Nyāya is as a process or cause of knowledge—hence our translation "knowledge source"—Uddyotakara below explains why Indian thinkers sometimes use the term* pramāṇa *to mean the instance of knowledge itself. There is an analogous usage in English, where terms for causes of knowledge are also used as knowledge: "According to my perception, that is Ann in the distance." Here "perception" means the resulting cognition, while also, more commonly perhaps, "perception" is used to mean the process that terminates in perceptual knowledge.*

Uddyotakara [27.2–6]: For all the *pramāṇas*, when the term *pramāṇa* is spoken in reference to itself, it has the sense of *knowledge* (*pramiti*). When spoken in reference to other objects, it has the sense of *knowledge source* (*pramāṇa*): "that by which something is known." The results of a *pramāṇa* in this sense are the ensuing ideas that "I should avoid, pursue, or remain indifferent toward this object," which arise only after the object is known.

Vātsyāyana considers next the way in which knowledge sources converge upon their objects. Various Indian schools of thought debated whether each knowledge source has its own domain of objects, or whether they converge upon the same objects. Vātsyāyana argues that both situations are possible. Here he relies on Nyāya's sister school of Vaiśeṣika, whose literature shows many positions shared with Nyāya, although there are important differences. Sometimes it is said loosely that Vaiśeṣika tends to focus on metaphysics and ontology, while Nyāya focuses on epistemology. By around 1000 CE, the Vaiśeṣika tradition becomes absorbed into Nyāya, with no separate literature to speak of. But its categories are explicitly endorsed and its treatises cited by the earliest Nyāya commentators, as we see with Vātsyāyana in the next passage.

Vātsyāyana [9.5–16]: Do the knowledge sources converge upon the same objects, or is each restricted to its own domain? We find it both ways. "There is a self (*ātman*)," is known from the teaching of a trustworthy authority, the testimony of the Upaniṣads. There is also inference: "**Inferential marks for the self are desire, aversion, effort, pleasure, pain, and knowledge**" (*Nyāya-sūtra* 1.1.10). Finally, there is a special kind of perception, born of deep meditation, which yogis possess: "Perception of the self arises from a distinct kind of connection between one's mental faculty of attention and one's individual self" (*Vaiśeṣika-sūtra* 9.13).

To take another example, fire is known from the statement of a trustworthy person: "There is fire over there." Then, getting closer, it is inferred when one sees smoke. Finally, the fire is perceptually apprehended when one is in range.

Regarding the restriction of a knowledge source to certain types of objects, we find scriptural testimony such as, "One who desires heaven should perform the Agnihotra sacrifice" (*Taittirīya Brāhmaṇa* 2.9). For ordinary people, there is neither perceptual experience nor an inferential mark by which they know of heaven. In another example, hearing the sound of thunder, one infers its cause; there is knowledge neither by perception nor by testimony. Likewise, when one is looking at one's hand, there is neither testimony nor inference for its existence.

Let us add that regarding knowledge, perception is preeminent. When someone learns something from the statement of a trustworthy testifier, he may still wish to understand it in another way (through inference, for example). Understanding the thing through inference, he may still wish to know it through direct experience. But upon seeing it directly, the desire to know ceases, as in the example of fire above.

Uddyotakara explains why perception is mentioned first in the list of pramāṇas.

Uddyotakara [28.4]: Perception is rightly listed first because all the *pramāṇas* are dependent upon perception.

Inference depends on perception because it is by perception that we discover the general connections that undergird inference, "Wherever there is smoke, there is fire," as well as the specific marks that trigger inference, "There is smoke over there." Testimony is dependent on perception, in that one must hear or read the testimonial statement that is the immediate vehicle or trigger for testimonial knowledge.

1.1.4: Perceptual knowledge arises from a connection of sense faculty and object, does not depend on language, is inerrant, and is definitive.

This "perception sūtra" lists four conditions that collectively must be met for a cognition to be genuine perceptual knowledge: (1) that it arise from a connection between sense faculty and object, (2) that it not depend on language, (3) that it be inerrant, and (4) that it be definitive. Commentators examine and elaborate upon each condition. Vātsyāyana and Uddyotakara explain that qualifications 1 and 2 provide the basic structure of perceptual knowledge, that is, that the knowledge is generated by sense faculties operating on objects and is not reducible to linguistic knowledge. And qualifications 3 and 4 serve to exclude error and doubtful cognition from the ranks of perceptual knowledge proper. Below, Uddyotakara discusses the first condition, that the knowledge be produced by a connection between sense faculty and object.

Uddyotakara [28.18–29.6]: Knowledge that arises from the connection between a sense faculty and an object is perceptual. The sense faculties will be discussed later,[1] as will the objects.[2] There are six kinds of connection between the two:

substance

1. conjunction (connection between a sense faculty and a substance; for example, seeing a pot where the visual organ contacts the pot there where it is);

1 *Nyāya-sūtra* 1.1.12.

2 *Nyāya-sūtra* 1.1.14.

2. inherence in what is conjoined (connection between a sense faculty and a property that inheres in a perceived substance; for example, seeing the color of a pot, the color inhering in the pot that is in contact with the visual organ);

3. inherence in what inheres in what is conjoined (connection between a sense faculty and a universal that is instantiated in a property inhering in a substance; for example, the smell of sandalwood in general that inheres within a particular trope or instance of sandalwood smell inhering in a piece of sandalwood);

4. inherence (connection that makes auditory perception possible);

5. inherence in what inheres (connection between the auditory faculty and a universal that inheres in a sound; for example, the loudness of loud music);

6. qualifier-qualified relation (connection involved in perception of an absence).

Among these, consider the visual organ: when a colored object such as a pot is known, the connection has to be conjunction, since the organ and the pot are by nature substances. In contrast, with something that is not a substance, such as a color, the connection is inherence in what is conjoined, since colors and the like rest in substances that are in sensory connection when they are perceived. The mode of "resting in" is inherence. In this way, the connection is inherence in what inheres in the conjoined in the case of universals such as those that inhere in particular bits of color and the like (for example, redness in a particular red trope). Similarly, the connection is conjunction in the case of the organs of smell, touch, and taste: conjunction of the organ with things that have smell or another sensible property such as touch or taste. With regard to odors and other properties themselves that inhere in the things that have them, the sensory connection is inherence in the conjoined. And for universals of odor, etc., it is inherence in what inheres in that which is conjoined. Universals are nested in—they rest in—such individuals. And for sound, it is inherence.

Note that types 1 to 3 and 6 occur for any sense faculty except hearing, while 4 and 5 are for hearing alone. The distinctions between types are not meant to capture phenomenology as much as catalog the power of perception directly to apprehend various kinds of objects, properties, and structural features of reality: substances (1), individual properties or tropes (2, 4), universals (3, 5), and absences (6). The need for distinct kinds of connection for hearing are due to Nyāya's notion that hearing involves a portion of ether that is located within the ears. Sounds are properties that inhere in ether, ether being the medium through which sound travels. Sounds that are heard have traveled to the portion of ether in one's ears, and hence the "connection" in play is the inherence of sound in the ether in one's ears. We perceive absences by noting that an object in perceptual range (e.g., the floor of a classroom) is qualified by the absence of some object in question (e.g., an elephant). A person knows there's no elephant in the room because she has looked and would have seen one if it were present. In his opening comments above, Vātsyāyana anticipates this idea by arguing that knowledge of unreal things is based on cognition of real things, coupled with the background notion, "If something were there, I would have noticed it." Below, Vātsyāyana and Uddyotakara consider the second condition for perceptual knowledge, that it be independent of language.

Vātsyāyana [10.11–20]: Some people have argued in the following way:

> There are names for every object of awareness, and proper awareness of objects is wrapped up in names. This fact is the basis of conventional practices (*vyavahāra*). Knowledge produced by a connection between a sense faculty and object would be something like, "There is this color," or "There is this taste." The words "color" and "taste" thus provide names for the content of cognition (*viṣaya*, "sense data," the interior objects of perception). We refer to cognition in this way, according to the name of its content, and as such, perceptual cognition is verbal in nature—this is a fatal objection to your view.

To reject this argument, the sūtra-maker claims that perceptual knowledge "**does not depend on language**." When one has perceptual knowledge of an object without knowing the name conventionally bestowed upon it, such cognition is not verbalized by a denotative term.

Uddyotakara [34.15–16]: When someone doesn't know the names of things he is seeing, perceptual knowledge still conforms to differences in the objects that are experienced. Even when someone does know the names of the objects being perceived, this is still the case. The name for the object is employed only after perceptual knowledge is produced.

Below, Vātsyāyana discusses the third condition, that perception is inerrant.

Vātsyāyana [11.3–6]: During the summer, the sun rays and the warmth radiating from the hot ground pulsate together and come into sensory connection with the visual organ of a person situated at a distance. In such a situation, the cognition "Water" arises for the observer owing to the connection between his sense organ and the object. So to exclude such false cognition from the definition of perception proper, the author of the sūtras includes the qualifier "**inerrant**." Error is to cognize something as other than it is, a cognition *deviating* from what is true. Perception, which is inerrant, cognizes something as it truly is, *undeviating* from what is true.

As noted earlier, Nyāya uses terms for knowledge sources and their results factively. Considering sight, for example, a perceptual illusion such as a mirage does not count as a proper or genuine instance of perception. It is rather a perception-imitator, a pseudo-perception. Below, Vātsyāyana, Uddyotakara, and Vācaspatimiśra discuss the fourth condition, that perceptual cognition is definitive.

Vātsyāyana [11.7–9]: A person looking at something at a distance is unable to determine precisely what it is, whether it is smoke or a cloud of dust. So to exclude from the ranks of genuine perception such unclear cognition which does arise from a connection between a sense faculty and an object, the sūtra-maker uses the qualifier "**definitive**."

Vācaspatimiśra interprets the word "definitive" in a different way than his predecessors and alters all subsequent Nyāya understanding of perception. He reads two criteria in the sūtra, "definitive" and "does not depend on words," as describing two separate kinds of perceptual experience, determinate and indeterminate, where the former is conceptually structured and the latter is not. By this, he allows indeterminate perception—long championed by Buddhist thinkers—a place within the Nyāya theory. By allowing some of the Nyāya theory of perception to accord with the Buddhist view, Vācaspati takes a big step towards Buddhist phenomenalism, which holds that conceptually rich experience is actually inferential, while real perception consists in raw, unconceptualized experience. These Buddhist thinkers hold that things such as the chairs and tables of our current experience are largely our own conceptual projections. But, crucially, Vācaspatimiśra is able to incorporate the notion of indeterminate perception into the Nyāya view without surrendering the commitment to realism, that such things do exist external to our perceptions. For Nyāya, external objects are causes of perception by entering into connections with sense faculties, and our object-directed concepts thereby originate in features of the external world. For the Buddhist, in contrast, we impose concepts on the world according to our desires. Thus, while Nyāya accepts and extols concept-laden perception, Buddhists hold that concept-laden cognition is not genuine perception, since it is we who make up and project concepts. The Buddhist view sees perception and conceptualized awareness as fundamentally incompatible and perception as only indeterminate. There is no determinate or "definitive" variety.

After laying out several Buddhist arguments in support of this view, Vācaspatimiśra answers with realist rebuttals and counterarguments. Note that he calls objects "efficacious" in order to express the idea that they are capable of acting as causes of perceptual knowledge by entering into relations with our sense faculties. They are also efficacious in the further sense that through our sensory experience they can satisfy our desires.

Vācaspatimiśra [111.9–21]: We have a reply to what was charged earlier, that there is incompatibility between (a) a genuine perception, produced directly from an efficacious object, and (b) a mental occurrence incapable of sensory relationship but which is expressed in words. Our answer is that there would be incompatibility if the object of perception were (as Buddhists propose) a *unique particular* (*svalakṣaṇa*). However, it is not that. For, as will be established, the object of perception that exists as ultimately real is endowed with universals or class properties, endures the passage of time, and is entirely capable of both producing sensory relationships and being expressed by words. Thus there is no incompatibility between (a) an instance of perceptual knowledge that is generated by an efficacious object, and (b) a mental occurrence that is itself admittedly incapable of a direct sensory relationship but which is expressed in words. And so our opponent's argument that relies on an alleged incompatibility (*prasaṅga*) proves to be dubious in its reverse form (since the object of perception produces both the immediate sensory relationship and the concept-laden perception).

Furthermore, it is wrong to hold that our thoughts are mere imaginations when we conceive of class characteristics and so on as distinct when they really are not distinct from what we call substances and so on; in other words, it is wrong to hold that such characteristics are not generated in conformity with real capacities of the object. For, as will be argued, there is a distinct difference between class characteristics and a substance (between Bessie the cow as a particular property-possessing substance and the properties or class characteristics such as cowhood that she possesses). And although there is this distinct difference, there are words for these distinct entities that all refer to the same individual (for example, "Bessie is a cow," where "Bessie," the proper noun, and "cow," the class term, both refer to the same individual), as will be shown later on.

And it is wrong to suppose that in the case of a distinct word such as "Ḍittha" used in a statement such as "That is Ḍittha" ("Ḍittha" being a common name for a person, like "John"), that the ideas we have about the thing are not generated by the object because the thing's unity is constructed imaginatively. We have already pointed out in introductory comments on the expression "**does not depend on language**" in the definition, that as objects do not contain within themselves the words that designate them, the two things (object and word) cannot both be in immediate sensory relationship with respect to an instance of perceptual knowledge if it is produced by a single sensory connection. Rather, at first something which possesses certain universals is immediately perceived (without the subject's thinking of the appropriate word). An individual, remembering his own previous experience, recalls the word that was used also at that time. All theories must accept this. But remembering the word is of no use whatsoever when it comes to generating perceptual awareness. Otherwise, such creatures as children and the mute would not have sensory presentations since they have no memory of words.

"Unique particular" translates sva-lakṣaṇa, *"that which is its own mark," which, according to Buddhist phenomenalism, is the true object of perception. Such completely unique entities cannot be conceptualized or captured by words for common characteristics.*

*The "reverse form" of a general rule in an argument is akin to what is called contraposition in propositional logic. To use a simple example, the correlation between smoke and fire (*wherever there is smoke, there is fire*) has a "reverse form" in the correlation between the absence of fire and the absence of smoke (*wherever there is no fire, there is no smoke*). The reverse form of the Buddhist's rule is: "Whatever is in immediate sensory connection, that is a unique particular free from concepts." Vācaspatimiśra argues the rule is wrong because the objects of perceptual experience are describable, talked about in common language. Technically, they are typically substances bearing universals and other properties capable of being linguistically expressed.*

In sum, Vācaspatimiśra allows a place for indeterminate perception by introducing into Nyāya a two-stage theory of perception that owes much to the Mīmāṃsaka philosopher Kumārila (c. 700), a fellow realist. In the first stage, perception is non-concept-laden, an unverbalizable sensory presentation that becomes in the second stage verbalizable and concept-laden. The concept typically comes from prior experience, for example, of cows, and memory for the bit of perceptual knowledge, "That's a cow." But for, say, a child's first-time perception of a cow, the concept comes purely from the world and perception's first stage, although the child does not know the right word.

Vātsyāyana now discusses the status of apperception, which is an "inner" perception of one's own mental states.

Vātsyāyana [11.15–21]: Objection: The definition of perception should allow for the experience of objects such as one's self (*ātman*) and awareness of one's own pleasures, but it does not. For knowledge of one's self or of pleasure, etc., is not generated by sense-organ connection with the object.

Answer: The faculty here is the "mind" (*manas*), which is an inner sensory organ. We shall take it up later separately from other sense organs because of their differences in nature.[3] . . .

Furthermore, we learn that *manas* is the sense organ for internal perception from the views of another system (the Vaiśeṣika). Reasoning within other systems is to be accepted if we have no view that contradicts it.

Our commentators argue that the "mind" (manas, *sometimes translated "inner organ" or "mental organ") must be accepted as an inner sense.* Nyāya-sūtra *1.1.16 says that a* manas *must be accepted if we are to account for the nature of selective attention. As mentioned here, it is also accepted as the "sense faculty" involved in an individual's self-knowledge and awareness of her own mental states. Note that the self is always the perceiver, not the internal organ, which is responsible for delivering cognitive and non-cognitive content to the self.*

Having completed a preliminary discussion of perception, Vātsyāyana follows the sūtra-maker in turning next to inference as a distinct knowledge source.

3 Under *Nyāya-sūtra* 1.1.16 in particular.

1.1.5: Next is inference, which depends on previous perception and is threefold: from something prior, from something later, and through experience of a common characteristic.

Vātsyāyana [12.4–16]: The phrase "**depends on previous perception**" refers to (i) perception of the relationship between an inferential mark and what it marks, as well as (ii) perception of the mark itself. Perception of an inferential mark and what it marks as bound together secures recollection of the mark as inferential. By such recollection, coupled with fresh perception of the mark, an unperceived object is inferred.

*An "inferential mark" (*liṅga*) is a sign or indicator that reliably indicates some other thing (*liṅgin*, the "indicated"). For example, dark billowing smoke pouring out of the windows of a house indicates fire inside. Inference is the capacity to gain knowledge by noticing the tie between inferential marks and the things they indicate. To use the same example, one seeing smoke knows there is fire through inference. In the context of argument and proof, an inferential mark such as smoke is called a "prover" (*hetu, sādhana*) and is cited to provide inferential support for a disputed thesis involving a "property to be proved" (*sādhya*), in this case, fire.*

"Property to be proved" is a cumbersome phrase, but there is no common English word that captures sādhya *effectively, and it will therefore be our standard translation of* sādhya *in this volume. Please see Chapter 9, "Debate," for detailed discussion of the five-step Nyāya proof.*

Vātsyāyana will now chart some of the major ways that an inferential mark and property to be proved are tied together according to the sūtra.

"**From something prior**" means an effect is inferred from its cause. For example, from swollen clouds one infers that it will rain. "**From something later**" means a cause is inferred from its effect. For example, seeing a formerly calm river brimming with rushing water, one infers that it rained upstream. "**Through experience of a common characteristic**" occurs, for example, when one sees something that was formerly in one place but is now in another owing to its movement. So from change of location, one infers the movement of the sun though one does not watch it move.

Alternatively, "**from something prior**" means inference of something currently unseen when observing something with which it was formerly found to be connected. For example, inferring fire from smoke.

Alternatively, "**from something later**" means argument by elimination. When, among various competing options, one remains unrefuted while the others succumb to untoward consequences, that one is the right view. For example, there are inferences like the following about something that exists and is thus impermanent: given doubt regarding the ontological category into which sound should be placed, it is concluded (in the *Vaiśeṣika-sūtra*[4]) that sound, since it is real, is impermanent and cannot be a universal, a "distinguisher," or inherence (these being eternal and not strictly real or existent). It must therefore be a substance, a quality, or an action (the remaining basic ontological categories according to Vaiśeṣika). But which of the three? Sound is not a substance, as it inheres in a single substance. It is not an action, as it is caused by another sound. One infers that sound is a quality, since that is the only option remaining.

Alternatively, "**from common experience**" means that when the relationship between an inferential mark and what it marks is not perceived, one infers an unperceived object through a mark that has similarity with something else. For example, one infers the existence of the self from desire and the like.[5] Desire and the like are qualities, and qualities inhere in substances. That substance in which desire and the rest are situated is the self. . . .

Perception targets existing things, while inference targets both things that exist and things that do not exist. How so? It's because inference ranges over the three times, past, present, and future. For objects in all three times are grasped by inference—"It will be," "It is," "It was"—and indeed things past and future are non-existent.

Vātsyāyana's argument takes the form of elimination of candidates drawn from the Nyāya-Vaiśeṣika categories. See the

---

4 *Vaiśeṣika-sūtra* 2.2.27.

5 The inference is elaborated at *Nyāya-sūtra* 1.1.10.

*chart provided in Chapter 5, "Substance and Causation," for a diagram of the Nyāya-Vaiśeṣika ontology. The substance in which sound is thought to inhere is called ether (*ākāśa*). Now, composite substances, such as a pot or a wagon, can inhere in things. A wagon inheres in its parts, and the parts in further parts down to non-composite substances, atoms. But all substances either inhere in nothing—such as atoms—or they inhere in two or more things—such as a dyad, which is something that inheres in two atoms. Sound inheres in ether, but ether is thought to be a non-atomic substance without parts. Ether, the medium of sound, is considered to be a single, all-pervading substance that inheres in nothing further. Sound thus inheres in a single substance and cannot be a substance. Sound cannot be an action either because actions have different causal powers than sound. "Quality" is the only remaining basic category on the Vaiśeṣika list. Thus sound must be a quality. Nyāya-Vaiśeṣika ontological positions often show a remarkable sensitivity to considerations of overall coherence, as is evident in the complexity here.*

In order to bring out the varied ways that inference relates to other knowledge sources, Uddyotakara begins his commentary by providing different, yet consistent, readings of the qualifiers in the inference sūtra.

Uddyotakara [41.5–7]: We can read the definition as saying "**depends on *them***" and in that case what is meant by "them" *is **all the*** **pramāṇas**, such that what is being taught is that inference can depend on prior input of any knowledge source. One may still say that perception is the foundation of inference, as Vātsyāyana has, since in one way or another all knowledge depends on perception.

*The sūtra reads "preceded by that," where "that" (*tat*) is a pronoun in a compound. As it is in a compound, the word is not explicitly declined, and its grammatical number must be unpacked according to context and its anaphoric referent. Here "that" is most straightforwardly read as referring to perception, the topic of the previous sūtra, and that is how Vātsyāyana understands the word. But the pronoun could in principle be understood differently. By reading it* *as plural in number, Uddyotakara takes the opportunity to make clear that the inferential marks that trigger inference need not be perceptually generated. They may be produced by any knowledge source. For example, we could infer fire upon seeing smoke over a hill, and then surmise that given such a fire it's likely that campers on the hill are cooking their midday meal. Below, Uddyotakara offers another way to read the "that" in the definition.*

[41.7–12] Or, "depends on previous perception" may be read to say "depends on two perceptions." Which two perceptions? The first perception would be experience of the relationship between the inferential mark and what it marks (for example, previously seeing smoke flowing from fire); the second would be the current experience of the mark itself (for example, seeing smoke currently without seeing fire). Consider a subject who desires to know something. By seeing the inferential mark in the second sort of perception, recollection is triggered through the arousing of a mental disposition formed by her previous experiences of the mark and what it marks together. This is immediately followed by the second sort of perception of the mark in view, another viewing of, for instance, smoke. This final perception, assisted by the recollection and previous experiences, takes the form of "reflection on an inferential mark" (*liṅga-parāmarśa*), in other words, inference.

To paraphrase, in the Nyāya view, both current perception of an inferential mark and memory of the connection between the mark and what it marks are included within inference, being necessary for inferential knowledge. But concerning the relative importance of all contributing factors, it is reflection on the mark that is the most crucial. Why? Because inferential knowledge follows immediately after such reflection. Above, Uddyotakara explains why it is commonly said that inference amounts to a triple perception, where the third perception is perceiving an inferential mark in just the right way, namely, as informed by prior knowledge of its connection to the object of the inferential knowledge to come (e.g., of fire). So, to summarize by using our stock example: an individual perceives smoke, and that triggers a memory formed by previous perception of smoke and fire together, which prompts her to finally see the smoke as indicating fire. *The third and final perception is "reflection on an inferential mark."*

Below, Uddyotakara interprets the declaration that "inference is of three kinds" to refer to three specific logical forms that remain important for much of Nyāya's later history. Let us review the inferential terminology. When discussing an argument or inference-for-another (see Chapter 9, "Debate," for exposition of the statement form), an inferential mark is called a "prover" (hetu, sādhana) *and the property that is marked is called the "property to be proved"* (sādhya).

Uddyotakara [43.7–12]: "**Inference is of three kinds,**" says the sūtra. These may be taken to be the "positive-negative" (*anvaya-vyatirekī*), the "positive" (*anvaya*), and the "negative" (*vyatirekī*).

Among these, the positive-negative inference has an inferential mark (for example, smoke) that is present in the subject targeted (yonder mountain) and possibly similar things (other mountains, etc., where there is fire) while being absent wherever the property to be proved (fire) is known not to exist (for example, a lake). For example,

> Sound is impermanent,
> because, while possessed of both universal and particular features, it is perceptible by external sense organs such as ours,
> like a pot, etc.

The positive inference has an inferential mark that is present in the subject targeted and similar things, while there is no example where the property to be proved is known to be absent. For instance, those who hold that all things are impermanent argue:

> Sound is impermanent,
> because it is produced.

For, to one who holds that all things are impermanent, there is no known example of a permanent entity.

The negative inference has an inferential mark that (a) is co-extensive with the subject of the inference, such that there are available no similar examples (no example in addition to the subject), and (b) is absent where the property to be proved is known not to occur. For instance,

> A living body is not devoid of a self,
> because that would entail the unacceptable
> consequence of its being devoid of life.

Here Uddyotakara introduces a classification of inference that in later Nyāya reflection supercedes other divisions. The most commonplace inferences are backed up by examples known to have both the prover, for example, smoke or smokiness, and the property to be proved, for example, fire or fieriness, present together, as well as by known absences of the property to be proved (no fire) correlating with known absences of the prover (no smoke). This type is called positive-negative.

The positive-only is backed up only by examples of positive correlations between prover and property to be proved. This type of inference occurs when there are no known instances of the absence of the property to be proved. For example, "Whatever is nameable is knowable," where there is no known example of something not knowable.

The negative-only is backed up only by examples of negative correlations between known absences of the property to be proved and known absences of the prover, there being no examples outside the inferential subject where the property to be proved is known to occur. In later in-house discussions as well as in controversies with Buddhists and others, it is the negative-only that is the most suspect. Only living bodies have selves, and having a self (or not being devoid of a self) correlates with being alive, but there is no example of something having a self (the property to be proved) and being alive (the prover) outside of the inferential subject taken to be all living bodies. But there are plenty of examples of negative correlations: wherever there is no self, for example, in a pot, there is no life.

Next is the sūtra on analogy. Vātsyāyana treats analogy as a knowledge source for learning word-meaning in certain circumstances. Analogy tends to have a secondary status for Nyāya. Often in his commentary, Vātsyāyana fails to mention it while listing the other sources: perception, inference, and testimony. Some Nyāya philosophers explicitly agree with Vaiśeṣika and others that it is not a separate pramāṇa. *However, mainstream Nyāya accepts it as an independent knowledge source along with the other three, arguing that the knowledge it produces could not be due to another kind of knowledge source.*

1.1.6: Analogy produces knowledge through similarity with something familiar.

Vātsyāyana [13.11–19]: The sūtra says that **analogy** produces knowledge of what is to be known through commonality with something already known. For example, it is said that a gayal (a rare kind of buffalo) is like a cow. What is being done by analogy here? If someone understands that the animal in question has properties that it shares with a cow, then upon seeing the creature he understands that *this* is the very animal. Thus the sūtra-maker says that the function of analogy is to learn the connection of something to its name. For example, if someone has learned from an analogical statement that a gayal is like a cow, then through perception of an animal that shares properties with the cow, she knows, "The word 'gayal' is the name of that animal." In this way, knowledge of the connection between the name to the named is produced.

To give another example, through analogical statements such as "The wild bean herb is like the mungo herb," or "The glycine bean is like the lentil bean," a person learning by analogy what is meant by such names may go on to gather the one or the other plant for the purpose of making a remedy. In this way, the province of analogy includes a good many other things in the world about which we want knowledge.

The fourth and last knowledge source on the Nyāya list is testimony. The nature and authority of testimony is hotly disputed among all the classical schools. Not only Buddhists but also followers of the Vaiśeṣika school and others would reduce testimony to a subspecies of inference, one based on a subject's knowledge that the testifier is trustworthy.

1.1.7: Testimony is instruction by a trustworthy authority.

Vātsyāyana [14.4–7]: A trustworthy authority (*āpta*) is someone who knows something directly, an instructor with the desire to communicate it faithfully as it is known. To be trustworthy (*āpti*) is to have direct knowledge of something. One who operates on this basis is a **trustworthy authority**. The criterion applies equally to sages, respected members of one's own community, and those outside the fold. And all people's practices of speech and action (*vyavahāra*) proceed on the basis of testimonial knowledge.

Uddyotakara [57.3–8]: (In order to reject testimony as a separate knowledge source, an opponent argues as follows.)

> Regarding the sūtra, "**Testimony is instruction by a trustworthy authority**," mustn't the veracity of such authorities be confirmed? Or rather would one independently have to confirm the truth of the claims about the object? If it is the former, that would come by inference. If the latter, that too would come otherwise than by testimony; it would come by perception.

> We reject this line of argument, as it does not properly grasp the meaning of the sūtra. This is not the meaning of "**Testimony is instruction by a trustworthy authority**." Rather, the sūtra means that the point of testimony is to produce understanding through uttering words, regarding objects within the range of sensory connection and for those beyond it (such as heaven). Thus the dilemma put forth is irrelevant.

Uddyotakara insinuates here the Nyāya view of the Veda as testimony about matters beyond the range of the senses, like heaven or liberation. The idea is expanded under the next

knowledge depends on testimonial knowledge that can't be verified.
↳ those knowledge itself provides basis for perceptual/inferential knowledge
↳ unless absurd consequences to knowledge, so far as we perceive/proceed in the world, accept testimonial knowledge as knowledge as testimony as a separate knowledge source

① objection
inference first that the person speaking is trustworthy

② testimony reducible to perception. because we have to double check ourselves.

Uddyotakara meaning of sūtra. focus on understanding rather than veracity

↳ as understanding is distinct from inference + perception (is a process) so too is testimony distinct.

sūtra. But first, as this sūtra is the final introduction of the concept of a knowledge source, Vātsyāyana says about the sources in general:

Vātsyāyana [14.6–7]: Practices and activities of gods, humans, and animals succeed through the operation of the knowledge sources as explained, and not otherwise.

1.1.8: Such testimony is of two kinds, because it has two kinds of object: that which is experienced (here in this world), and that which is not experienced (here in this world).

Vātsyāyana [14.10–14]: Something **experienced** is an **object** of which there is experience here in this world. Something **not experienced** is an **object** which is discerned elsewhere. Thus (a) statements made by sages (statements about heaven for instance) and (b) statements made by ordinary folk are distinct.

What is the point of mentioning this? It is that a person should not hold that the **instruction of a trustworthy authority** is a knowledge source only with respect to something **experienced**, thinking that in such a case alone is the object definitively known. No, with respect too to that which has *not* been experienced, testimony *is* a knowledge source, because there could be inference (for example) to such an (unexperienced) object.

Just as one could in principle come to perceive directly something in this world that in fact one knows by testimony (e.g., "There is a crack in the Liberty Bell"), so sages and yogis can make authoritative statements about things not experienced by ordinary folk because they have extraordinary perceptual experience—"yogic perception" (yaugika-pratyakṣa)*, which is to include, by Nyāya's lights, special auditory experience of sages who have "heard" Vedic verses. Indeed, ordinary people can make inferences about things that they have not personally experienced insofar as the inferences would be based on what they have learned from such authorities. In other words, there can be inferential support for the existence of otherworldly objects (such as heaven), taking as* *premises what sages have said based upon their extraordinary perceptions. Similarly, in our own era there are scientific and historical claims we take to be true on the basis of expert testimony, but which we could never verify by our own direct experience. We may nevertheless make supporting inferences in such cases, appealing to the authoritativeness of the speakers who provide our premises.*

Uddyotakara [57.10–14]: The point of saying **testimony is of two kinds** is to provide a fixed categorization. Authoritative traditions which are in many ways different are sorted into two basic categories according to their content as perceptual or inferential.

Alternatively, the sūtra says that there are two kinds of *speaker* since some talk about experienced objects while others talk about unexperienced objects. . . . The criterion for authority is the same, whether with regard to **sages, respected members of one's own community, or those outside the fold**. No separate rules have been expressed, because we see that everyone's activities and practices proceed according to traditions transmitted by testimony.

Suggestions for Further Reading

Purushottama Bilimoria, "Jñāna and Pramā." *Journal of Indian Philosophy* 13 (1985): 73–102.

Arindam Chakrabarti, "On Knowing by Being Told." *Philosophy East and West* 42 (1992): 421–40.

Arindam Chakrabarti and B. K. Matilal, eds., *Knowing from Words: Western and Indian Philosophical Analysis of Understanding and Testimony*. Dordrecht: Kluwar, 1994.

S. C. Chatterjee, *The Nyāya Theory of Knowledge: A Critical Study of Some Problems in Logic and Metaphysics*. Calcutta: Calcutta University Press, 1939.

B. K. Matilal, *Perception: An Essay on Classical Indian Theories of Knowledge*. Oxford: Clarendon Press, 1986.

B. K. Matilal, *The Character of Logic in India*. SUNY Series in Indian Thought. Albany: State University of New York Press, 1998.

J. N. Mohany, *Reason and Tradition in Indian Thought*. Oxford: Clarendon, 1992.

Pradyot Mondal, "Some Aspects of Perception in Old Nyāya." *Journal of Indian Philosophy* 10 (1982): 357–76.

Stephen Phillips, *Epistemology in Classical India: The Knowledge Sources of the Nyāya School*. New York: Routledge, 2012.

Study Questions

1. Write out the definitions of the following, according to the text:

   pramāṇa
   perception
   inference
   analogy
   testimony
   inferential mark
   reflection on an inferential mark
   pervasion (sometimes translated as "correlation")

2. Explain the role of "success in action" in Vātsyāyana's discussion of the importance and nature of knowledge sources.

3. What does it mean to claim that a knowledge source is factive or inerrant? How, then, do Naiyāyikas explain false cognition or error?

4. What innovation does Vācaspatimiśra introduce into Nyāya theory of perception by his novel explanation of the phrase "does not depend on words"? How does he argue that perception can generate true, propositionally structured awareness, opposed to the view of his Buddhist adversaries?

5. In Uddyotakara's discussion of inference, why is "reflection on an inferential mark" sometimes called "the third perception"? What are the other two perceptions, and how do all three work together?

6. Explain the following inference patterns discussed by Uddyotakara: "positive-negative," "positive," and "negative."
7. What does it mean to say that testimony "is of two kinds"? Is this a defensible position?
8. What qualifications make a person a trustworthy authority according to Vātsyāyana? Does one have to know that the testifier is trustworthy, or must he simply be trustworthy? What is the Nyāya view, and is it correct in your estimation?
9. Give an example from your own life of things you know from each of the three *pramāṇas*: perception, inference, and testimony. Could you know it in another way? How about analogy? Is analogy the only way to learn what a word means?
10. What does it mean to say that Nyāya's *pramāṇa* theory is not robustly "internalist" and focuses instead on the role of causation in generating positive epistemic status?

Chapter 2

Doubt and Philosophical Method

Scholars speculate that the origins of Nyāya lie in the coaching needed to present a public plea—whether legal or for funds for a school or community—to a king or another powerful person. Over time, Nyāya methods of debate and reasoning became central in Indian jurisprudence as well as in other fields such as aesthetics. The entire fifth book of the Nyāya-sūtra *and many sūtras elsewhere concern canons of debate and inquiry. One of the great insights of Gautama, the "sūtra-maker," was to assimilate a view of everyday processes of knowledge generation to a debate theory and higher-order methodology applicable to philosophical disputation. Things that are disputed in this context include the question of life's ultimate purpose, the nature of self and consciousness, reincarnation, the external world, God, karma, and other weighty topics.*

This chapter presents the Nyāya view of doubt, the conditions that give rise to it, and the school's program for doubt resolution. Such conditions include controversy, and of course philosophy thrives on controversies of a highly abstract nature. Details concerning controversies over issues of metaphysics will occupy us in later chapters. In this one, we shall see how Nyāya's philosophical method grows out of its pramāṇa *theory supplemented by a theory of reasoning called* tarka. *Gautama directs us to understand how second-order employment of the knowledge sources makes them methods of inquiry to be supplemented by rational refutations. This program is called "*nyāya,*" the school's technical term for philosophical method. That the word is made the label for the entire philosophy underscores the significance of the methodology. The word is also used for a formal presentation of an inference, "inference for another," and the* *double usage may be the reason that some people—according to Uddyotakara—claim that all certainty (*nirṇaya*) requires inference. Our philosophers deny this claim, however. Perception by itself can make for certainty. These matters are straightened out by our commentators. (For the Nyāya syllogism, i.e., a* nyāya *as a formal "inference for another," see Chapter 9 of this volume.)*

Our first topic is doubt, which for Nyāya is the catalyst for critical reflection and formal philosophical investigation.

1.1.23: Doubt is deliberative awareness in need of details about something particular. It is produced (1) from common properties being cognized, (2) from distinguishing properties being cognized, (3) from controversy, (4) from non-determination by experience, and (5) from non-determination by lack of experience.

Vātsyāyana [25.6–11]: "**Doubt is deliberative awareness in need of details about something particular, which is produced (1) from common properties being cognized.**" For example, a post and a person have properties in common. A subject who has experienced both post and person in the past sees something in the distance with a certain height and width and desires to know which it is. Wondering, "Is it the one or the other?" he is unable to decide. Such cognition, which does not provide definitive ascertainment, constitutes **doubt**. The subject experiences a property common to two things, but does not experience something distinct to either one. So the experience requires further information if he is to have knowledge. This provokes doubt. Thus **doubt is deliberative awareness in need of details about something particular**.

A second type results from **distinguishing properties being cognized**. . . .

The first kind of doubt is easy to understand from Vātsyāyana's comments, but the second is complicated. In short, Vātsyāyana says that while a special property may serve to distinguish something from other things, doubt may remain about the general kind to which it belongs. For example, an archaeologist could discover a stone tablet with a unique kind of script. The script, let us say, distinguishes the makers of the tablet from people in other ancient cultures, but given the uniqueness, doubt would remain about its larger cultural milieu and indeed how to read it.

Next is doubt due to controversy or disagreement.

Vātsyāyana [25.18–26.2]: "**From controversy**." **Controversy** amounts to conflicting views about a single thing or topic. To be in conflict is to be opposed, incompatible. One view is "There is a self (*ātman*)." Another is "There is not a self (*anātman*)." Furthermore, it is not possible that the thing could both exist and fail to exist at the same place. And no reason is found that would definitively prove the one side or the other. In such a situation, there is **doubt**, an absence of ascertainment of the truth.

Uddyotakara [91.16–18; 92.4–5]: "**Doubt . . . is produced from controversy**." The meaning of the word "**controversy**" is discussion where there are contradictory views. Doubt arises for a subject becoming acquainted with a topic under discussion when there are contradictory views—given that our subject knows something about the thing or topic of dispute and it is undecided whether the assertion or denial is correct. . . .

The cause of doubt that arises **from controversy** depends on there being speakers or advocates. "Which side is proposing the correct view and which is proposing the incorrect view?" Such doubt arises for someone listening to the dispute. This kind of doubt is thus mentioned separately from the first two because of this difference. (The first two need not stem from conflicting statements by other parties but can arise from a person's own perceptual uncertainty, for instance.)

In the translation above, we have represented the interpretation of Vātsyāyana, who takes the current sūtra to specify five separate kinds of doubt. However, Uddyotakara (and following him, Vācaspatimiśra) argues that there are only three, with the last two as descriptions applicable to every kind of doubt. Uddyotakara says that doubt always involves non-determination by either experience or non-experience. On his reading, the sūtra would be translated as follows: ***Doubt***

> ***is deliberative awareness in need of details about something particular. It is produced (1) from common properties being cognized, (2) from distinguishing properties being cognized, or (3) from controversy, all three of which are beset by non-determination from experience or lack of experience.*** *In our opinion, his reading is more compelling than Vātsyāyana's. What were understood as separate doubt-triggers by Vātsyāyana (4 and 5) are merely conditions that allow doubt to arise according to Uddyotakara. Doubt may be triggered by any of the conditions 1 through 3, and as long as there is "non-determination from experience or lack of experience" such doubt cannot be dismissed. For example, if two reasonable people disagree about the claim that the president is visiting our campus today, and I am not in a position to remove the doubt by either* seeing him (4) *or* seeing that he isn't there (5), *my doubt will continue.*
>
> *Next, Vācaspatimiśra dispels the presumption that doubt from controversy involves a second party directly at hand. No, it could be a matter of internalizing a dispute.*

Vācaspatimiśra [215.9–11]: Although the word "**controversy**" (*vipratipatti*) derives from a prefix meaning "conflicting" (*vi-*) and a noun meaning "understanding" (*pratipatti*) (such that we might think at least two persons are involved), Uddyotakara indicates that the so-called "discussion" could be internal to the person having the doubt, since it would not be possible if the proposing and opposing which generate doubt were entirely remote.

> *A stretch of sūtras at the beginning of* Nyāya-sūtra *chapter two is devoted to analysis of doubt and the resolution of certain philosophic worries about it. There the commentators stress that investigation is triggered by doubt. Vātsyāyana (commenting on 2.1.7) [57.18–58.2] notes that "Whether in pursuit of science or in debate, investigation is preceded by doubt. . ." and Vācaspatimiśra (commenting on 2.1.7) [314.4–7] agrees: "Every type of investigation is preceded by doubt. . . . When Vātsyāyana says, 'Whether in pursuit of science or in debate,' he means that kind of debate (*vāda*) whose purpose is to determine the truth, not that which is just for victory."*

We proceed now to sūtra 1.1.40, on tarka, *sometimes translated "philosophical reasoning." More precisely, it is a kind of hypothetical reasoning meant to draw out untoward consequences of an opponent's view, or to supplement the findings of knowledge sources used in support of one's own view. It results ideally in the resolution of controversy and in the production of reflective knowledge or higher-order certainty,* nirṇaya.

1.1.40: *Tarka* is reasoning that proceeds by considering what is consistent with knowledge sources, in order to know the truth about something that is not definitively known.

Vātsyāyana [36.6–37.10]: Desire to know arises, in the first instance, when the truth about something is not known. "This thing should be understood." And the thing being considered has two contrary properties attributed to it, such that one wavers, thinking, "Maybe it is this way, maybe not." Granting that there is a means to establish one of the two properties, he holds that there is a *pramāṇa* that would settle which is possible. One side is possible, given the evidence of knowledge sources, and not the other.

In the example that follows, "knower" is a general term for a conscious being. To say the knower is "produced" means that it is created when it is born in this life, and that there is no immortal self. To say it is "unproduced" means that there is an immortal self, which pre-exists birth and takes on a new body when born. The likely opponent in this passage is a Buddhist philosopher who holds that a conscious being does not endure the passage of time, and that there is a stream of conscious beings that are created and destroyed constantly within the life of a single person. Since classical Buddhists and Naiyāyikas both accept the law of karma, to prove that the Buddhist view would contradict it would be grounds for dismissing the Buddhist theory.

Here is an example. Someone is curious: "I would like to know the true nature of the knower who grasps the objects that are known." The consideration on her part would be:

"Is the knower something that has been produced or has not been produced?" And she grants that the knower that is under consideration does have a nature that could be found to be consistent with the findings of knowledge sources.

She thinks: "If the knower is unproduced, then one could experience the fruit of one's own action (karma in a previous birth accounting for one's lot of pain and happiness in this life). On this supposition, there could be both the cycle of birth and rebirth (*saṃsāra*) and final beatitude (*apavarga* = *mokṣa*, 'liberation') in that pain, rebirth, purposive action, vice, and wrong understanding, each of which is caused by the next item on the list, and done away with successively, such that final beatitude would ensue upon the last being removed. In contrast, if the knower is produced, then neither the cycle of rebirth nor liberation would be possible. Indeed, a knower who had been produced would be intrinsically tethered to a body, sense faculties, a mind along with its thoughts, and feelings, such that it would not be possible that one would be experiencing in this life the fruit of his actions in a previous lifetime. And having been produced, one would not endure, such that he could not enjoy the fruit of action done by himself previously, as such karma would either be non-existent or destroyed. So in this way a single being could not maintain a connection with a plurality of bodies over time, nor could there be an ultimate disconnection in the form of liberation."

By reasoning suppositionally like this, one would come to see that no explanation consistent with knowledge sources is possible for the view that the self is produced, which she would then not accept. This sort of reasoning is *tarka*. . . .

Objection: Why is it said that *tarka* is aimed at the truth, but that it doesn't directly produce true cognition?

Answer: Because it doesn't produce definitive knowledge of something's positive nature. It provides grounds for approval by illustrating that one of the competing properties being considered is consistent with knowledge sources. By itself, it does not provide definitive knowledge of something's positive nature, settling it or making it certain: "This thing has such a nature."

Objection: How is *tarka* even *aimed* at the truth?

Answer: As we have characterized it, this lucid process of reasoning suggests that something is consistent with knowledge of the truth, and it is then followed by knowledge of the truth, as supported by some knowledge source. In this way, *tarka* is aimed at knowledge of the truth.

Tarka presupposes the knowledge sources in that its method is to suppose that there is a source. It is sanctioned for use in debates aimed at the truth (*vāda*) as an auxiliary to the citation of knowledge sources.

In the statement of the sūtra, "**when the truth about something is not definitively known**," the mention of "truth" amounts to something's being understood as it is, known without falsity, in accord with its reality.

And while on the topic of *tarka* (we have the next item in the first sūtra's list of topics):

1.1.41: Certainty (*nirṇaya*) is determination of something through deliberation about alternatives, by investigation of theses and countertheses.

Vātsyāyana [37.12–38.15]: To establish something is to prove it. To rule something out is to refute it. These two, proof and refutation, depend upon theses and countertheses. The two are called theses and countertheses because they work interrelatedly, connectedly. For, dismissal of one or the other of the two unavoidably amounts to substantiating the opposite, as that would be entailed. ***Nirṇaya*, certainty**, is the substantiation of a view such that its topic is definitively settled. . . .

The words in the sūtra "**through deliberation**" mean "having engaged in deliberation." Such deliberation makes clear the thesis and counterthesis, and initiates *nyāya* ("philosophical method"). For this reason, it is mentioned in the sūtra. And **deliberation** may be understood as recognizing the attribution of two opposed properties or natures—both of them—to a single property-bearer. . . .

There is no rule, however, that the definitive ascertainment which constitutes **certainty** must follow from deliberation about a thesis and a counterthesis. Why so? Determination of an object's nature, which is certainty, can also arise perceptually by the functioning of the sense faculties upon their objects. But in the context of careful, expert investigation, certainty consists in definitive determination of an object through consideration of theses and countertheses. . . .

Uddyotakara [136.21–137.3]: Some claim that certainty amounts to inference, describing it as nothing more. We deny this. For, inference depends crucially on the relationship between the inferential mark and that which it marks, whereas that relationship is absent in some cases of certainty—which can arise from any knowledge source.

Furthermore, inference is a *pramāṇa,* a source or cause of knowledge, whereas certainty is the result or product. Certainty has its own specific content and nothing more, whereas inference involves both immediate content (smoke) and content directed to something else (fire). For example, when seeing smoke, insofar as one's perception precisely determines that it is smoke in view, such is a bit of certainty, not an inference at all. And when one uses such precisely determined smoke to then infer that there is fire, that would be is a case of inference. . . .

Vācaspatimiśra [268.15–19]: If we were to say that inference was nothing more than certainty, then it would never at all depend on memory of the relationship between the mark and marked (and that is false). Conversely, if certainty amounted to reflection on an inferential mark as described, then it would depend on memory of the relationship between the mark and marked (and it does not, at least not when produced by other knowledge sources such as perception).

As seen above, sūtra 1.1.41 provides a definition of nirṇaya, *"certainty," which is prototypically the result of careful, reasoned examination of both sides of a dispute. Such examination is reputed to be far and away the dominant procedure by which philosophical positions are arrived at throughout the* Nyāya-sūtra *and indeed in other schools. But by suggesting that certainty may be produced by perception, the commentators assert an empiricism and a commitment to perception as the most basic knowledge source, in that at least normally perceptual evidence is all that is needed to decide a dispute. In such cases, knowledge of even the highest grade need not be justified through argument.*

*Doubt is viewed as the main catalyst for cognitive review and critical reasoning, as it triggers a second-order concern that may be called reflective inquiry or attempted certification. With this in mind, Uddyotakara claims that doubt is an essential component of investigation: "While there is no rule that doubt must precede certainty (*nirṇaya*), it must precede investigation" (2.1.1). Vātsyāyana notes that self-conscious reasoning is not directed to unknown things nor to things ascertained definitively, but to things that are apprehended in an uncertain way (1.1.1). The later commentators point to his multiple mentions of doubt in his comments on sūtra 1.1.1 as underscoring the position that it is doubt that sparks inquiry.*

In that opening stretch of commentary, Vātsyāyana also provides a vision of Nyāya's philosophical methodology in a nutshell:

Vātsyāyana (under sūtra 1.1.1) [3.11–14]: What then is *nyāya*? It is examination of an object or topic by means of knowledge sources. And it is especially the use of inference based on perception and testimony. It is critical review (*ānvīkṣā*)—in other words, reflective investigation into something already cognized through perception or testimony. Since it proceeds in this way, as *subsequent* investigation into the findings of perception and testimony, it is understood to be critical examination. It is the science of demonstration, of systematic study. However, an inference that is contradicted by perception or testimony is illegitimate, a mere pseudo-demonstration.

*As mentioned, the word "*nyāya*" is also used for a formal inference, but here Vātsyāyana uses it for philosophical method as a whole, which includes* tarka, *"suppositional reasoning." Thus philosophy flows out of the findings of* pramāṇas *supplemented by reasoning. The findings of* pramāṇas *have to be put together, however. They have to interlock into a coherent system of generalized truths. In other words, the* knowledge sources *provide planks for one's science or theory. These planks are called* siddhānta, *"accepted* *positions," but only so long as they fit well with other accepted views. This is brought out by Vātsyāyana in a stretch of sūtras about* siddhānta, *another of Nyāya's core topics.*

Vātsyāyana [27.12–30.2]: Next, accepted position is considered. Something accepted is something objective that has been recognized to be true, "This is of such and such a nature." Something that has been accepted, which is deemed important, becomes a "stable view." It is called *siddhānta.* A stable view that settles something as being such and such is a fixed determination of its properties. Thus we have the following.

1.1.26: From a system of thought, from a topic, and from a supposition, the stable view that emerges is an accepted position (*siddhānta*).

Vātsyāyana: A stable view **from a system of thought** (*tantra*) is a stable view about something within a system. An example is a scientific text (*śāstra*) that teaches a collection of things as mutually bound up together into a coherent system. A stable view **from a topic** is a stable view about something implicated in a topic. A stable view **from a supposition** is a matter of conceiving a view about something not previously ascertained. An accepted position emerging from a supposition is for the purpose of close examination of details about something.

But because of differences among systems, the sūtra-maker says the following.

1.1.27: There are four types of accepted position (*siddhānta*) because of the differences among stable views: (1) accepted in all systems, (2) accepted in a single system, (3) accepted from a topic, and (4) accepted on the basis of a supposition.

Vātsyāyana: . . . Of these:

1.1.28: A position accepted in all systems is something that is accepted within at least one system while not being opposed in any other system.

Vātsyāyana: For example: "The sense organs are the olfactory and the rest." "Smells, tastes, etc. are objects of the sense organs." "Earth and the rest are material elements."

"Apprehension of something arises by means of knowledge sources."

1.1.29: A position accepted in a single system is accepted by one school of thought but not others.

Vātsyāyana: For example, on the part of adherents to the Sāṃkhya system, there is the following. "The non-existent does not come into existence." "The existent does not fall into non-existence." "Conscious beings are not different in kind." "Distinctness holds only regarding bodies, sense organs, minds, their objects, and their causes."

And on the part of adherents to Nyāya we have the following. "The creation of the world is caused by such factors as people's karma." "Vices give rise to karma." "And (so) there is activity." "Conscious beings are distinguished by their own peculiar qualities." "Something non-existent can come into existence." "Something produced can be destroyed."

*In the above comparison between Sāṃkhya and Nyāya, a central contrast involves causation. Sāṃkhya holds that creation does not bring anything new into existence but rather only that which exists already in a potential form within primordial matter (*prakṛti*). This is called* sat-kārya-vāda *(the doctrine of the pre-existence of what is created). Likewise, it holds that nothing is ever really destroyed. Nyāya champions the opposite view,* asat-kārya-vāda, *which holds that creation brings new things into existence and that created things are indeed destroyed. This theory of causation will be discussed at length in Chapter 5, "Substance and Causation."*

1.1.30: When one thing is accepted because it is entailed by something else that has been established, it is a "position accepted from a topic."

Vātsyāyana [29.7–11]: When something, some expressible fact, has been accepted, other things come along as presupposed. Without them, this fact, would not be accepted. They are then things that are based on it. Any of presuppositions would then be a **position accepted from a topic**.

For example, there is the inference, "The knowing subject is distinct from the body and the sense organs, *since* there is apprehension of a single thing simultaneously through the organs of sight and touch."[1] Here, things that are presupposed include (a) other objects, (b) differences among the sense organs, (c) the sense organs' having each its own type of phenomenal object (the eyes have visible forms, while the faculty of touch has tactile objects, for instance), (d) the senses being uniquely characterized by their apprehension of their several proper objects, (e) their being instruments of knowledge for a knower, (f) that a substance is distinct from qualities such as smells, (g) that a substance is the locus or substratum of qualities, and (h) that conscious beings are not likewise restricted concerning the nature of their objects (*viṣaya*). When the prior thing is accepted, these other things are accepted too. Without them this thing could not be true.

Here we have an important inference that is restated and elaborated in detail by our commentators in Nyāya-sūtra *chapter three and in this volume in Chapter 4, "Self." The point now is that while the existence of the self is what the inference proves, many other propositions considered systematically are accepted as presupposed, including some about other objects and facts about the sense faculties. In current philosophical language, such things are necessary conditions that are required for the conclusion of the inference to be true. Therefore, accepting the latter demands acceptance of the former.*

1.1.31: When, for the sake of careful examination of the details of a view, there is the suppositional acceptance of something that has not yet been examined closely, this is a position accepted on the basis of supposition.

Vātsyāyana [29.15–30.2]: Something objective, which has not been examined closely, is provisionally accepted. For example, let it be assumed that sound is a substance. But is it permanent or impermanent? Then as a substance, whether it is permanent or impermanent gets closely examined down to **the details**. Such is **a position accepted on the basis of a**

1 *Nyāya-sūtra* 3.1.1.

supposition. One proceeds thereby to make known the excellence of one's own thesis and to condemn the thesis of another.

Accepted positions are thus the solid building blocks of a school's entire system of thought, and as the core tenets of a tradition of thought, they serve to structure philosophical investigation and disputation.

For the final installment of this chapter on certification and philosophical methodology, we again turn to what the classical commentators take to be a challenge by Mādhyamika Buddhists (modern scholars, in contrast, disagree about who the opponent is that Gautama may have had in mind). Here, the opponent puts forth a challenge to the pramāṇa *epistemology as a whole. The stretch of sūtras, 2.1.16–20, contains one of Nyāya's most important anti-skeptical arguments. It ranks alongside the defense of the reality of the world found in Chapter 3, "In Defense of the Real," in this volume, and a response to "destructive debate" found in Chapter 9, "Debate." Here, Nyāya must answer the charge that it faces a regress of justification: any attempt to justify our knowledge of* pramāṇas *would rely on further pramāṇas, ad infinitum. We may note that sūtras 2.1.17–19 have clear parallels in Nāgārjuna's* Vigrahavyāvartinī (Refuting the Arguments) *verses 31–33.*

The discussion begins with the question of how we can know the pramāṇas *themselves. Vātsyāyana argues that the correct methodology here is first to identify instances of cognitive success and then to theorize about what sorts of processes or conditions give rise to them. Earlier in his commentary (sūtra 2.1.11 [59.13]), he expresses the idea as follows: "Since there is no rule about the exact way that knowledge sources and their objects are connected . . . we identify the ways they are connected through reflection upon common experience." Commenting on 2.1.16, he expands on the idea by pointing out that knowledge sources can themselves be objects of knowledge, should we choose to reflect on them. A skeptical challenger argues that this leads to a dilemma: We would either have an infinite regress where* pramāṇa-*token*$_2$ *is used to justify* pramāṇa-*token*$_1$, pramāṇa-*token*$_3$ *is used to justify* pramāṇa-*token*$_2$, *and so on, or one must try to stop the regress with a mere assumption that one has knowledge without proof.*

Vātsyāyana [62.17–63.2]: The technical terms "knowledge source" and "object of knowledge" may refer to the same thing according to the occasion for use of the terms. The occasion for using the term "knowledge source" is when something is a means of knowledge. The occasion for using the term "object of knowledge" is when something is an object of knowledge. And thus a single object may be called *pramāṇa* or *prameya* (object of knowledge) according to whether it is a means of knowledge or an object of knowledge from a particular point of view. The following sūtra is meant to illustrate the point.

2.1.16: And knowledge sources may be objects of knowledge, like a measuring scale.

Vātsyāyana [63.4–64.12]: A scale is a source of knowledge, as it produces knowledge of something's measurement of weight. Things with weight, such as bits of gold, are then the objects of knowledge, the things known. But when a second scale is calibrated by using gold already weighed, the gold is the knowledge source, producing knowledge about the second scale, and the second scale would be the thing known. . . .

Objection: Fine. Let's accept the following: A single thing can be referred to by words indicating its different functions according to the occasion of use, that is, whether the thing is talked about as an object, an instrument, a location, and so forth. And perception and the rest are sources of knowledge insofar as they are causes of knowledge, and they are objects of knowledge insofar as they are the content of knowledge. Moreover, that they are commonly known as such is illustrated by statements such as, "It is by perception that I know it," "It is by inference that I know it," "It is by analogy that I know it," "It is by testimony that I know it," and "My knowledge is perceptual," "My knowledge is inferential," "My knowledge is analogical," "My knowledge is testimonial." Then they are grasped in individual instances.

Furthermore, we understand them in specific ways through technical analyses, like the definition of perceptual knowledge (at *Nyāya-sūtra* 1.1.4), "**knowledge that arises from a connection of a sense faculty with an object**." But regarding the knowledge that takes perception and the rest as its object: (a) Would it be established by another *pramāṇa*, or (b) would it not be established by another *pramāṇa*?

Response: What is the difference between these alternatives?

2.1.17: (Objector:) On the view (a) that knowledge sources are themselves established by knowledge sources, the unwanted consequence would be that still other knowledge sources would have to be proved.

Vātsyāyana [64.15–19]: (The objector continues:) If perception and the rest are themselves known through knowledge sources, then that by which they are known would have to be a different knowledge source, implicating, as an unwanted consequence, the existence of still further knowledge sources. The sūtra-maker is talking about an infinite regress: "This is known by another, which also is known by another, and so on." But such a regress would be unacceptable, because that is not a coherent possibility.

What if instead we accept that a *pramāṇa* need not be established by another?

2.1.18: (Objector:) Or if we say (b) one *pramāṇa* need not be established by another, then, in the same way, we should accept objects without reasons.

Vātsyāyana [65.2–3]: (The objector continues:) If we can claim knowledge of perception and the rest without having to admit further knowledge sources, then we can do the same for supposed objects of knowledge such as a self. There is no relevant distinction between the two.

Now since the very notion of a knowledge source would thus be undermined, the sūtra-maker says next:

2.1.19: (Answer:) No, *pramāṇas* are established like the light of a lamp.

Vātsyāyana [65.7–10]: For example, the light of a lamp can be a knowledge source as part of the process of perception when something visible is apprehended by sight, while it itself would be known through another instance of perception through its connection with the visual organ. That the lamp is a cause of perception is also known through inference, since our ability to see or not conforms to its presence or absence. We could also know it through the statement of an authority, "In the darkness, use a lamp." In the same way, there is knowledge of perception and the rest just by other instances of perception and the others, as the case may be.

The "lamp" analogy seems naturally to support a foundationalist *response to the problem of regress: in the very act of illuminating other things, light—similarly knowledge—makes itself known without requiring yet another source of illumination. But this is not how Vātsyāyana understands the matter. A Mīmāṃsaka or Vedāntin or indeed a Yogācāra Buddhist—opposed to Nyāya's view of "certification by another,"* parataḥ prāmāṇya*—might use the lamp example to illustrate a view of "self-certification,"* svataḥ prāmāṇya, *a kind of self-justification for the knowledge sources. Thus our knowledge of them would be the foundation of all the rest of our knowledge. According to this idea, knowledge sources generate knowledge of themselves as they generate knowledge of their objects. This would effectively be a third option, "self-justification," passing through the horns of the skeptical dilemma: there would be no need for another knowledge source, nor would there be postulation without proof. But in his comments, Vātsyāyana interprets the lamp analogy in a way that underscores the fact that* pramāṇas *support one another. This resonates with a modern family of views called* coherentism, *which holds that interlocking consistency within one's belief system is what provides justification for any particular belief. It is not that some foundational beliefs are justifiers while others are dependent and justified. Rather, they are all interdependent; the beliefs generated by* pramāṇas *can be employed by us in different ways, as justifier or justified, according to circumstances. By reading the sūtra in this way, Vātsyāyana sets a distinct trajectory for subsequent Nyāya epistemology.*

Rejecting self-certification as what the sūtra-maker meant with the lamp analogy, our commentator now takes up the Mādhyamika charge of infinite regress.

2.1.20: Sometimes we find that no further source is required, while sometimes we find that another source is required. There is no fixed rule.

Vātsyāyana [67.10–16]: . . . (The objector has claimed:) "If perception and other knowledge sources are made known by other perceptions and so on, then you face an infinite regress (which undermines your entire theory)." We say that this is wrong. If knowledge of perception or of another knowledge source as a source landed us in infinite regress, then everyday action and discourse would not go on with respect to certifiably known things and the knowledge sources that support them. However, everyday action and discourse do proceed for someone comprehending known things and their identifiable knowledge sources: When I grasp an object by perception or by inference or by analogy or by testimony, the certificational cognition that occurs goes like this: "My knowledge is perceptual," or "My knowledge is inferential," or "My knowledge is from analogy," or "My knowledge is testimonial."

And motivation to seek righteousness (*dharma*), wealth, pleasure, and liberation proceeds through these comprehensions, as likewise motivation to reject what is opposed to them (whereas if there were still doubt, no such goal-directed activity would occur). Such discourse and action would cease to be possible if the alleged regress were indeed to occur. And it is not the case that there is action and discourse other than this that would land us in infinite regress whereby the alleged lack of a stopping point would really occur.

To summarize the Nyāya epistemology, we may say that Gautama and Vātsyāyana begin by looking for kinds of processes that generate knowledge, identifying four irreducible pramāṇa *types: perception, inference, analogy, and testimony. These produce knowledge automatically, without a need for conscious reflection or oversight. But when legitimate doubt or controversy arises, a responsible epistemic agent typically shifts to careful sorting through the evidence to adjudicate the status of belief, what we have called "certification."*

Certification involves the various pramāṇas *working together to produce a web of interlocking beliefs, some of which are certified, where we know that we know certain truths.*

In response to the challenge to the whole of the Nyāya approach, which alleges that the theory is beset by an infinite "certification" regress, Nyāya argues that we trust cognition that is apparently true. This trust is supported on pragmatic grounds. We rely on knowledge sources to guide us in our practical pursuits, and with especially important pursuits we do so self-consciously, Vātsyāyana stresses. Our need to act requires us to trust cognition if there aren't good reasons to doubt, or else we would hardly achieve anything. Then if there is reason to doubt, we look to other knowledge sources for support, and such certification can restore confidence and return us to default trust. This trust is demanded on pragmatic grounds. Here, we may say that Nyāya has a foundationalist *element to its epistemology, in that such default trust serves as a basis for thought and action that is secure, so long as there are no good grounds for doubt. But it is a "soft" foundation, always reviewable and revisable in principle, should the need arise.*

Chapter 3, "In Defense of the Real," will bring up other reasons in support of default trust in cognition, reasons that underpin Nyāya's realism.

Suggestions for Further Reading

Sitansusekhar Bagchi, *Inductive Reasoning: A Study of* Tarka *and Its Role in Indian Logic*. Calcutta: Munishchandra Sinha, 1953.

Piotr Balcerowicz, "When Yoga Is Not Yoga: The Nyāya-Vaiśeṣika Tradition and the *Artha-śāstra*." In *World View and Theory in Indian Philosophy*, ed. Piotr Balcerowicz, pp. 173–245. Delhi: Manohar, 2012.

Matthew Dasti, "Vātsyāyana: Cognition as a Guide to Action," *Oxford Handbook of Indian Philosophy*, ed. Jonardon Ganeri. New York: Oxford University Press, 2017.

Nirmalya Guha, "Tarka as Cognitive Validator." *Journal of Indian Philosophy* 40.1 (2012): 47–66.

J. N. Mohanty, "The Nyāya Theory of Doubt." *Visva Bharati Journal of Philosophy* 3 (1965): 15–35.

Stephen Phillips, *Epistemology in Classical India: The Knowledge Sources of the Nyāya School*. New York: Routledge, 2012.

Karin Preisendanz, "Debate and Independent Reasoning vs. Tradition: On the Precarious Position of Early Nyāya." In *Harānandalararī: Volume in Honour of Professor Minoru Hara on His Seventieth Birthday*, eds. R. Tsuchida and A. Wezler, pp. 221–51. Reinbek: Inge Wezler, 2000.

Mark Siderits, "The Madhyamaka Critique of Epistemology I." *Journal of Indian Philosophy* 8 (1980): 307–35.

Study Questions

1. What are the major ways that doubt arises according to Nyāya?
2. Explain the idea that for Nyāya our default attitude is to trust apparently true cognition, and to shift to reflective analysis when doubt arises.
3. What is *tarka*? How does it function? Why is it called an assistant to the *pramāṇas* but not a full-fledged knowledge source itself?
4. Provide your own example of *tarka* resolving a disputed issue.
5. What is the difference between certainty (*nirṇaya*) and mere belief? And what does it mean to say that certainty is not always inferential?
6. What are the four kinds of "accepted positions"?
7. What is the skeptical dilemma considered in *Nyāya-sūtra* 2.1.18–20?

8. What is Nyāya's response to the problem of skeptical regress? In this regard, what does it mean to say that we have pragmatic grounds to trust apparently true cognition?

9. What are *foundationalism* and *coherentism* as approaches to epistemological justification? Identify both foundationalist and coherentist elements in Nyāya's approach to knowledge and justification.

Chapter 3

In Defense of the Real

Nyāya is one of classical India's most stalwart proponents of philosophical realism. Realism is the view that certain features of reality (e.g., external objects, selves, universals) exist independently of consciousness. Where an anti-realist or idealist would claim that something we take to be real is rather a product of our own mental projection or our conceptual or linguistic conditioning, the realist would argue that it is a genuine part of the furniture of reality irrespective of our participation. Realists need not accept that everything we encounter in the world is real; indeed, Nyāya recognizes various things like illusory perceptual states where what we apparently see in the world has to do with our own state of mind. But it does hold that much of the world as we experience it consists in mind-independent realities that may be categorized according to certain fundamental types. In Chapters 4 through 6, we will examine specific elements of Nyāya's realist metaphysics: self, God, substances, and causation. In this chapter, we reflect on Nyāya's defense of realism in general.

In Indian philosophy, opposition to realism has been closely associated with two schools of Buddhism, a skeptical tradition that follows Nāgārjuna (c. 200 CE) and a phenomenalist and idealist school inaugurated by Vasubandhu (c. 350 CE). Vasubandhu's tradition, whose key figures include Dignāga (c. 480 CE) and Dharmakīrti (c. 525 CE), is spoken of within Nyāya as vijñāna-vāda, *"the view that there is only consciousness." Various opponents presented in the* Nyāya-sūtra *resonate with the thought of Buddhist thinkers, and, indeed, both of the Buddhist schools are explicitly identified by Vācaspatimiśra in the section covered in this chapter,* Nyāya-sūtra *4.2.26–37. Probably, however, Gautama, the sūtra-maker, was familiar not so much with these specific Buddhist schools but with broad ideas under the banner of* śūnya-vāda, *"the view that all is empty," which connects with the Buddha's teaching of* nirvāna *as the supreme good.*

*We have seen that a skeptical-regress objection (*Nyāya-sūtra *2.1.17–18) has close affinities to Nāgārjuna's attack on* pramāṇa *epistemology in his work entitled* Refuting the Arguments. *In* Nyāya-sūtra *4.1.37–40, a view is presented that is also akin to Nāgārjuna's notion of emptiness (*śūnyatā*), as an objector claims that "**everything is devoid of genuine existence, because we can establish things' mutual non-existence**" (4.1.37) and "**everything's own nature is established as dependent on other things**" (4.1.39). In our selections here, we find an opponent who argues that worldly objects are akin to objects experienced in dreams and therefore lack genuine reality. In commentary on 4.2.35, Vātsyāyana characterizes the challenger as holding that nothing is real and that there is no true nature to things. These views may be characterized as anti-realism and skepticism of decidedly Buddhist varieties.*

Nyāya responds by defending what we may call a baseline realism, the view that at least some features of the world are real. This is supported by a parasitism thesis. Error is said to be parasitical upon knowledge. To claim that error exists presupposes there are things known to be true, just as not all coins could be counterfeit. Real coins must exist to provide the standard for what is genuine. Because of this argument, global skeptics and anti-realists are said to have contradictory or self-defeating positions.

Our first selection comes after a discussion of mereology *(the area of philosophy concerned with the part-whole relation, 4.2.4–17) and the existence of atoms (4.2.18–25), where a challenger puts pressure on Nyāya's conception of material objects. The conversation has two major sections. The first focuses on the reality of specific types of object, and the second on the reality of the entire world. The scope of the conversation changes after Gautama and company appeal to the evidence of* pramāṇas. *At that point, the challenger seeks to undercut* pramāṇa *epistemology entirely by comparing the world to a dream.*

Immediately below, the challenger argues in a way that resonates with Buddhist positions. He claims that we cannot separate the objects of cognition from cognition itself. Therefore, we shouldn't hold that external objects are mind-independent.

4.2.26: (Opponent:) But when we examine things closely through cognition, we do not find true objects, just as we do not find a cloth when we distinguish the threads.

Vātsyāyana [271.8–10]: (Opponent:) When a bunch of threads are closely examined—"Here is this thread," "Here is that thread"—through cognition of them one by one, nothing over and above these is found that is cognized as a cloth. Since we do not find real objects, there is no awareness of truth, and the cognition of a cloth is an error. This holds for everything.

Uddyotakara [487.9–12]: (Opponent:) . . . In this way, parts may be closely examined as they occur in cognition, and the parts of the parts, all the way down to atoms. And even atoms can be conceptually divided portion by portion such that whatever is identified dissolves. Thus, because in this way nothing exists, cognitions of such things as cows and pots too are errors.

4.2.27: (Answer:) That is not a reason, since it is self-defeating.

Vātsyāyana [271.13–15]: When we closely examine things, it is not that we fail to find any truth about them. Conversely, if we fail to find any truth about any of them, we have not examined them closely. The sūtra-maker has already rejected the view that we fail to find any truth about anything when we examine things closely, when he said (at *Nyāya-sūtra* 4.2.15): **"And the unwanted consequence of such part-whole analysis is that in that way all these things would dissolve."**

Vātsyāyana argues that "to examine objects carefully" as implored by the opponent would be to try to apprehend their true nature. To deny that it is possible would be to say that "careful examination" is impossible too, since the goal of careful examination is to discover the truth. The opponent's argument is thus incoherent, as Gautama says in the sūtra cited. A similar idea is found at Nyāya-sūtra *4.1.37, in response to a proto-Mādhyamika claim that "all is void"* (sarva-abhāvaḥ).

The next sūtra also focuses on the part-whole relationship, called "mereology" in contemporary philosophy. More general rebuttals follow.

4.2.28: (Answer continued:) Objects are experienced as unified, because a whole inheres in its parts.

Uddyotakara [488.6–8]: Substances that are effects are not perceived separately from the causes in which they inhere (as the cloth is not seen separately from the threads in which it inheres). For, when something is grasped as separate, this relationship does not exist. That is to say, two substances can be grasped as separate only when they do not stand in the relationship of one inhering in the other.

"Substances that are effects" are composite substances that are built up out of smaller parts, such as a piece of cloth that is made up of threads. Their parts are their cause in the sense of "material cause"—or, more precisely according to Nyāya, "inherence cause"—the substrata or stuff out of which the composite substance is composed and in which the composite substance inheres. Uddyotakara is thus arguing that there is a good explanation for the fact that a cloth is not separable from its threads, but this does not mean we should deflate the reality of a cloth to that of the threads. The whole is more than the sum of its parts. Composite substances will be discussed at length in Chapter 5, "Substance and Causation."

4.2.29: (Answer continued:) Your argument also fails because objects are established through knowledge sources.

Vātsyāyana [272.9–13]: We find out the truth about things by **examining them closely through cognition**: "Such and such exists," and "It has a certain character"; "Such and such does not exist," and "It does not have a certain character." All of these findings are established through *pramāṇa*-generated knowledge. This knowledge is what is meant by "**close examination of objects through cognition**." All sciences, all activities, and the conventional speech and practices of all living beings depend on the findings of knowledge sources. For things are determined, "This is the case" or "This is not the case," after they have been investigated through cognition. In the course of such investigation, we do not find that things cannot be explained.

4.2.30: (Answer continued:) And because of the possibility and impossibility of knowledge sources (*pramāṇa*).

Vātsyāyana [272.16–273.3]: And, accordingly, there is no possibility of the thesis, "Nothing exists." "Why?" It's wrong **because of the possibility and impossibility of knowledge sources**. If the thesis, "Nothing exists," were supported by a *pramāṇa,* then that *pramāṇa* would contradict the claim, "Nothing exists." But on the second option, if there were no *pramāṇa* in support, then how would the thesis, "Nothing exists," be proved? If the proof were to be by another *pramāṇa,* then why wouldn't this establish the thesis, "Everything exists"?

Vātsyāyana's last remark is not to be taken as an assertion that everything exists, but rather as the dialectical point that if we are allowed to invent a new pramāṇa *when it suits our purposes, then we could prove anything and indeed prove the very opposite of the Buddhist thesis. This is a textbook example of* tarka, *suppositional reasoning, as discussed in Chapter 2, "Doubt and Philosophical Method."*

With the next sūtra of the section, we are treated to a famous dream argument. After Gautama invokes pramāṇas *in support of accepting some things as real, he has an objector try to undermine his epistemology in a single stroke. How can we be sure that ordinary life is not like a dream? Or, as the sūtra after that suggests, it could all be like a perceptual illusion, a mirage. Nyāya's answers follow in a set of five sūtras and ideas that articulate the core of the school's commitment to realism.*

4.2.31: (Opponent:) Your conception of things known through knowledge sources is akin to conceptions of objects encountered in dreams.

Vātsyāyana [273.6–7]: (Opponent:) In dreams there are no real objects of cognition but there are conceptions of them as real. In the same way, there are no real knowledge sources or objects of knowledge, although we do have conceptions of them as real.

4.2.32: (Opponent continued:) Or, it's like magic, cities of Gandharvas (castles in the sky), or a mirage.

Vācaspatimiśra [624.12–15]: Objection: Let it be granted that presentations and experiences in dreams have a certain dream character. Now, should it be taken for granted that what we experience when awake, such as "It's a pillar" or "It's a wall," is of an entirely different sort? Thus the opponent says, "**Or, it's like magic, cities of Gandharvas, or a mirage**." In thousands of cases, waking presentations and experiences are seen to be similar in character to such error. And therefore the presentations we have of columns and walls are not different.

A common response to the dream argument is to remind the skeptic that dreams are neither as vivid nor as consistent and coherent as waking experiences. The challenger, as imagined by Vācaspatimiśra, accordingly supports the dream analogy by pointing to mirages and other illusions as additional ways we get things wrong. These have the vividness of waking experience and yet mislead us all the same. They are also sometimes consistent across perceivers' experience and coherent with other things we presume to know. A city of Gandharvas is the Indian equivalent of a castle in the sky, a cloud formation in the distance that looks like a castle or a city. And it is not just on a single occasion that we seem to see such things.

4.2.33: (Answer:) This is unproven, because you haven't provided a reason to accept it.

Vātsyāyana [273.12–274.6]: Your assertion—that knowledge of objects in the waking state along with **the conception of things through knowledge sources is akin to conceptions**

of objects in the dream state—is **unproven because you haven't provided a reason to accept it**. That is to say, no good reason appears in support of your claim. Furthermore, you have given us no reason to accept that objects experienced in the dream state do not themselves exist.

Opponent: The reason is that upon awakening we no longer see them.

Response: On your view, one has no resources to deny the reality of dream objects by comparison with the objects of waking experience. If dream objects do not exist because they are not experienced upon awakening, then those very objects we find in waking life must exist, as they are in fact experienced. Your reasoning supports the opposite of what you claim. Non-experience of something can prove that it is absent only when positive experience of it can prove that it exists. But if nothing is true in either case, then not having an experience of something could not be evidence for its absence in the way that an absence of a lamp prevents one from seeing visible objects. Here, determining an absence—the absence of visible objects—depends upon a presence, the presence of visible objects that do in fact exist.

Vātsyāyana begins his core response to the skeptical challenger by arguing that unless we admit that some things are real, we lose all basis for claiming anything is not real. Knowledge of an absence of something depends upon what our experience would be like if it were present. I don't expect to find my glasses in the dark, but I know what it would be like to find them. I can know that they are right there on the table and that my not seeing them is due to the darkness. Similarly, if I can say that something is unreal, I have to know what it would be like for it to be real. If everything were unreal, we'd be unable to distinguish between truth and error.

Vātsyāyana continues now by arguing for another realist consideration: dreams and illusions are produced through discernible causal mechanisms.

Vātsyāyana [274.7–10]: Furthermore, you should provide a reason for the variety of things found in the dream state. That is, since you accept that there are **conceptions of**

objects in dreams, you should identify the cause for such a variety of dream states. Some dreams are fearful; others joyful. Some are the opposite of both. And at other times we sleep without experiencing any dream whatsoever. But if it is admitted that **conceptions of objects in dreams** have causes, then it should be that the variety is explained as due to the variety in the causes.

> *Even if dreams are themselves fictitious, they depend upon real causes. It's not that everything can be false.*
>
> *Next, Vātsyāyana reiterates the point that our ability to recognize the unreality of dream objects depends on our being able to contrast them with objects we know in the waking state. If all we had were dreams, then we'd be in no position to claim that their objects did not exist. And if the very distinction between reality and unreality is undermined, we'd have no basis to claim dreams present things that are unreal.*
>
> *Following this, we are treated to another motivation for realism: illusion and all cognitive error depends, like dreaming, on previous inputs. Dreams and errors take things we've experienced as preserved in memory and project them into situations where they don't actually exist. I see something resembling my friend Mike in a dream (which in the dream I take to be Mike), because I project memories of Mike I've gained from real-life experiences into the dream state. Error thus requires veridical cognition, which provides the raw materials for false cognition. Error states involve misplacement, projecting something where it isn't. Thus they depend upon encounters with real things. In the terms of a stock example, one could not project the idea of a person on a post that is misperceived in the distance (thinking, "It's a person" when it's really a post) unless one had experienced persons in the past.*

4.2.34: And our conception of objects in dreams is like memory and imagination.

Vātsyāyana [274.13–275.6]: Their content comes from previous experience. The objects of memory and imagination are supplied by previous experience such that the two cannot be used to deny their objects' existence. The same holds in the case of dreams. Experience of objects in dreams is dependent on things experienced earlier. Dreams cannot be used to deny the things' existence. In this way, a visible object encountered in the dream state is furnished by the waking state.

The person who when asleep dreams of certain things is the one who recognizes them once awake, thinking, "I saw this." Conceptions of objects in dreams are determined to be false because of the character of waking experience. And when one recognizes a dream object, the conception of the object in the dream is determined to be false by the character of some specific waking experience.

But even if the two states weren't different, your argument would not establish anything. If you find no distinction between dreaming and waking states, then your claim that knowledge sources and their objects are **akin to conception of objects in dreams** would have no probative force, since you've rejected the very foundation of your argument.

Furthermore, the erroneous determination of an object as something it is not depends on a precondition. For example, the determination, "That's a person," when the thing is not a person but a post, has as precondition of the concept "person" (acquired from previous experience of persons). In this way, determinations of dream objects in the form "I saw an elephant" or "I saw a mountain" become possible by depending on a precondition (of earlier experiences of elephants or mountains).

And this being the case:

4.2.35: The destruction of a false perception results from knowledge of the truth of things, akin to the destruction of conceptions of dream objects upon waking.

Vātsyāyana [275.9–276.3]: The determination "That's a person" when the object in view is a post is a false perception. It is a cognition of an object as something it is not. Determination of a post as a post is knowledge of the truth about the thing. And by such knowledge of the truth, the false perception is removed, but not the real object, which has characteristics that are common to both persons and posts. Similarly, cognitions of **magic, cities of Gandharvas (castles in the**

sky), or a mirage, are determinations of an object as something it is not. Here, too, according to the same principle, destruction of a false perception results from knowledge of the truth about things. However, the existence of the actual thing is not to be denied.

Furthermore, false cognition in magic and the rest has a basis in material fact. For example, magic occurs when a capable person, employing an object that is similar to what she wants us to think we see, creates in us a false cognition. And when from afar there is mist or the like whose appearance is similar to a city, one gets the idea of a city, and in absence of the former (the causal cognitions that produce error), the latter (the false impression of a city) would not arise. Moreover, when the sun's rays pulsate in combination with hot earth, one has a notion of water because he sees something similar. For one close by, in the absence of such conditions, the illusion disappears. Error occurs on account of specific conditions in terms of where, when, and for whom. It does not occur without causes.

We also find a difference between the cognitive state of a magician capable of tricks and the cognitive state of her audience. A similar difference holds for those nearby and those at a distance regarding **cities of Gandharvas (in the clouds) or a mirage**. Likewise, there is a difference regarding dream objects between those who are awake and those who are dreaming. If you hold that nothing truly exists, then you will be unable to explain these distinctions and differences. If nothing has an intrinsic nature, then nothing can be explained.

Uddyotakara [492.3–6]: A false perception projects the idea of a person onto a post. And knowledge of the truth about the thing makes the false projection cease. But it does not make the object itself cease, the thing that has characteristics common to both persons and posts. We do not conclude that the post does not exist. It's the same with projections of things experienced previously into dreams, projections that are removed by waking experience. But the object itself, which is characterized by common content of experience, is not made to cease. The rest is clear in the *Commentary*.

4.2.36: Cognition itself is also real, since we apprehend its causes and its existence.

Vātsyāyana [276.5–6]: And like objects themselves, cognition—your false cognition as cognition—cannot be denied. Why? Because we apprehend its causes and because we apprehend its true existence. . . .

Uddyotakara [492.8–10]: . . . "What then are the causes of false cognition?" Experience of something similar without noticing distinguishing features, along with projecting specific features where they don't occur, provides an example of such causes. Moreover, this explanation could be given to the person subject to the false cognition, and by comprehending the causes of her error she would come to view the object as it is.

Uddyotakara explains what happens in the stock example of misperception of a post in the distance, where one mistakes it for a person. Persons and posts share some general characteristics that explain the mistake's possibility. Further, the subject fails to notice any feature that would make it obvious that it is a post, such as an absence of fingers and toes, while projecting features of persons onto it. False cognition has intentionality; it is object-directed. Indeed, in all our examples it is directed towards real things albeit they are mispresented. The wrongness of false cognition shows a kind of divided intentionality, the misplacement explained above. And in their comments on the next sūtra, our Naiyāyikas will argue that such misplacement—mistaking something as an F when it is not an F—requires that in general there are things that are F.

4.2.37: And because of the difference between the real thing and what is supposed, false cognition is to be explained as having a twofold nature.

Vātsyāyana [4.2.11–17]: The cognition of the truth about the thing is "Post." What is supposed is "Person." Error, seeing a post as a person, occurs when their differences are elided while their similarities are grasped. One likewise sees a streaming flag as a row of cranes, and a lump of earth as a pigeon. It is not true that all cognitions that are false converge in their content, because there is diversity in what we take to be similar. Yet one who holds that there is no true nature to things—that nothing can be explained—would have to embrace the unwanted consequence that it all converges in that way.

And further, grasping sense objects (specific odors, colors, etc.) with respect to things that actually possess them would end up being mistaken as is any other cognition. This, along with the fact that there would be no way to grasp similarities between a real thing and what is supposed, entails that some cognition would be true. Therefore, it's wrong to hold that all cognitions of objects through knowledge sources are false.

In other words, if specific errors were not caused by real causal mechanisms, which produce distinct sorts of mistakes, then all errors would converge, being equally groundless. But Vātsyāyana observes that we can recognize that specific mistakes depend on specific causal conditions. Often the key factor is similarity between the real object and what is mistakenly taken to be the case. He argues that a denial of an underlying basis for cognition (error and knowledge alike) prevents his challenger from distinguishing between error and true cognition. Hence, the challenger cannot deny that some cognitions are true.

This is a central passage for Nyāya's defense of realism. Earlier, the argument was that in order to be wrong about something, to mistake something not-F for something F (to see a post as a person), we must be able to deploy the concept of the "F" in question. I could not mistakenly see a person in the distance if I didn't have the concept of a person, and Nyāya argues that in order to have such a concept, I must have had knowledge of persons in the past. In this the final sūtra of the section, we find an allied argument that we could not explain error if there were not something real underlying the "F" (namely, the post in the distance) that we misperceive. Since error is to take something in some way that it is not, there has to be a something to be mistaken about—what later comes to be called the viśeṣya*, the "property-bearer" or* "qualificandum"*—along with the* viśeṣaṇa*, "qualifier,"* *the F or, in the current example, being-a-person. I cannot make a mistake unless there is something that I am wrong about. Thus error—and by generalization all cognition—has a dual nature, presenting something as qualified by a property. Perceptual illusion presupposes that there is something that is misperceived. This is yet another argument for realism presented in this section of the text.*

To sum up and apply the Nyāya point to the contemporary debate between realists and anti-realists, it is a common strategy for anti-realists to point out that two people can see the same thing in radically different ways according to their conceptual schemes, language use, and cognitive conditioning. But, as Nyāya argues, one cannot even formulate such a case without helping oneself to the notion of a real thing that the two people are looking at differently. One has to presuppose a realist conception of the object of disagreement in order to formulate the anti-realist argument!

Suggestions for Further Reading

Matthew Dasti, "Parasitism and Disjunctivism in Nyāya Epistemology." *Philosophy East and West* 62.1 (2012): 1–15.

Joel Feldman, "Vasubandhu's Illusion Argument and the Parasitism of Illusion Upon Veridical Experience." *Philosophy East and West* 55.4 (2005): 529–41.

B. K. Matilal, *Perception: An Essay on Classical Indian Theories of Knowledge.* Oxford: Clarendon Press, 1986.

Pradyot K. Mukhopadhyay, *Indian Realism.* Calcutta: K. P. Bagchi, 1984.

Stephen H. Phillips, *Classical Indian Metaphysics: Refutations of Realism and the Emergence of "New Logic."* Chicago: Open Court, 1995.

Jadunath Sinha, *Indian Realism.* New Delhi: Motilal Banarsidass, 1999.

Study Questions

1. Define realism and anti-realism as discussed in this chapter.
2. What does the imagined Nyāya challenger mean by claiming that the notion we have of knowledge sources and their objects is like the notion we have of dreams and their objects?
3. There are at least four ways that Nyāya argues that realism is required to account for the fact that error can occur. Explain all four, and in each case elucidate a sūtra or commentary where it is discussed.
4. What does it mean to explain error as a misplacement or misfire? How does this misplacement occur according to Nyāya? Explain using an example not given in the text.
5. Explain the Nyāya argument that error requires realism because we have to be wrong about something when we make mistakes.
6. Nyāya gives examples of mirages of water, magician's tricks, and cities seen in the clouds to explain perceptual illusion. Provide your own example of a perceptual illusion and explain the causal and conceptual bases of the illusion according to Nyāya's analysis in this chapter.

Chapter 4

Self

As much as any topic broached in the Nyāya-sūtra, *Nyāya's views on the self and consciousness need to be understood in the context of teachings of other schools. The early Nyāya position is flanked by opposition both by Buddhists who champion a doctrine of "no-self,"* anātman, *and by the Sāṃkhya tradition, which argues that the real self is a source of awareness without the capacity to act, which comes from "materiality,"* prakṛti. *As Nyāya matures, another opponent is the Advaita Vedāntin who views the apparent plurality of individual selves as illusion in the face of the reality of a single cosmic self.*

Nyāya-sūtra *1.1.1 lists the major topics of the school, the second of which is* prameya, *"object of knowledge." The principal objects or types of objects are listed at sūtra 1.1.9. Heading that list is "self,"* ātman. *Sūtra 1.1.10 gives a concise statement of the principal Nyāya arguments for the existence of selves, arguments that are fleshed out and supplemented by other arguments in a long stretch of sūtras in* Nyāya-sūtra *chapter three. There we find not only extended examination of the rival Buddhist theory but also refutation of a materialist theory of self and consciousness advocated by Cārvāka.*

Udayana comments on 1.1.10 that although Nyāya views the self as known in part by apperceptions expressed by the word "I" (aham), *as in "I am seeing a pot," some take the word in such sentences to refer to the body, or in another way try to confute the evidence of self-awareness. For this reason, he says, Gautama tells us right away what the inferential marks are that prove the self's existence. Later we learn that the self that is proved is an individual amongst other individuals and not Vedānta's cosmic self, and this despite Nyāya's insistence that the Upaniṣadic scriptures championed by Vedānta give us testimonial knowledge that a self is a real and enduring entity.*

Nyāya's arguments take place against a background of Buddhist challenges to Nyāya's realism about enduring objects, and especially Buddhist denial of self as a special sort of enduring object. Buddhists put pressure on the notion of a self by deploying a theory of momentariness: things exist for only a instant, and what we take to be enduring substances are rather "streams" of countless entities in causal sequences. According to this view of momentariness, what many Hindu philosophers take to be an enduring—indeed eternal—self is rather a stream of cognition-instances that is mistakenly taken to be an enduring entity. In their commentaries, our Nyāya philosophers devote much effort to refuting this position.

1.1.10: Inferential marks for the self are desire, aversion, effort, pleasure, pain, and knowledge.

Vātsyāyana [16.5–20]: From sensory contact with a certain type of object, pleasure arises and is experienced by a self. Observing another object of the same type, the person desires to have it. The **desire** to have, "This is the kind of thing I experienced before"—on the part of a single observer seeing multiple objects of the same type and recognizing them as such—is an **inferential mark for the self**. For, such a desire would not be possible if there existed only a series of distinct cognitions each with its own fixed content, just as it would not be possible with a body different from one's own.

Caused by pain, **aversion** also arises from such recognition, by putting together various experiences on the part of a single perceiver of many objects.

A person makes effort to have something, perceiving that it is the same type of thing as that which she knows causes pleasure. This is the **effort**, which would not occur without a self as a single perceiver of many objects of the same type over time (that is, without that which puts together the various experiences). For, again, such would not be possible if there existed only a series of distinct cognitions each with its own fixed content, as with a body different from one's own. With this, **effort** motivated by pain or suffering is also explained.

Furthermore, a person remembering pleasure along with pain secures the relevant means to gain pleasure and to avoid pain. She experiences pleasure and she experiences pain. Remembering such experiences, she puts herself in a position to understand matters of pleasure and pain. The reason for this is just as was stated above. A person wanting to know something reflects, "Just what is that?" And she can know her own deliberation through introspection, "This deliberation." So that kind of **knowledge** requires the same agent that is continuous between the desire to know and the deliberation; such being grasped, there is an **inferential mark for a self**. The reason for this is just as was stated above (that is, that there is a self that puts together information from different occasions of experience).

Here the idea, "as with a body different from one's own," requires analysis. Proponents of the view that there is no self would admit that a series of distinct cognitions, each with its own fixed content, could not recognize previous experiences generated in connection with *bodies* other than one's own. Similarly (in the absence of an enduring self), distinct cognitions with content restricted by connection with one's own body could not be the basis of recognition, because the two scenarios are fundamentally the same.

It is well known that remembering belongs to the one who had some precise earlier experience, a single creature. One does not remember something experienced by another or something he himself has never experienced before. In the same way, it is well known that for all sorts of creatures one does not remember the things found in another's experiences. Proponents of the "no-self" view cannot account for either of these occurrences (the fact that one remembers things from one's own past experiences and that one does not remember things from the experiences of other people). In contrast, matters as we have presented them, namely, that there is a self, accords well with the phenomena described.

The core concern of all the commentaries under this sūtra is to refute the Buddhist theory that all we have are diverse sense experiences without an enduring subject who possesses and ties them together. The body is in constant flux, and, to use Buddhist language, even in the "stream" of momentary cognitions I mistakenly take to be myself, the "me" of back then is something other than the "me" of right now. Uddyotakara also hints in the next passage at the further argument that on the Buddhist view it would be impossible to recognize a single object presented through two different sense modalities. This will be discussed later at length in this chapter.

Uddyotakara [60.14–61.17]: Since the items mentioned in the sūtra come to be fused with fixed content provided by memory, they all prove that there is a single subject. For, recognition could not occur if there were a plurality of subjects, a plurality of cognitively fixed contents, and a plurality of causes for the ideas put together. The ideative flows of sights, tastes, smells, and touches are not made to come together to form a recognition on their own. Nor is it true that my visual experience in the past is something I am able to touch later. And it is also false that my tactile experience from the past is the sight I see now.

Furthermore, it is wrong that when something has been seen by Devadatta that very thing seen is recognized by Yajñadatta. Nor do we find it said, "Whatever Devadatta has directly experienced in the past, I, Yajñadatta, have thusly experienced." What's the reason for all this? It's because distinct cognitions have fixed content of their own. Having fixed content of their own, cognitions mutually exclude one another by nature. This is accepted by those who deny the self's existence. On their view, we should not expect any acts of recognition. Therefore, that which brings together contents into a recognition is precisely a self.

Opponent: Such recognitions happen because of causal relationships.

Reply: Then you hold that a recognition does not involve a single subject. How could that be?

Opponent: Because of the causal relationships. From each individual prior cognition comes a successor cognition, because the latter conforms to the causal power of its predecessor. In this way, a whole bundle of causal powers are strung together into a comprehensive whole. Recognition is thus produced by causal relationships alone, causal relationships among cognitions, even though there is a plurality of individual experiencers (in a single "stream" that comprises a person). It's like such things as a seed. It is only a distinct sort of sprout that appears immediately after a succession of rice globules, which is determined by what has preceded it in conformity to rice capacity (the capacity of rice as opposed to, say, the capacity of wheat). Later, it is again rice seed that is produced if the elements have been favorable, not wheat seed, because that is not what preceded it causally. Similarly, a recognition occurs from a determination through causal relationships among cognitions belonging to a single stream (*santāna*). They do not belong to another cognitive stream because they do not have those other cognitions as their predecessors. The operative principle is what immediately precedes what. It is false, let us repeat, that a recognition occurs because there is a single enduring subject or agent, since none is found. Therefore, such a recognition as you describe can occur otherwise than by your explanation, and it cannot be used to prove that a self exists.

Reply: Wrong, because you haven't given up the idea of a plurality of distinct individuals (that is, diverse cognitions). When you say that a recognition comes about from causal relationships, you haven't freed yourself from the idea of a plurality of distinct individuals. Why is this? It's because causal relationships presuppose such pluralities. Indeed, a causal relationship is based on a plurality of distinct individuals. And it is understood in common by both our sides that no recognition is found if there is only a plurality of distinct experiencers. How so? Because what has been experienced by one is not remembered by another. And no one is able to recognize an object of which she has no memory. . . .

A common strategy in early Buddhist philosophy is to argue that the roles commonly attributed to substances in maintaining continuity over time can be reduced to cause-effect chains. Uddyotakara has his opponent suggest this very point to explain how recollection may take place even without a self that endures. Causal continuity between cognitive events in a "stream" of multiple experiencers that we mistakenly call a single person is all that is needed to account for recollection. The example of a seed employs the stream notion, where in Buddhist terms a seed right before sprouting and at the time of sprouting are two different things, united only by causal continuities between them.

Next we have Vācaspatimiśra pointing out that certain cases of cause-effect relationship do not generate recollection over time. Causal relationships are thus not sufficient to underwrite the sort of psychological events described in the sūtra. He imagines an opponent arguing that we don't always see the causal connections but that they are operative all the same. Vācaspatimiśra counters with an example of a small piece of fruit being replaced by another, such that a cause-effect tie between the object of cognition need not even be necessary, much less sufficient, for recognition of similarity.

Vācaspatimiśra [176.22–177.5]: . . . And it is not true that in spite of the differences among cognitions causal relationships alone could make possible recognition such as we have described. For, where there is a causal relationship very clearly evident, such as between threads and a piece of cloth, or between pot-halves and the pot they compose, even there, there is no putting together of experiences over time. There is nothing like a recognition in the form of , "Those threads previously experienced are this very piece of cloth," nor, "That which was a pot-moment is this moment of a pot-half."

Opponent: In truth, we often fail to observe the differences between the things that stand in a causal relationship. Yet we find that, being divided every moment, they are the basis for the experience of recollection.

Answer: Wrong. If you take away one piece of *āmalaka* fruit and put in its stead another *āmalaka,* you can *recognize* it as of the same type. And between the two pieces of fruit there is no causal relationship. . . .

Next is a different sort of argument by Uddyotakara that begins with the idea that qualities reside in substances. There is no free-floating "red"; the color exists only as nested in substances such as this red scarf or that red apple. And things such as desire and aversion are qualities that require an appropriate, psychological sort of substance in which to rest. It is a self who plays the "supporting" role. Nothing short of an enduring substance can house such things that, like other qualities, require a support. That is to say, they need something to serve as their substratum and location.

Uddyotakara [64.12–18]: Some say that alternatively the sūtra "**Inferential marks for the self are desire, aversion, effort, pleasure, pain, and knowledge**" can be interpreted in another way. These items, desire and the rest, are qualities (*guṇa*), and qualities demand things other than themselves in which to reside. This is the reasoned position.

. . . (Thus) a self can be proved by means of an eliminative argument: because desire and the rest are impermanent, they are not self-supporting. Another reason they depend on things other than themselves is that they are effects. They are like color and other material qualities, which depend upon the substances in which they inhere. Furthermore, these are not qualities belonging to the body, since they do not inhere in material substances. And material substances being ruled out, we identify these as qualities of a self, a psychological substance. Thus, a self is proved.

The next sustained argument for the self is from Nyāya-sūtra *chapter three. It focuses on cross-modal cognition, our ability to grasp objects through multiple sensory channels.*

3.1.1: Because one grasps the same object through sight and touch, there is a self that is distinct from the body and sense organs.

Vātsyāyana [135.14–136.4]: Some particular object is grasped by sight; the same object is also grasped by touch: "That very thing which I saw with my eyes I am now feeling through my sense of touch," and "That very thing which I felt through my sense of touch I am now seeing with my eyes." The two instances of mental content that are each directed towards one and the same object have—in being comprehended—a single subject. And it is not the case that the subject comprehending the two is simply the aggregate of bodily parts. Nor does there come to be a single subjectivity through the activity of any particular sense organ. Thus the grasper of one and the same object by the visual organ and the organ of touch comprehends two instances of mental content about one and the same thing, two instances of mental content that have distinct causal complexes and distinct instrumental causes, but have no other subject than the grasper. That one, in a special category, is a self.

Question: How, again, is it that the mere functioning of the sense organs cannot bring about a single subjectivity for both instances of content?

Answer: It is true that a sense organ is capable (in a sense) of comprehension in terms of grasping and repeatedly transmitting its peculiar content itself to a subject who endures the passage of time. But it does not grasp the other content which belongs to another sense faculty.

Question: Why is it that an aggregate of bodily parts cannot bring about a single subjectivity for both instances of content?

Answer: Because he is one and the same who is *conscious* of the two instances of mental content that have distinct instrumental causes but one and the same self as subject. No aggregate could be *conscious* of them.

Question: Why?

Answer: Because each item within such an aggregate of bodily parts would continue to fail to comprehend the other instances of mental content, like the case of a sense organ (which, as pointed out, cannot grasp another organ's content).

3.1.2: Objection: This is wrong. (There is no self that is distinct from the body and sense organs) because sense organs are restricted to their own proper content.

Vātsyāyana [136.7–17]: Objection: Other than the aggregate of body and the rest (the sense organs), there is no consciousness. Why? **Because sense organs are restricted to their own proper content.** That is to say, the sense organs have objects or content that is strictly demarcated. When there is no organ of sight, no color is grasped.

And we accept the following rule: if x is absent when y is absent, but present when y is present, then x belongs to y. Thus, the grasping of color belongs to the visual organ. The two eyes are what see color. The other organs also work in this way on their own objects, the olfactory and the rest. Just these several sense organs are conscious, because what is grasped is content restricted to specific sensory modalities. The reason is that specific content is grasped because of the presence or absence of the separate sense organs. And so, what's the point in positing something else as the experiencer?

Response: You haven't given a good reason, since it's a dubious point. You contend that the nature of grasping content is fixed according to the presence or absence of the sense organs, and that, given this principle, the inference for a self as the conscious experiencer fails. But your contention remains doubtful, since there is an alternative: there is a conscious self *because* the sense organs are instrumental for conscious awareness but not themselves sufficient for the conscious grasping that occurs. Since there is this alternative view, a doubt remains.

And what you said, "**because sense organs are restricted to their own proper content**," is addressed in the following sūtra.

3.1.3: (Answer:) The very restriction of sense organs to their own proper content is a reason to suppose the existence of a self—thus, the self's existence is not contested.

Vātsyāyana [137.1–13]: If, let us suppose, a sense organ did not have content that was restricted to one sensory modality, then as an all-cognizing, all-content-grasping, conscious thing, we wouldn't have to infer a conscious being over and above that. But no, it is *because* the sense organs are restricted in content that there has to be something else, a conscious being capable of cognizing anything, a grasper of content of whatever sort, transcendent to that which is restricted in content. This is our inference.

It is easy to illustrate that such undeniable recognition as we have sketched out occurs in a conscious being. A person who sees something (such as a ripening fruit) that has a certain shape and color can infer its taste or smell based on previous experiences. And someone cognizant of something's smell can infer its color and shape or taste as well. The same is to be said for the rest of the types of specific content. . . . Hearing letters ordered sequentially, one is able to recognize a word in a sentence, and cognizing a fixed verbal arrangement in a sentence, one grasps complex content produced by it, content which none of the sense organs could grasp working independently. All this, which spans various arrangements and modalities, must be cognized by a being capable of cognizing anything, and not just through one specific mode of presentation. On the heels of this argument, you cannot just turn our point on its head. A simple case is all that is needed for illustration. Thus, what you put forth, that given that there is consciousness in the sense organs there is no use of positing a conscious being over and above them, is wrong.

A further argument in this section of the Nyāya-sūtra *focuses on the need for moral, or "karmic," continuity. Nyāya argues that the Buddhist view that reduces the self to a stream of fleeting states cannot account for moral continuity. Normally, we hold that one who commits an act carries moral implications of the act long after it is completed, since she is the same person over time. But on the Buddhist view of momentariness, at every instant, when the current body/mind aggregate is destroyed, the current "me" would be annihilated. The later "me" instance is a different thing entirely, and should not be bound by the acts of another. Moreover, if at each moment the "self" is destroyed, why should an individual strive for a future salvation that she will not experience? Or for anything at all? The Nyāya complaint is that the Buddhist view not only undermines morality, but makes the struggle for enlightenment farcical. Note that the term "results" in the passage below refers to the moral or karmic consequences of one's own actions.*

Vātsyāyana [137.17]: From what has been established (in sūtras 3.1.1–3), it follows that the self is distinct from the body and the rest. It is not simply the aggregate of the body and so on.

3.1.4: When a living body is harmed, no sin would be incurred (if there were no self).

Vātsyāyana [137.19–138.10]: Use of the word "**body**" in the sutra is meant to express the aggregate of body, senses, cognition, and awareness that make up a living being. One who (for example) burns a living body causes harm to the living being, committing a wicked act called sin. "**No sin**" means that (for those who deny a permanent self) there would be no connection between the agent of sin and its results; conversely, there would be a relationship between the results and someone other than the agent. Indeed, in the flowing series of body, senses, cognition, and awareness, one aggregate would arise while another is terminated. And that there is a *sequence* in the form of a stream of arising and terminating would not mitigate the problem of the agent's otherness, since each individual aggregate of body, etc., would stand distinct from every other aggregate. For, the fact that each stands distinct from every other is widely understood. And so, this being the case, the living being in the form of an aggregate of body, etc., who causes harm would not be the one connected to the karmic fruits of harm, and the one who would be connected would not be the one who caused the harm. Thus, on the view that there are distinct beings (in a series, as opposed to a single enduring self), there results the unacceptable consequence of losing what one has done and acquiring what one has not done.

Further, if it is true that an (entirely new) being arises and is terminated (constantly), individuals would not be shaped through the causal influence of karma. And religious ways of life such as celibacy for the sake of liberation would be meaningless. So if the living being were merely an aggregate of body, etc., when a person was burned and harmed, no sin would be incurred by the one who did the burning. This view is unacceptable. Therefore, the self is something other than the aggregate of body, etc., and it endures the passage of time.

Uddyotakara [333.11–15]: On the Buddhist view, there could be no effort for liberation, since it would be achieved without effort. "Simply by being born, one would be liberated (as each self-instance is immediately annihilated)." Celibate religious life, undertaken for liberation (according to the Buddha's own teachings), would be meaningless. Nor would there be the religious inquiry whereby *bhikṣus* (monks) respond to questions made by the Buddha himself (as recorded in the sacred texts). . . .

Among several arguments in favor of a self in Nyāya-sūtra *chapter three, we have reviewed three: (a) diachronic recognition of one thing at two times, (b) synchronic perceptual synthesis concerning one thing through two distinct sensory transmissions, and (c) moral or karmic continuity. A fourth, somewhat less prominent line of argument opposes the view that the body itself, with all its parts in "intimate association," is the seat of consciousness. One argument against this view is (d) a corpse has all the material elements and properties that a living person has without consciousness. To account for consciousness, there has to be something else. The arguments from diachronic recognition, from synchronic perceptual synthesis, and from karmic continuity occur in the passages translated above, but the fourth is more diffuse, running through several sūtras involving peculiar ideas about the body. At the end of our chapter, the antimaterialist argument will be presented and reviewed.*

We turn now instead to arguments that aren't concerned with the existence of the self but with its nature. Along with other schools under the umbrella of Vedic culture, Nyāya views a self as "eternal" or "constant." The relevant Sanskrit word, nitya, *means "continuous," not necessarily "time-transcendent." While a self experiences temporal succession, it is never threatened by non-existence. The main idea in the Nyāya arguments is that the continuity of the self stretches indefinitely into the past, because otherwise we wouldn't be able to explain features of our psychology. That it extends indefinitely into the past is then our reason for thinking that it also extends indefinitely into the future. The issue here is reincarnation. If there were no previous life, a new-born child would not express emotions such as happiness or fear, for which she gives every indication.*

Vātsyāyana [146.3–8]: Question: This conscious being that is something other than the body and the rest, as has been argued, is it eternal or is it non-eternal? Now we have this doubt "because both ways of being are found to occur."[1] That is, existent things exist in both ways; some are eternal, others non-eternal. And by our having learned that there is a self, this doubt is not yet resolved.

Answer: The arguments that establish that there is a self do indeed themselves establish that there is a state of the self prior to incarnation, because it is different from the body. Thus there is also one afterwards (that is, after death), because the self is different from the body. How so?

3.1.18: Because happiness, fear, and unhappiness are experienced by a new-born appropriately, through connection with what was previously practiced and remembered (a self endures beyond death).

Vātsyāyana [146.11–14]: A **new-born** is a child who has not in this lifetime experienced things that cause **happiness, fear, and unhappiness**. These emotions are nevertheless experienced by the new-born, since the baby shows signs by which these feelings may be inferred. And such experiences come about only through connection with memories. Such connection with memory does not come about without prior practice and experience. And in the case of a new-born, the prior practice and experience can only be during a previous lifetime. In this way we establish that there is a state of the self afterwards too, because the self is different from the body.

Uddyotakara [344.2–5]: Objection: The existence of a self has been proven by reasons that also establish that it endures even when separated from the body. Since that has been proved, there is no need for further discussion.

---

1 *Vaiśeṣika-sūtra* 2.2.22.

Answer: This discussion must take place. Why? That there is a single enduring being from birth until death has been established by the arguments so far. However, it has not been established that the self continues after the body's destruction. This is what remains to be proved by the sūtras at hand. The current section is directed to making this known.

Vācaspatimiśra [471.11–18]: Uddyotakara refutes an objection against embarking upon another section of text by means of the current sūtra. . . . By having been made to see that the body, senses, cognition, and pain (or feeling in general) are not identical to the self, and, by implication, having been made to understand that recognitions belong to a single self that is the same through changes of childhood, adolescence, maturity, and old age, we also find that the self exists after the destruction of the body. Such is the motivation for us to open a new section. The question put concerns what remains to be done; that is, given what has been settled already, the doubt concerns whether the work of the new section has not already been done—this is Uddyotakara's meaning. He puts the question to rest with the words, "This discussion must take place." Even though it has been proved that the self is different from the body and so on, and that it is continuous from childhood through old age, there is doubt about just what it is. Is it that a self endures from the birth of the body until death such that it only supervenes on the stream of those things such as the body that exist from birth to death? Or is it that even when those things have passed away, the stream of the body and the rest, it would really continue? This is the examination that is to be undertaken now. It has not been ruled out. To put such doubt to rest, a new section is opened. This is what Uddyotakara says.

Uddyotakara [344.6–17]: Here is the meaning of the sūtra. . . . As may be inferred from its smiling, thrashing about, and crying, a new-born child is found to have appropriate experiences of happiness, fear, and unhappiness. But the sense organs by themselves are not capable of generating such content (the child being newly born). And these feelings are produced through connection with memories. Connection with memories, furthermore, would not be possible without there having been a previous incarnation. The connection to one's body, cognition, and feeling constituted by this birth demands a relationship with things that have been previously experienced. Such emotions are quite real and expressed by the child.

Happiness is pleasurable experience that happens when one gets whatever is the intended object of hope or expectation. **Fear** comes from an incapacity to avoid what one would like to avoid when causes of unwanted experience are about to coalesce. **Unhappiness** amounts to the expectation that it will be impossible to have again some desired experience which has been closed off. Possessing these emotions in accordance with how they are defined is what is meant by saying that they are held **appropriately**.

Practice and experience (which produce memory) require repeated cognition of the same content, or at least content of similar form or shape. For example, rice eaten by a subject on different occasions produces memory of such eating. Memory consists of cognitive content that is comprised of previous perceptions or thoughts when their objects have ceased to be present. Recognition amounts to cognitive content—content of previous perception or thought—that informs present content, thanks to the previous cognitions. The connection that is the cause of memory is the mental disposition (*saṃskāra*) subject to a kind of reawakening or triggering. By remembering content produced by something desirable, the child smiles, from food, for example, or a present being brought. By remembering content produced by something unwanted, the child cries, thrashing his limbs about, making particular sounds and shedding tears, indicating that he feels the presence of that which he wants to avoid.

*All this and other phenomena—in particular, a new-born's action of reaching precisely towards its mother's breast for nourishment (sūtra 3.1.21)—are taken to show that the mental dispositions (*saṃskāra*) responsible for the memories have to have an enduring receptacle to make possible both the emotions and the purposive action of reaching. Like smiling, etc., goal-directed action requires previous cognition of the goal. The objection (sūtra 3.1.19) that the smiling, etc., could be like a flower opening and closing according to* *the presence or absence of the sun, is met (sūtra 3.1.20) by the observation that in common experience smiling and the like have previous experience as part of the causal complex responsible for bringing them about.*

Next, an objection is put forth (sūtra 3.1.22) that a newborn's reaching for the breast is instead like iron filings being pulled by a magnet, without need of conscious direction or purpose. This is answered (sūtra 3.1.23) by the observation that the child shows a certain flexibility and range within first-time action, whereas filings move only towards a magnet. These considerations are taken to prove that a conscious self exists prior to birth. And if one's current life has been preceded by events from a past life, which belong to a self that has retained the dispositions that the prior life's experiences formed—as in what is colloquially called "muscle memory"—then it stands to reason that our current lives will be followed by others or at least other states of a self (in case one achieves "liberation," mokṣa*).*

Nyāya-sūtra *chapter three has many more sūtras devoted to the self in relation to other items of our psychology, in particular the physical body as well as perception and the sense organs. The second "daily lesson"(each chapter has two; see Appendix A) opens with the transitory nature of occurrent cognition, which is changing all the time. After an excursion to refute the Buddhist view that not only cognition but everything is momentary, the topic becomes the location of occurrent cognition. While this has been discussed before, the current context allows Vātsyāyana to review and refine the view that the self is the locus of awareness, and not any particular cluster of physical elements or non-sentient intermediaries.*

3.2.39: Cognition is a property of the self, since alternatives have been eliminated and undefeated reasons have been given above.

Vātsyāyana [197.1–18]: The current topic is the proposition that cognition is a quality belonging directly to a self. There has indeed been **elimination** of alternative candidates. Through elimination of alternatives shown to be unfit, the correct view will be that which remains because it has not fallen to difficulties. Certain candidates for locating cognition, (a) the material elements that make up the body, (b) the sense organs, and (c) the mind, *manas*, have been eliminated. Another substance has not been eliminated—it remains—and that is (d) the self.

The words "**along with undefeated reasons given above**" mean that cognition is a property of the self also because the reasons that establish the existence of a self have not been ruled out, such as (sūtra 3.1.1) **Because one grasps the same object through sight and touch, there is a self that is distinct from the body and sense organs**. The expression "**undefeated reasons given above**" has two purposes: to establish that the self remains a candidate for the location of cognition, and to know how the topic at issue is resolved.

Alternatively, the words "**undefeated reasons**" may be taken to mean that this sūtra is simply presenting another reason. Being constant and continuous in its existence, the self we have been discussing would *emerge* on separation from the body, in a heaven among gods if righteousness (*dharma*) has been practiced. In contrast, if unrighteousness (*adharma*) has been done, the emergence on separation from the body would be in a hell. The word in the sūtra means "emergence" on this reading, emergence characterized by obtaining another body. Furthermore, given that the self exists constantly, the emergence would be its becoming a container or location of properties. But this would not be possible if there were merely a connected series of cognitions without a self, without a container or substratum. . . .

And if there were nothing but a stream of cognitions, everything produced from the everyday activity of living beings would become disjointed, because a being would be divided in itself. Nothing would be distinguishable, and nothing effected (since an act begun by one would be completed by another). This would follow because there would be no remembering. The principle is: no one remembers the content of another's experiences. Moreover, remembering really amounts to a grasping—by one and the same knower—of something previously known, "This thing I know now is something I cognized previously." It is this one-and-the-same knower who grasps whatever it is that was known previously. And such grasping on her part amounts to remembering. Therefore, it would not be possible if there were merely a connected series of cognitions without a self.

It is commonly thought in Hinduism (as well as Buddhism and Jainism) that an individual emerges in another world—a heaven or a hell or a psychic holding-ground—before taking another earthly incarnation. Where she emerges depends on the righteousness or unrighteousness of her actions in this life, as does also her situation, talents, etc., in her next birth in this world. See Chapter 8, "The Right and the Good," for further discussion of soteriology and its connection to morality.

Below, Vātsyāyana continues to engage with a materialist who holds that consciousness is a property of the body, not of a non-physical self.

Vātsyāyana [203.3–7]: Opponent: Consciousness is a quality of the body, because it exists when there is a body but not when there is not.

3.2.46: (Opponent:) There is doubt whether cognition is a property of a self, because substances exhibit their own qualities as well as the qualities of other things.

Opponent: That the one thing is present when the other is present leads to doubt. In the case of water, we find its own qualities occurring, such as fluidity, but also the qualities of other things like heat (when water is mixed with fire atoms). The doubt about consciousness runs as follows: Is it that consciousness is found to occur when there is a body because it is a quality of the body, or is it that consciousness belongs to another substance (a self)?

Response: Consciousness is not a quality of the body. Why not?

3.2.47: (Response continued:) (Consciousness is not a property of the body) because as long as the body lasts there will be properties like color, but not consciousness.

Vātsyāyana [203.11–16]: A body is never found to lack color or the like. But a body without consciousness (e.g., a corpse) is known to occur. The situation is like water which in itself lacks warmth (but can be heated by the inclusion of fire atoms). Therefore, consciousness is not a quality of the body.

Objection: It could work like a dispositional property (*saṃskāra*).

Answer: Wrong, because its triggers could never cease (and thus it would always be manifest).

Objection: They would cease according to the type of substance that has the dispositional property.

Answer: No. On your view, if there were complete cessation of the triggers, there could be no dispositional property thenceforth. Whatever kind of substance the body is, such that it could locate consciousness, it would be exactly that kind of thing when consciousness ceased completely. Therefore, the response that consciousness is like a dispositional property is incorrect. . . .

Here Vātsyāyana has an opponent say that consciousness could be a dispositional property of the body, a property that exists even when it is not manifest, as water's capacity to freeze at certain temperature exists even when the water is in a liquid state. The idea reverberates with much contemporary philosophy of mind, and so the Nyāya response—that consciousness would be constantly triggered or never at all—is particularly interesting. In other words, the opponent has no theoretical resource to view a body as conscious or as not conscious, since its physical makeup would be the same in both instances. And if consciousness were a dispositional property, it would either be triggered even in death or never triggered even in life, since the bodily material would be the same in both instances.

Suggestions for Further Reading

Arindam Chakrabarti, "The Nyāya Proofs for the Existence of the Soul." *Journal of Indian Philosophy* 10 (1982): 211–38.

Arindam Chakrabarti, "I Touch What I Saw." *Philosophy and Phenomenological Research* 52 (1992): 103–17.

Kisor K. Chakrabarti, *Classical Indian Philosophy of Mind: The Nyāya Dualist Tradition*. Albany: State University of New York Press, 1999.

Matthew R. Dasti, "Nyāya's Self as Agent and Knower." In *Free Will, Agency, and Selfhood in Indian Philosophy*, eds., Matthew R. Dasti and Edwin F. Bryant. New York: Oxford University Press, 2014.

Jonardon Ganeri, "Cross-modality and the Self." *Philosophy and Phenomenological Research* 61.3 (2000): 639–58.

Jonardon Ganeri, *The Self: Naturalism, Consciousness, and the First-Person Stance.* Oxford: Oxford University Press, 2012.

C. Ramaiah, "The Problem of Personal Identity—Nyāya Vaiśeṣika Perspective." *Indian Philosophical Annual* 20 (1987): 68–84.

John Taber, "Uddyotakara's Defense of a Self." In *Hindu and Buddhist Ideas in Dialogue: Self and No-Self*, eds., Irina Kuznetsova, Jonardon Ganeri, and Chakravarthi Ram-Prasad. Farnham, Surrey; Burlington, Vermont: Ashgate, 2012.

Study Questions

1. Both *Nyāya-sūtra* 1.1.10 and 3.1.1 present arguments for a unified, *sui-generis* self based on certain psychological features that we observe in ordinary life. Explain each argument in brief.

2. What does it mean to say that a psychological state such as aversion depends on recollection, which in turn requires an enduring self? Is this correct?

3. Nyāya arguments against a Buddhist no-self theory rely heavily on the notion that one individual cannot have another's memories. How is this used against the no-self view? Is Nyāya's objection a reasonable extension of the principle, which seems obvious in common life?

4. Why can't unified consciousness be produced merely by individual sense organs working independently or by an aggregate of bodily functions, according to Nyāya?

5. What is Nyāya's argument for reincarnation and the pre- and post-existence of a self? Is it a strong argument? Why or why not?
6. Explain the principle that certain emotions and all purposeful action require the input of memory to occur. Does this concur with our common experience?

Chapter 5

Substance and Causation

Nyāya's metaphysical picture is closely aligned with the realist, category-based schema of its "sister school," Vaiśeṣika. Nyāya and Vaiśeṣika are generally considered to have merged during the time of Udayana (c. 1000 CE), but even from the earliest commentary of Vātsyāyana, Naiyāyikas consistently employ both the Vaiśeṣika categories and the school's theory of causality. The principal categories identified are: substance, quality, action, universal, individuator, inherence, and absence (this last, absence, was the latest to be recognized as an irreducible part of the ontology). The work of the great Vaiśeṣika Praśastapāda (c. 550 CE), who articulates both the major categories and the theory of causation in ways far more systematic than the early Nyāya-sūtra *commentators, comes to be of central importance for later Nyāya efforts in metaphysics.*

This chapter focuses on substances and causation, two fundamental elements in Nyāya's conception of the world. For universals, another important category, please see Chapter 7 of this volume, "Word and Object." We start with an overview of sorts. Nyāya-sūtra *1.1.9–22 lists and defines certain primary "objects of knowledge" (*prameya*), which become the major metaphysical topics with which the school is concerned. Examinations of several of these spill over from metaphysics into value theory, soteriology, and epistemology. It is noteworthy that in their commentaries on this sūtra, early Naiyāyikas make a point of noting that the Vaiśeṣika categories are also "objects of knowledge."*

1.1.9: Self, body, sense faculties, objects (of the senses), cognition, mind (*manas*, the "internal organ"), purposive

action, vice, rebirth, fruit of action, suffering, and final beatitude are the objects of knowledge.

Vātsyāyana [15.6–18]: Among these, the **self** (*ātman*) is the perceiver of all objects of experience. It feels them, is aware of them all, and experiences them. The seat of its experience is the **body** (*śarīra*). The **sense faculties** (*indriya*) are instruments of experience. What are to be experienced are **objects** (*artha*) of the senses. **Cognition** (*buddhi*) is experience.

The senses are not the operative instruments in every case of experiencing something (such as knowledge of our own thoughts). Thus we infer that there is a **mind** (*manas*), an "**internal organ**," that can take anything as its object.

And next, **purposive action** (*pravṛtti*) and **vice** (*doṣa*) perpetuate one's embodiment and connection with senses, sense experiences, cognition, happiness, distress, and reflective experience. Having a body is preceded by earlier embodiments and will be followed by later ones. There is no beginning to the series of previous bodies. Final beatitude would be the end of successor bodies.

Thus there is **rebirth** (*pretyabhāva*). Enjoyment of pleasure along with pain including the means whereby they are brought about is the **fruit of action** (*phala*).

The mention of **suffering** (*duḥkha*) here in the sūtra should not be understood to exclude the experience of pleasure that conforms to one's comforts. What then? Taking birth is what allows one to experience pleasure, but even that is included within the sūtra's mention of "suffering," since it is inevitably conjoined with suffering in the form of various harassments and obstacles. Suffering is described in this way to aid reflection and yogic meditation. One deeply reflects on these facts and becomes detached. **Final beatitude** (*apavarga*) comes about for someone who has become in this way dispassionate. It amounts to the removal of pain and suffering (*duḥkha*) of every kind by cutting one's ties to the cycle of repeated birth and death.

There is also another way to understand **objects of knowledge**: substance, quality, action, universal, individuator, and inherence (the basic ontological categories according to Vaiśeṣika). And according to this division, the knowable objects would be innumerable. But the sūtra lists the particular items mentioned because knowing about *them* leads to final beatitude (*apavarga*) and having misconceptions about *them* perpetuates the cycle of reincarnation.

A note on the term "mind," which translates manas*: The* manas *is a psychological faculty that is connected to a self, part of the self-mind-body complex. It governs selective attention, mnemonic retrieval, and introspection. While* mind *is sometimes taken to be a synonym for* self *in Western thought, here it refers to a psychological faculty distinct from the self, and is sometimes spoken of as a mental sense faculty ("inner sense") by our thinkers.*

Uddyotakara [59.1–8]: The meaning of the sūtra is that knowing the **self** and the other items listed is particularly conducive for liberation. It was not written to deny the other kinds of objects (discussed in other treatises). . . . Since universals, individuators, and inherence function as the grounds for mutually distinguishing **self** and other types of object, it is understood that universals, etc., qualify self and the rest.

In their comments above, Vātsyāyana and Uddyotakara not only affirm the Vaiśeṣika categories but underscore the ties between their analytic methodology and a professed "yogic" objective to achieve ultimate liberation. Ties to yoga also appear elsewhere: see Chapter 8 of this volume, "The Right and the Good."

Below is a representative passage from Vātsyāyana's commentary on sūtra 4.1.38, which further affirms the Vaiśeṣika categories within Nyāya's realism. The sūtra is responding to an anti-realist critique that echoes Nāgārjuna's Buddhist claim that all things exist interdependently and thus lack substantial existence.

4.1.38: No, (the anti-realist position is untenable) since it has been proven that existing things have an inherent nature (*sva-bhāva*).

Vātsyāyana [237:3–9]: It is not the case that everything lacks substantial existence, since things genuinely exist in accord with their inherent natures. That is to say, things exist along with their own peculiar properties, as proposed earlier in the sūtras. "What does it mean then for things to have their own peculiar properties?" (The *Vaiśeṣika-sūtra* provides the answer:) **To substances, qualities, and actions belong universals such as *being*. . . .**[1] **Substances possess actions (and qualities).**[2] Here, examples are given of distinctive properties. And further, **Earth has the qualities of taste, color, odor, and touch.**[3] Individual differences are endless, as we apprehend distinctive features belonging to universals, individuators, and inherence. Because if there were nonexistence (as alleged by the Buddhists) things would be indescribable and featureless, they would not have distinctive properties captured in common ideas about *being* and so on. But we do find such properties. And thus it is not the case that everything lacks substantial existence.

The following diagram charts early Nyāya's categories as adopted from Vaiśeṣika:

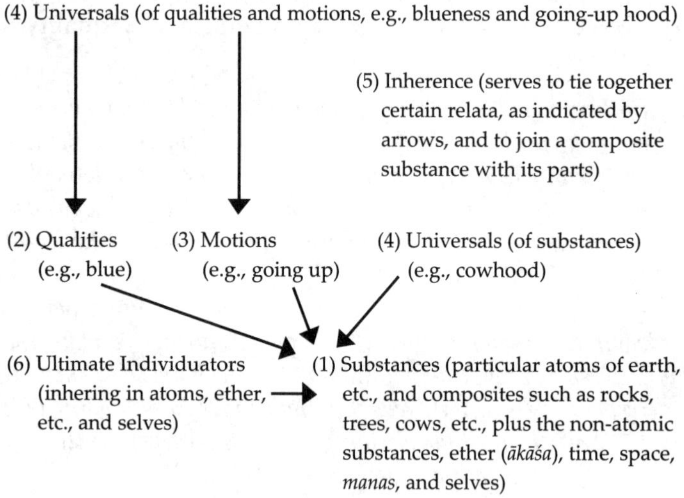

*We will focus now on substance (*dravya*), a bedrock metaphysical commitment within Nyāya's conception of reality. In*

1 Compare *Vaiśeṣika-sūtra* 1.1.7.

2 Compare *Vaiśeṣika-sūtra* 1.1.14.

3 Compare *Vaiśeṣika-sūtra* 7.1.1.

*general, substances are things that possess qualities (*guṇa*) and actions, and are capable of maintaining their identity as their qualities and actions change. Nyāya recognizes different kinds of substance: non-composite atoms of four types (earth, water, fire, and air), and composite macro objects such as trees, rocks, and the tables and chairs of common experience. Other substances include ether, which is a single ubiquitous substance that is the medium of the transmission of sound, as well as time, space, minds (*manas*), and non-material selves, which bear psychological qualities such as knowledge and desire. Much of our investigation will be concerned with composite wholes, substances that are built up out of smaller parts. We will consider first a defense of the irreducibility of composite wholes, and then an argument in support of the atoms that are considered their fundamental constituents.*

In the next excerpt, an opponent argues that what Nyāya takes to be macro objects with their own distinct reality (such as pots and trees) are rather metaphysical "heaps" or aggregates without a genuine, coherent identity. Nyāya responds by offering reasons why certain things though composite are nevertheless irreducibly unified entities. Their existence depends upon parts that are their "inherence causes," but they are nevertheless united single things over and above the atoms, dyads, etc., that comprise them.

2.1.33: (Objection:) There is doubt about the composite whole, since it remains to be proved.

Vātsyāyana [75.6–8]: Objection: What was assumed in the immediately preceding sūtra, 2.1.32, that the composite whole made of parts is real, is unsupported, since it **remains to be proved**. What remains to be proved is, first of all, that there is a separate, distinct substance existing over and above its material causes. It has not been shown that this is tenable. And that being the case, we are left with nothing but controversy over the point, and therefore there is doubt **about the composite whole**.

Uddyotakara expatiates on Nyāya mereology under this sūtra for almost twenty pages of Sanskrit, rebutting more than a dozen reductionist arguments. Responding to an objector, he suggests that central to the debate is the status of conjunction, the relational quality that links substances. He claims that conjunction accounts for the configuration or material arrangement of causes and is itself metaphysically distinct from the substances it relates. How else could threads become a cloth? Here the opponents appear to be Buddhists, but not anti-realists of a Mādhyamika type. Rather, here we have reductionists who view apparent macro objects as nothing more than clusters of smaller entities.

Uddyotakara [210.1–4]: You (the Buddhist reductionist) suggest that things are nothing more than a "particular arrangement" of their parts (that a cloth is nothing more than a particular arrangement of threads, for instance). But is this particular arrangement itself something distinct or not? If you say, Yes, there has come to be some other thing beyond the parts themselves, and so you should tell us what it is. Then if you say, No, there is not another thing, and so your statement about a "particular arrangement" is meaningless. For us, in contrast, conjunction (*saṃyoga*) accounts for the particular arrangement, and it itself is something else.

The next sūtra continues the main line of debate and argues that we need to accept composites to make sense of all the things we are capable of knowing.

2.1.34: (Reply:) If the composite whole is not accepted, there would be no knowledge of anything.

Vātsyāyana [75.11–17]: If there were no composite whole, then it would not be possible to know anything.

Objector: What do you mean by "anything"?

Reply: We mean anything in any of the categories: substance, quality, action, universal, individuator, and inherence.

Objector: Why should we think in this way?

Reply: An atomic substance is not perceptible, since atoms are beyond the range of the senses. On your reductionist view, there is no new thing, no composite whole that could be the object of experience over and above the collection of atoms. Qualities and other properties are capable of being perceptually grasped because they inhere within perceptible objects. They could not be apprehended without being grounded in something. But they *are* apprehended, for example, when we know and say, "This is a pot," "This is black," "There is just this one," "It's large," "It's sitting on something," "It is vibrating," "It is made of clay," and so on. And these properties mentioned exist, these qualities and the like. Because of this, we are able to grasp everything that we do. We are able to perceive things. Thus the composite, the whole, is an additional substantial reality beyond the parts.

Uddyotakara [227.16–228.8]: If there were no composite whole over and above its parts, there would be the unacceptable consequence that nothing at all could be known.

Opponent: How so?

Reply: First of all, as noted by Vātsyāyana, we find that ultimate atoms do not enter into experience, for they are beyond the range of the senses. And you (the reductionist opponent) do not recognize the existence of composite substances. Given this, for you there would be no knowledge of substances, such as, "This is a pot," nor knowledge of qualities, such as, "This is dark," nor of actions, such as "This is moving," nor of universals, such as, "This exists," nor of particulars, such as "This is a pitcher," nor of inherence, such as, "*In* this pot there is color and the like," and so on. The same holds for other instances of knowledge, such as, "This is a single thing," "This is large," "This is connected to something," "This is disconnected from something," "This is separate," "This is earlier," and "This is later." And yet we do grasp all these things, substances, qualities, actions, and so on—the whole worldly display. Thus Vātsyāyana says, "Because of this, we are able to grasp everything that we do. We are able to perceive things. Thus the composite, the whole, is an additional substantial reality beyond the parts."

Alternatively, "**There would be no knowledge of anything**" may be read as "**There would be no knowledge through any of the knowledge sources**."

Opponent: How so?

Reply: In order for something to be perceptible, it must have sufficient size and exist concurrently with the perceiver. If something exists concurrently and is of sufficient size, then it is fit to be perceived by the external organs. And if one rejects composite wholes such as pots, then there would be nothing fit to be perceived by the external organs. And because there would be no perception, inference and the other *pramāṇas* could not work. Each and every *pramāṇa* would be finished. And yet objects are known by means of *pramāṇas*, perception and the rest. By them we grasp what we grasp. We perceive. Thus the composite, the whole, exists in its own right. The intention with the current sūtra is to point out the impossible contradictions we land in if we fail to accept the composite whole. These impossible contradictions would lead to the implosion of all the knowledge people have acquired.

2.1.35: (Reply continued:) And because holding and pulling are possible, there is a composite whole beyond the mere parts.

Uddyotakara [228.10–17]: . . . **Holding** occurs when one part of a thing is grasped and by dint of this the entire thing is prevented from moving to another place. That is, we have holding when, by grasping only a part of a whole, a person grasps the entire thing. And thus she prevents it from moving to another place. **Pulling** occurs when a thing that has been grasped in one part is moved as it is to another place by dint of moving that single part.

Objection: Where do these definitions come from?

Reply: From common usage. People commonly use the words in this way for holding and pulling. And such holding and pulling do indeed prove the existence of the composite whole.

Objection: How so?

Reply: Because the properties of holding and pulling are not found in either non-composite things or in parts (by themselves, e.g., in atoms). For, holding and pulling are not perceived in non-composite things or in parts, and yet holding and pulling are found to occur. So they must be features of composite wholes.

Vācaspatimiśra [347.20–348.3]: These two, holding and pulling, prove the existence of a composite whole which is experienced in things such as cows and pots.

Objection: How is this?

Reply: We see that non-composite things—such as the mental state of awareness, also ether, as well as ultimate atoms which constitute things' non-composite parts—are not physically apprehended in this way.

Thus, Uddyotakara puts forth an argument to the following effect: There are things that are experienced as composite wholes, such as cows and pots, but are under dispute regarding the question of whether they are mere aggregates of atoms. If these things were not composite wholes, then holding and pulling them would be impossible. Whatever is not a whole with parts cannot be held or pulled, like knowledge, etc., and unlike cows, pots, and so on. The latter are not like that. Therefore, they are wholes with parts.

*Ether (*ākāśa*) is an all-pervading, non-composite substance, the medium of the transmission of sound. Awareness (*vijñāna*) is a psychological quality that is partless as well. An ultimate atom (*paramāṇu*) is the smallest, non-composite substance, the indivisible building block of macro objects. Neither ether nor atoms are composite substances, and neither can be gripped and pulled. Thus both ether and atoms stand as negative examples in support of Nyāya's argument.*

All of our commentators, from Vātsyāyana on, give voice to an objector who argues that there is no need to posit a separate entity that unites parts. Rather, all that is needed is the property, "adhesion," which binds micro objects such as atoms together. And Vātsyāyana has the objector provide counterexamples of things not metaphysically unified and yet capable of being held and pulled, as well as of things that seem metaphysically unified but are incapable of being held and pulled, all under this same sūtra, 2.1.35.

Vātsyāyana [76.5–6]: Objection: If being able to be held and pulled were due to something's merely having parts, then we would have found that a heap of dust is capable of being held and pulled. And further, when straw, rocks, and wood are stuck together with glue, they should not be held together or move as a unit when pulled, since no new substance has been produced.

The glued cluster of oddities is a counterexample to Nyāya's argument. The idea is that a cluster of things stuck together haphazardly isn't a genuine composite whole, and yet something like this can be held and pulled. A pile of dust is built up out of smaller parts but can't be held or pulled. Uddyotakara shows that he sees the force of the counterexamples, but instead of disputing them, he makes a fundamental clarification about the Nyāya position.

Uddyotakara [228.18–229.2]: Objection: Pulling and holding are due to nothing but a conglomeration of parts, not the existence of a composite whole. In the case of a pile of dust, for instance, there is no pulling or holding. In cases such as straw, rocks, and wood stuck together with gum, we do find pulling and holding.

Reply: This is wrong, because you have not understood our position. We do not claim that every composite whole is capable of being held and pulled. Rather, our view is that holding or pulling do not occur for things that are not composite wholes. And no contradiction is observed with respect to any composite whole. You say that things put together by gum such as straw, rocks, and wood are capable of being pulled and held. Yes, we say those are indeed cases of composite wholes. If we said one could catch hold of something, however, and pull it although it were neither a composite whole nor a part of something else, then we would land in impossible contradiction.

In contemporary terms, Uddyotakara is claiming that being a composite whole is necessary, not sufficient, for the capacity to be held or pulled. If there is holding and pulling, then there is a composite whole. And without composite wholes, there would be no possibility of holding or pulling. Thus properties such as holding and pulling establish the existence of the composite whole.

Vācaspatimiśra [348.4]: Uddyotakara notes that his argument is not contradicted. Contradiction is a fault that besets arguments when its prover is found to deviate.

By claiming that there is no contradiction or deviation in the argument, Vācaspatimiśra, following Uddyotakara, implies that the prover, "being held and pulled," correlates with composite wholes and does not deviate by occurring with anything that is not a whole.

The core question of the next sūtra is whether our experience of macro objects might not be erroneous. Nyāya takes such experience to be veridical, and thus solid evidence that macro objects have a reality of their own, beyond the parts that comprise them. An opponent argues that our experience of single, unified things is rather a mistake. From a distance, a forest or an army looks like a unified, single thing, but when we get close, we realize that it is nothing more than a cluster of trees or a mass of soldiers. It is alleged that the same holds for our experiences of tables, chairs, pots, and so on. Following Gautama, Vātsyāyana responds that, again taken to its logical conclusion, this has to be a false analogy.

2.1.36: If one contends that composite wholes are experienced like an army or a forest, that would be wrong, since atoms are beyond the range of the senses.

Vātsyāyana [77.2–3]: Atoms are different from the things you assume to be examples of separate individuals misperceived as unities, for some reason. Unlike such things, atoms are beyond the range of the senses. It is thus wrong to claim that our knowledge of objects as single unities is a mistake caused by our failure to grasp the components individually.

In lengthy commentary, Uddyotakara follows Vātsyāyana by arguing that the opponent provides a false analogy. The mistake alleged is not possible with respect to atoms. Even the opponent's reasoning implies that individual soldiers and trees are real, unitary entities.

Uddyotakara goes on to argue that it makes little sense to say that we project errors upon imperceptible clouds of atoms. This is in response to an imagined objector's challenge that the illusion of the whole goes all the way down. Here, he draws upon Nyāya's standard account of perceptual error, which we examined in Chapter 3, "In Defense of the Real." Generally, when we mistake x *for* y*, this is because there is some* *commonality between them. We see a post in the distance as a person because they are both roughly five to six feet tall and two feet wide. And we make the error because we fail to notice the particulars that would distinguish one from the other. But in the case currently under discussion, since we cannot see atoms, we are in no position to see any commonality between a cluster of atoms and macro substances that would lead us to mistake the former for the latter.*

Uddyotakara [230.5–7, 231.3–7]: One cannot claim that every cognition of a single, unitary object is mistaken. After all, "the many" is nothing more than a collection of single things. This is true even when we are experiencing many as one, as with an army, such that we get the idea there is something single and undifferentiated because we fail to notice differences. For, there is a reason why failure to notice differences has to come to an end (in knowledge of unanalyzable units). . . .

Opponent: The cognition of unity projected upon a plurality is an error.

Reply: The error is caused by perception of commonality while failing to notice particulars. One projects a contrary property onto something by way of not seeing the particulars. But there is no perception of commonality regarding atoms, as they are beyond the range of the senses. With no perception of commonality, how could it be that one fails to notice the particulars? And in the absence of both of these (in the case of atoms), there could be no projection of a false property. And it is wrong to hold that an erroneous cognition could arise without a cause or reason.

As we saw briefly at the beginning of the chapter, in these debates about the status of macro objects, conjunction, *a relational quality that links substances, is crucial to Nyāya. Since conjunction is what allows smaller substances to unite, it is central to Nyāya's view of composite wholes. In the next passage, Vātsyāyana imagines an opponent proposing a deflationary understanding of conjunction: it is nothing more than a description of the position of atoms as being close to one another. Vātsyāyana responds by arguing that conjunction is real and metaphysically significant. It has the power to produce things that are genuinely new.*

Vātsyāyana [78.22–79.1]: Opponent: Conjunction is nothing more than proximity culminating in contact. It is not some additional thing.

Reply: Wrong, since conjunction causes new entities. Conjunction causes the vibrations that produce sound (for example, when a percussion instrument is struck), color (for example, fire atoms coming into conjunction with earth atoms comprising a pot change its color), and so on. And we would not find causes for the vibrations producing sounds, changes of color, etc., unless there is a special quality connecting the substances. Thus, conjunction is a distinct sort of quality.

We should add that not only is conjunction crucial to our world of macro objects, qualification by universals is also crucial. The reality of a cow includes its instantiating the universal cowhood as well as qualities such as color and weight. Bessie is not just peculiar conjunctions of atoms but a cow. The battle over the reality of universals and the like is fought, however, in a different arena (see Chapter 7, "Word and Object").

Wrapping up his long commentary, Uddyotakara offers four formal arguments in support of composite wholes. For analysis of the structure of such formal arguments, please see Chapter 9, "Debate."

Uddyotakara [236.18–21]:

(1) Yarn is different from the cloth made from it,
Since the yarn is a cause of the cloth,
Like the weaver's loom and other causes of the cloth (all of which are clearly different from it).
Yarn is a cause of the cloth—this is a matter of experience and so our reasoning applies.
Therefore, it is different from the cloth.

(2) Yarn is different from the cloth made from it,
Since the two have different causal capacities (*sāmarthya*),
Like poison and antidotes.

Yarn and cloth have different causal capacities.
Therefore, yarn is different from the cloth.

(3) Yarn is different from the cloth made from it,
Since the two are objects of distinct cognitions,
Like sight and touch.
Yarn and cloth are objects of distinct cognitions.
Therefore, yarn is different from the cloth.

(4) The color of yarn and the color of cloth have different causes,
Since the two have distinctive features,
Like sight and touch experiences.
The color of yarn and the color of cloth are distinct.
Therefore, they have different causes.

Each of these inferences provides reasons for metaphysical distinctness. The first argues that a cause and effect are not identical. Therefore, even material causes such as threads are not identical with their effects. The second argues that two things with different causal capacities are distinct. The idea that having a distinct causal capacity is a sure sign of a distinct existence is a thesis promoted by Buddhists themselves, and Yogācārins in particular, whom Uddyotakara identifies as his chief adversaries. The third argues that objects of distinct cognitions are distinct. Cognitions are distinguished by their contents, and clearly, "It's yarn" and "It's cloth" are distinct in content. The fourth argues that different qualities such as different colors have different causal conditions. This is one step removed from the earlier point that two things with different causes are not identical.

Next we look at a few sūtras on atoms, the eternal, non-composite building blocks considered the ultimate stuff of composite wholes. A barrage of objections is voiced in the section, from the fourth chapter of the Nyāya-sūtra, *following another, mainly repetitive discussion of composite wholes. Nyāya's central contention concerning atoms is that the idea of infinite divisibility makes no sense. There must be a stopping point.*

4.2.16: Things cannot be divided down to an ultimate dissolution, for there must be atoms. . . .

4.2.25: These opposing considerations do not refute our notion of the atom, for they would lead to an infinite regress and that is impossible.

Vātsyāyana [270.17–19]: And if there were an infinite regress of divisibility, every substratum would have an unending number of parts that would themselves be substances, and it would be impossible to settle differences of size or weight. There would also be the absurdity that the part (the atom) and the whole (the composite made of atoms) would be equal in size, because the "ultimate" atom would be divisible into parts.

In all this discussion of composite wholes and their relation to their material substrata, a background consideration is the nature of causation, the way the various factors come together to produce something new. Nyāya's view of causation is deeply embedded in its view of reality, so deeply that it tends to function as a presupposition that is articulated only piecemeal as contextually required.

While searching for causes, Nyāya concerns itself more with clusters of necessary conditions than with a single sufficient condition. To use the example of a clay pot, causal conditions that give rise to it include the clay, various qualities that inhere in the clay, time and space, the potter who puts the clay together along with the potter's knowledge of how to make a pot, and all the instruments used such as the wheel and the stick. Within this cluster of conditions and factors, Nyāya uses a threefold typology to capture the primary types of cause.

The "inherence" cause. *This is the pre-existing stuff or objects in which effects inhere. For physical objects such as pots, this would be potshards or clay, for example. As discussed above, the most fundamental cause of this kind would be atoms. Philosophers of other schools sometimes think that this should be called the "material cause," especially when atoms are the substratum. But there are many cases where an inherence cause is simply the location of an effect or* *property without being material that is molded, like clay, to produce an effect. For psychological effects such as perceptual knowledge, the inherence cause is the self, which is the substratum of psychological states.*

The "co-inherence" cause. *This is a feature of the inherence cause relevant to the emergence of the effect. While the threads are the inherence cause, the color of the threads that make up a cloth is the co-inherence cause of the color of the cloth. In the case of physical objects, the special conjunctions of the parts are co-inherence causes of the emergent objects. For example, a dyad has as a co-inherence cause the conjunction that joins two ultimate atoms. In the case of psychological effects such as perceptual knowledge, the connection between the mind and the self, which brings information into focus, is a co-inherence cause.*

The "efficient" or "instrumental" cause. *This is any of a number of factors that are necessary to the causal process. In the example of the pot, the potter and all the tools used to shape the clay into a pot are instrumental causes. In the case of psychological effects such as visual awareness, the visual sense organ and practically everything involved in perception as a knowledge source are instrumental causes. In Chapter 6, "God," we will see that Nyāya argues that God acts as an efficient cause of just about everything by organizing atoms into coherent structures.*

*Of course, in English we often use the word "cause" to mean the most proximate and immediate causal factor, ignoring other necessary factors. We say that the switch causes the light to come on, ignoring the energy from the power plant, the cables that carry it, and so on. For this most immediate factor, Nyāya has in Sanskrit a different word (*karaṇa*), which means "trigger." Triggers include* pramāṇas *as causes of knowledge, for example, in that they bring together pre-existing causal conditions to produce instances of knowledge.*

Nyāya's approach to causation puts it at odds with various competitor schools. By stressing that causality involves a cluster of necessary conditions, Nyāya is comfortable with things having dispositional properties. For example, liquid water in a glass has the disposition to change into ice, but that occurrence requires other factors, something to bring the temperature down, a freezer, for instance. This approach contrasts with the mainstream Buddhist tradition, which focuses on sufficient causation. For Yogācārins in particular, a cause is that which is sufficient to produce an effect. The position famously underpins the Buddhist doctrine of momentariness, which holds that a seed-instance that has not yet sprouted is something entirely different from the "same" seed-instance a moment later. Indeed, even while lying dormant, each temporally distinct seed instance is a different thing from the instance that preceded it.

Nyāya attacks the view in Nyāya-sūtra *4.1.14–18. Our commentators insist on continuity between cause and effect. In the case of the seed and the sprout, several necessary factors—warmth from the sun, earth, water—come together to trigger a disposition within the seed to sprout. Without continuity between the inherence cause that houses the disposition (the seed) and the effect that is triggered (the sprout), there would be no regular causal patterns, Nyāya contends. Momentariness cannot explain this coherently.*

Nyāya holds that causes bring new things into the world, things that did not exist previously. But what exactly is new about an effect, especially given that a macro physical product does depend upon a pre-existing material substratum? In answering this question, Nyāya is opposed by several camps. On one side is the Sāṃkhya school, another Vedic tradition, one that claims that effects exist in their material nature in a latent state. Sāṃkhya holds that in reality effects pre-exist within their causes. What we call causation (e.g., crafting a pot out of clay) merely "manifests" a latent effect. The pot was already there in the clay and need only be brought forth. On another side are the aforementioned Buddhists, whom Vātsyāyana and company tend to label "nihilists." These philosophers argue there is no continuity between cause and effect. Nyāya defends middle ground between the two extremes.

Below, with Nyāya-sūtra *4.1.49–50, we are treated to arguments against Sāṃkhya. What seems to be Uddyotakara's best argument comes in a quip: If effects pre-exist as Sāṃkhya holds, why go to all the trouble to grind seeds to get oil?*

Vātsyāyana [242.16]: Something produced does not exist prior to its production—this is certain. Why?

4.1.49: Because production and destruction are observed.

Uddyotakara [458.5–459.2]: Something that was unperceived earlier is perceived later, and this makes sense if the thing produced did not exist before its production. Furthermore, destruction accounts for something that was by nature perceptible no longer being seen. These occurrences would not be possible on the (Sāṃkhya) view that things are permanent. On that view of effects as pre-existent, there would be neither production nor destruction. And if the concepts of production and destruction were rejected, everyday practices would be abandoned. Why do people do what they do everyday? Is it not because they think, "Doing this, I will gain that," or "Doing this, I will avoid that"? This is why people act. However, on the view of the prior existence of the effect (*sat-kārya-vāda*, the Sāṃkhya view), there would be nothing for people to gain or avoid. . . .

Sāṃkhya objector: The chief cause, the material cause, has a purpose embedded in it, the purpose of *manifesting* latent individual effects.

Reply: What is it really, this "manifestation" of yours that is brought about by your material cause?

Objector: It's what you call an effect, something to be brought about.

Reply: You contradict your own view (as something new is brought about).

Objector: Well, it's an effect as a property of the pre-existing cause.

Reply: Still the contradiction remains.

Objector: The manifestation is of objects that, as effects, are perceived. These are what are brought about (not new objects but experiences of the newly manifested things).

Reply: The contradiction remains; you have not escaped it (since you still admit things that are new).

Objector: The manifestation is a situation, a condition of the pre-existing cause, the situation being the effect.

Reply: Even with that conception, the contradiction has not ceased, because the situation, as you say, of being the effect is the coming to be of that which did not exist previously.

Objector: The manifestation is a distinct configuration of the cause.

Reply: There is still a contradiction, in that the "distinct configuration" would be something new that comes into being.

Objector: No, it is already there.

Reply: Then, your proposition that (as you say) "The chief cause, the material cause, has a purpose embedded in it" is meaningless.

Objection: The manifestation is the flourishing of the cause's essential nature.

Reply: No such flourishing of the cause's essential nature can be seen prior to the time of production. Thus it is empty to claim it's already there in identifying your so-called material cause. And since this so-called flourishing of an essential nature comes into existence having been previously non-existent, you have not been freed from contradiction.

To sum up, in whatever way one conjures up meaning for the idea of "manifestation," in just that way the notion of a pre-existent effect will be blocked.

A principal argument for Sāṃkhya's sat-kārya-vāda *is that we need some way to account for causal regularity.*[4] *For example, sesame seeds produce sesame oil and not olive oil. Sāṃkhya argues that there must be a deep tie between the nature of the effect and the nature of the material cause to account for this fact. In the next sūtra, Nyāya counters that this story still requires one to understand effects as genuinely new entities. Here Nyāya returns to the notion of capacity, the potentiality to bring about certain effects in the appropriate conditions.*

4.1.50: What is proved, however, by our understanding is the prior non-existence of the effect.

Uddyotakara [451.4–10]: Sāṃkhya objector: This sort of thing is preceded by that sort of thing. Because of such laws

4 *Sāṃkhya-kārikā* 9.

or regularities involving a material cause, it's not true that the effect is absent in the cause.

Reply: **What is proved, however, by our understanding is the prior non-existence of the effect**. It is not that causal regularities occur because of the pre-existence of the effect, but rather because of the *capacity* of the cause to produce the effect. "This is capable of being caused by *x*, but not by *y*"—in this way **by our understanding an effect is proved**: If something is capable of producing something else, that thing is designated the chief cause of the other. It's not that anything, or "everything," can produce anything and everything. That anything or everything could give rise to anything and everything is not experienced.

Objection: Regularities of production lead us to discover the lawful ties between causes and effects.

Reply: Here, too, we have to ask: What do you mean by the words "causes" and "effects"? What is a cause as you speak of it? And what is an effect as you speak of it?

Objection: We say that a cause is that which makes something and an effect is that which is made.

Reply: If you hold that this "making" is nothing but manifestation, there would be the unacceptable consequences laid out above.

*Causal capacities undergird laws and regularities of nature, according to Nyāya. The Sāṃkhya opponent has a point: only banana seeds have the capacity to make banana plants. Such capacity (*sāmarthya*) may be called a dispositional property, a capacity triggered when the situation is right, that is to say, when other necessary conditions come to be in place, for example, moisture, warmth, and soil in addition to the seed or material cause in the case of a sprout appearing. As pointed out, Nyāya's view of causation supposes a background cluster of necessary conditions that together produce specific effects.*

Suggestions for Further Reading

Wilhelm Halbfass, *On Being and What There Is: Classical Vaiśeṣika and the History of Indian Ontology*. Albany: State University of New York Press, 1992.

Bimal Krishna Matilal, "Causality in the Nyāya-Vaiśeṣika School." *Philosophy East and West* 25 (1975): 41–48.

Umesh Mishra, *Nyāya-Vaiśeṣika: Conception of Matter in Indian Philosophy*. Delhi: Bharatiya Kala Prakashan, 2006.

Harsh Narain, *Evolution of the Nyaya-Vaisesika Categoriology*. Varanasi: Bharati Prakashan, 1976.

Stephen Phillips, *Classical Indian Metaphysics: Refutations of Realism and the Emergence of "New Logic."* Chicago: Open Court, 1995.

Study Questions

1. What is a substance? Provide examples of the following according to Nyāya's view of the world: composite wholes, non-composite substances, and psychological substances.
2. What is meant when Naiyāyikas argue that we couldn't know anything if composite wholes didn't exist? Reconstruct the argument.
3. Explain the "holding and pulling" argument in support of composite wholes.
4. What is conjunction? Why does Nyāya need to defend its reality in order to defend the reality of composite wholes?
5. Consider Uddyotakara's four arguments for the reality of composite wholes. Which do you think is the strongest? Why? Which do you think is the weakest? Why?
6. Why must there be atoms according to Nyāya?
7. Summarize Uddyotakara's arguments that are meant to refute the Sāṃkhya idea of the pre-existence of the effect within the cause.
8. Explain the Sāṃkhya view that an effect must preexist within its material cause. What is Nyāya's alternative proposal to address this concern?

Chapter 6

God

*A noteworthy feature of the Nyāya tradition is its rational theology, the effort to prove the existence of God (*īśvara*) by argument. To use the language of Nyāya, it attempts to establish God's existence and some general sense of his nature through* inference (anumāna)*, the second of the four knowledge sources, in contrast to sacred texts, which are one subtype of testimony (*śabda*). In the early school, a few theistic arguments are developed by commentators in connection with sūtras 4.1.19–21, the "theistic sūtras." Beginning with Udayana, a separate, complex literature emerges, with dozens of arguments. Since in the* Nyāya-sūtra *itself, not including the commentaries, the Lord is not invoked outside the theistic sūtras, some modern scholars have speculated that Nyāya was originally atheistic or at least agnostic. The entire classical tradition, however, takes the sūtras to endorse a brand of theism, and our commentators use them to launch a rational theology centered on the notion of* īśvara*, a being who assembles the manifest world out of eternal, indivisible atoms and governs it according to the karmic merit of individual selves.*

Vātsyāyana, our earliest commentator, reads the sūtras as devoted to showing compatibility between God's power and karma. He does not argue in any detail to establish the existence of īśvara*, although he does sketch out the creator's nature. But Uddyotakara and all later classical commentators argue explicitly and elaborately that God exists while also articulating in broad outline what they see as the divine nature.*

Nyāya's theology seems rather minimalist compared to, say, Vedānta's notion of Brahman, the Absolute. The Nyāya principle seems to be to avoid theological pronouncements beyond what is necessary for its explanations, and we may suspect that there were many Naiyāyikas who, to one degree or another, had more robust theological commitments than are expressed here. Some were Vedāntins, such as Vācaspatimiśra who wrote a brilliant commentary within the school of Advaita Vedānta.

Inference is the main knowledge source in Nyāya discussions of Īśvara. *While our philosophers sometimes cite sacred texts, in particular certain Upaniṣads, and some hold that there is possible a mystical awareness of God as a kind of yogic perception, the mainstream attitude is that when trying to prove something within metaphysics and the deepest truths of a world view, inference must be the knowledge source that plays the crucial role. Thus, Nyāya's rational theology is dominated by a concern to find the best provers of God's existence. The one that comes to receive the most attention is sometimes called the argument from producthood: earth and the like are products, like a pot. As a product, earth and the rest require a conscious agent capable of putting their parts together, down to atoms, which do not naturally join up. Naiyāyikas conclude that the only being fit to bring about the order that we know as the world is God, an all-pervasive, unembodied spirit or self.*

Our theistic sūtras are embedded within a long discussion of causation and the origins of the world as we experience it (see the outline of the Nyāya-sūtra *in Appendix A). The topic of causation is introduced through a concern with rebirth and the karma caused by action. Our sūtras, 4.1.19–21, then take up the role of* Īśvara, *God, in relation to factors that influence the unrolling of an individual's life. The issue is the relationship between dispositions made by past human action (karma) and the power and grace of God (*Īśvara*) when it comes to one's future lot. However, Uddyotakara takes the opportunity here to talk about a wider scope of God's activity, to include God as a causal factor for practically everything. Nevertheless, our commentators agree minimally that the first two sūtras voice competing claims, respectively that God has exclusive determinative power, and that no human action does. A third position synthesizes the two and presents* *the accepted Nyāya view: one's actions shape one's future birth through the creation of karma but only if the karma is actuated by God.*

4.1.19: God is the sufficient cause, since we find that human action sometimes does not come to fruition.

4.1.20: No, that is wrong, since in the absence of human action there is no fruition.

4.1.21: That, too, is not a good reason, since fruition is actuated by God.

Vātsyāyana [228.3–16]: God grants causal power to what has been done by human beings. That is, for an individual who is acting for a certain karmic fruit, God makes that fruit come forth. If God did not, human action would be karmically fruitless. Thus, what humans do is not sufficient for karmic fruition, **since fruition is actuated by God**, and yet **in the absence of human action there is no fruition**.

God is distinct from other selves owing to his special qualities. God is most akin to a self; it doesn't make sense to think of him as something else. But he is different from other selves in that demerit (*adharma*), mistaken cognition, and delusion are absent, while he is perfect in merit (*dharma*), knowledge, and yogic concentration and accomplishment (*samādhi*). As a consequence of his merit and concentration, he possesses lordliness in the form of the eightfold yogic powers (*siddhi*), such as the ability to make oneself as small as an atom. His merit (*dharma*), which conforms to his intention, activates the merit and demerit collected in each individual self as well as gross elements such as earth. And so God's irresistible will in creating should be understood as enacting what individuals have themselves done; that is to say, it is not insulated from the influence of what individuals themselves have done.

God is a trustworthy authority. His relationship to creatures is like that of a father to his progeny. His nature is not to be thought of as something other than that of a self. None of his properties aside from knowledge could serve as an inferential mark proving his existence, and from sacred tradition we know that God is a perceiver, a knower, and omniscient. And if the Lord were entirely beyond the range of perception, inference, and scripture, who could ever demonstrate that he was not knowable through a characteristic like knowledge?

If one proposed that God's creative actions occur without being influenced by what individuals have themselves done, this proposition would be refuted for all the reasons we have given against the view that bodies are born independently of karmic merit.[1]

The Yoga-sūtra *and other yogic texts mention eight powers or perfections* (siddhi) *that a yogically perfected being may possess. By describing God's greatness with yoga terminology, Vātsyāyana shows close affinity between Nyāya and Yoga, which will be shown again in chapter four of the* Nyāya-sūtra *(see Chapter 8, "The Right and the Good," of this volume) when yogic* samādhi *(perfected concentration) is taken up.*

Commonly, karmic merit is thought of as adṛṣṭa, *"Unseen Force," which, according to the Mīmāṃsā school of Vedic exegesis, is a factor influencing absolutely everything that happens. Nyāya and other schools appear to have a similar view, except that a role for God as overseer is thought to be demanded.*

Uddyotakara [432.14–433.3]: We do not claim that God creates independently of karmic merit and the like. Rather, the Lord grants human action causal power. What is meant by *grants* here? When the time comes for what anyone has done to fructify karmically, the Lord accordingly apportions causal power at that moment. Anyone who would suggest that God acts with indifference to karmic histories would face unacceptable consequences such as the impossibility of liberation. But such consequences are avoided on the view we have advanced, namely, that God's creative action is in accord with karma. The rest is made clear in Vātsyāyana's *Commentary*.

When the sūtras say thus "**fruition is actuated by God**," the Lord is taken to be an efficient cause. An efficient cause is that which grants causal power to two other kinds of cause,

1 *Nyāya-sūtra* 3.2.60–72.

the inherence and the co-inherence causes, as a shuttle or the like works on threads and their connections to make a piece of cloth.

> *The idea here is that an efficient cause (the weaver along with his weaving tools) works on threads (the inherence cause) and the thread's own properties, which include connections with other threads (the co-inherence causes). By working with the other two causes, the weaver arranges things such that the threads and their properties give rise to a newly produced piece of cloth.*

Uddyotakara [433.3–16]: And so it may be asked, "If God is an efficient cause of the universe, then what is its immediate material cause?" The answer is that for earth and the like it is the manifest material cause in its most subtle form—what we call "ultimate atoms."

There is agreement about what is the manifest material cause, but the distinct nature of the efficient cause is yet controversial. While we propose that it is God's activity, various views are disputed by philosophers. Some say the efficient cause is time, others God, and others that it is nature itself. So given the disagreement about the specific cause, what then is the reasoned view? We say that it is God, for the knowledge sources support this view irrefutably.

Objection: But the existence of God isn't proven.

Answer: By this you appear to be trying to confound our position by suggesting that one must first prove God's existence and then by refuting rival views establish that he is the efficient cause. But we deny that this is the case. God's existence is implicit in the proposition that he is the world's efficient cause. The reasoning that establishes God's causality also establishes his existence. Something that doesn't exist cannot function as a cause.

Objection: What then is the proof of God's causality?

Answer: The following may be put forth:

1. Primordial matter, atoms, and karma have to be directed by a conscious agent before they can function,
2. Since they are insentient,
3. Like an axe.

4. As axes, due to insentience, cut only when directed by an axeman, so too do insentient things, such as primordial nature, atoms, and karma, come to function.
5. Therefore, they too are directed by a conscious agent as a cause.

Having provided now a fundamental argument—namely, that insentient causes demand sentient guidance—Uddyotakara goes on to reject competing proposals for an efficient cause of the universe. One is Sāṃkhya's primordial matter (pradhāna)*, which is claimed to unfold of its own accord for the sake of the selves that populate creation. Another is atomicity, the atoms themselves considered simply to come together under the influence of Unseen Force (karma) without need for a superintending God. Uddyotakara's refutations delve into details of each proposal. Here let us note only that the general principle motivating his refutations is that structured effects require conscious agency within the causal complex sufficient to produce them. He often repeats that the problem with the alternative proposals is that they identify only insentient* (acetana) *causal factors. Even Unseen Force or karma is insentient, as it is a kind of informational state and moral vector that is generated by the efforts of conscious beings. As such, it cannot function without superintending intelligence.*

Next, Uddyotakara responds to questions and objections that allow him to develop his theology and, in particular, answer the question of why God creates the world. His position is close to that of the British philosopher Alfred North Whitehead: It is God's intrinsic nature to create. Here he explicitly differentiates his view from Vedānta, in its contention that the world is God's līlā, *"play."*[2]

Uddyotakara [437.14–438.13]: Objection: What purpose could the Lord have in creating the world? For we find that in everyday life people act out of some particular concern, thinking, "I will gain this," or "I will avoid that." God, however, need not avoid anything, as he is free from pain and suffering. Nor need he gain anything, as he has complete self-mastery and control.

2 *Vedānta-sūtra* 2.1.33.

Reply: Some say that creation is for the sake of play, that the Lord creates the universe as a kind of sport or pastime. But this is wrong. For play is done for the sake of enjoyment by those who would lack enjoyment without it. And it is false that the Blessed One would seek enjoyment in this way, since, as has been said, he suffers no unhappiness. Those who are unhappy engage in amusements to become happy.

Others say that creation is for the sake of revealing the glory of the Lord. They think that God creates the manifold universe as a testament to his glory. This is similarly wrong. For the Lord would not gain even a hint of distinction by means of his glory being revealed (to the likes of us), nor would he lose anything by not revealing it.

Why, then, does he create? The proposal that cannot be faulted is that he does so because that is his very nature. As elements like earth function by their own nature in acts such as providing support, the Lord is also active in accord with his nature. The fundamental truth about him is that it is his intrinsic nature to act.

Objection: Then because of his intrinsic nature God would have to be always active (and there could be no *pralaya*, no periodic dissolution of the world, along with other unacceptable consequences). . . .

Response: Our view does not suffer such a fault, because we understand God to possess intelligence. Being intelligent, as we have explained, is included in the Lord's intrinsic nature. And to be intelligent means to act with sensitivity to specific factors. Such sensitivity ensures that God does not do everything all at once nor the same thing all the time. . . . Something happens when all the causal factors sufficient for it are in place. Something whose causal conditions are not all present does not happen. Not everything has its causal factors in place simultaneously with everything else. Thus our view does not face the unfortunate consequence that everything would happen all at once. In acting, the Lord looks to the proper time for the manifestation of karmic merit and demerit. That is to say, he looks to the conditions sufficient to bring something about. This includes the creatures who have accumulated karmic merit, the right time for the ripening of the merit and demerit that belongs to individuals, and the absence of conditions that would block such manifestation.

Later portions of Uddyotakara's long commentary on sūtra 4.1.21 consider where God would best fit within Nyāya's categories. He argues that the theistic proof presupposes that God possesses knowledge, and is thus a property-bearing substance and specifically a self. Uddyotakara further considers the uniqueness of God's knowledge, arguing that it is not produced by any kind of physical or mental mechanism and is thus unlimited, as is required for the creative function. He also considers whether it is better to regard God as liberated or bound, concluding that these terms do not neatly apply to a being who has never been bound to begin with. God is a unique self, with special properties, although there are properties, such as number—God has the property of being a single *being—that God shares with other beings and individual selves.*

Uddyotakara [438.22–440.6]: Question: . . . Is God a substance or in another category such as quality, or is he something entirely different?

Answer: God is a substance, since he possesses the quality of knowledge, like other quality-possessing substances.

Question: Since he possesses knowledge, is he just another self?

Answer: No, he is a special self because of his distinct qualities. As earth and the like are substances yet not selves because of their special properties, so there is a distinction between the Lord and ordinary selves. He is not just another self.

Question: What are his distinct qualities?

Answer: Some say that (he has the qualities of a perfected yogin). . . . In any case, he excels other selves by having eternal knowledge. It is this quality that makes him unique. Other qualities like number, are shared with other beings. God has six main qualities (number, extension, pervasiveness, distinctness, conjunction, and disjunction), like ether.

Question: What evidence (*pramāṇa*) is there that God has *eternal* knowledge?

Answer: The inference already provided, that atoms come to function as they must because an intelligent cause superintends them.

Question: But that proves an intelligent cause. What proves that the knowledge is eternal?

Answer: That it's not possible that God's attention be restricted to individual objects. Cognitions such as ours that are restricted to individual objects depend upon a collection of causes, including a body, in order to come about. But we see that the Lord's knowledge cannot be restricted to individual objects when he produces various effects simultaneously, such as the simultaneous production of enormously variegated vegetation. This wouldn't be possible if the Lord's knowledge were restricted to individual objects. . . .

Question: But if God has knowledge, wouldn't this mean he also has a body?

Answer: If we posited that to be the case, we could not avoid declaring whether such a body is eternal or non-eternal. If we said non-eternal, that would entail that God is subject to karmic merit and demerit (which govern the production of bodies), and that would not be the "God" we accept. If, on the other hand, we were to accept that the body God had is eternal, we would propose something contrary to experience (all bodies we have encountered being non-eternal instead). Better than this is to posit eternal knowledge (which, being uncaused, doesn't necessitate having a body). . . .

. . . And without the Lord's having such knowledge, the world could not have been created. Moreover, this knowledge, grasping all things, past, present, and future, is perceptual in character, not inferential or testimonial. For the Lord does not infer or rely on testimony. Nor is it a matter of memory and mental dispositions, as the Lord's knowledge is eternal.

Vācaspatimiśra [563.7–9]: When Uddyotakara says that the Lord's knowledge is perceptual in character, he means that it is unmediated and direct. It is not that it is produced by eyes (etc.), since the Lord's knowledge is eternal. To call it "perceptual" is an analogical extension of the term.

On the question whether God should be considered liberated or bound:

Uddyotakara [440.11–12]: Is the Lord bound or liberated? He is not bound, as he is entirely free from pain and suffering. And since he is not bound, he cannot be liberated either. It is only the bound who are liberated, and the Blessed One is not bound in any way. Thus he is not liberated.

Next let us look at some of Vācaspatimiśra's development of themes and concerns introduced by Uddyotakara. A prime worry is to show that one can reasonably employ inductive reasoning to infer a unique type of being. A challenger is made to argue that if Nyāya's God is a self who knows and acts, then like all selves who know and act, God must have limitations. Chief among these is reliance upon a physical body. Vācaspati denies that this must be the case. What is crucially at stake in the controversy is the power of inductive reasoning to discover unique and novel truths, while relying on correlations known through common experience. Vācaspati devotes himself to defending the possibility of inferring a unique creator God without violating basic rules of inference.

First, however, he introduces his own formulation of the argument for God's existence from producthood, putting it alongside Uddyotakara's—which is, as we have seen, that primordial nature, atoms, and the like are insentient, like an axe, and require a conscious agent to function.

Vācaspatimiśra [563.11–19]: This is what our revered teacher (Uddyotakara) is saying: . . . there are three kinds of things in this universe: (a) those known to have an intelligent maker, such as palaces, watchtowers, gates, and arches; (b) those known not to have an intelligent maker, such as atoms and ether; and (c) those for which having an intelligent maker is in doubt, such as bodies, trees, earth, and mountains. There is doubt about this third group's having an agent as a cause, because it is something that is yet to be known or because it is disputed, and no *pramāṇa* or defeater that would settle the matter has been identified. And it is not the case that mere non-perception is enough to refute God's existence, as there may be existing things that by nature are imperceptible, such as atoms. And so we argue:

1. Things that are the subject of dispute, such as bodies, trees, mountains, and the ocean, have a maker who is knowledgeable about their material cause,
2. Since they are produced; alternatively, since their material cause is insentient.
3. Whatever is produced—and whatever has a material cause that is insentient—is, like a palace, preceded by a maker who is knowledgeable about the material cause.
4. Things that are the subject of dispute, such as bodies, trees, mountains, and the ocean, are produced and have insentient material causes.
5. Therefore, they too are preceded by a maker who is knowledgeable about their material cause.

Vācaspatimiśra proffers here two different provers within one argument: that the material objects in question are produced, and that they have insentient material causes. He goes on to argue that his proof is not beset on either alternative by logical defects or faults. Then he has an interlocutor claim that the nature of the supposed creator is incompatible with the materials to be used in creation being known, since having a body is a condition required to have knowledge.

Vācaspatimiśra [564.9–12]: Opponent: Knowledge, whose object is a material cause such as earth[3] or the like, would have to be produced (like all knowledge) by causal factors that include a self/*manas* connection and a body. In the absence of any of these, cognition would be absent. Therefore, your argument should be rejected. Furthermore, my point, which is established, is not defeated by any consideration that you have advanced. If the collection of causal factors including a body, etc., were not in place, then such knowledge too would not occur, as necessarily when heat is absent there is no fire, as the source of the burning is absent.

3 Reading *kṣiti* instead of *kṣipta* (564.9).

Arguments for God's existence that begin with our experience of agential creation seem subject to the objection that all such agents have features that God should not have but would have to have if the argument is sound. This is, for example, a major strategy in David Hume's Dialogues Concerning Natural Religion, *which is famous for refutations in this vein. In India, both Buddhists and Mīmāṃsakas contend that having a body is a necessary condition for knowledge, as found in common experience, as heat is necessary for combustion. In our experience, all agential causation involves the agent's having direct experience of the materials upon which he or she works. A potter sees and touches the pot she crafts. And all such producers or creators have bodies without which knowledge would not arise. Nyāya's God would thus have to have a physical body if the argument is to be consistent with the supporting evidence.*

In classical Indian logical discourse, the common term for entailment is "pervasion" (vyāpti). *To say that* x *is pervaded by* y *means that every* x *instance is also a* y *instance. Being a cow is "pervaded by" being a mammal. Immediately below, Vācaspatimiśra accepts a challenger's claim that when ordinary knowledge is produced, a body/mind complex is required. But God's knowledge is unlike ours in that it is uncaused and eternal. Since it is not produced, God's knowledge does not need a body/mind complex. It and thus knowledge in general is not "pervaded" by the knower having a mind and a body. That God would have to have a body is thus not entailed.*

Vācaspatimiśra [564.12–15]: Answer: No. It is not true that denial of a non-pervasive factor requires one to deny something that is not pervaded by it. If something could be counted a cause when it is not pervasively associated with a certain effect, then behold, our entire practice of inferential reasoning—which depends on the pervaded / pervader relationship—would be destroyed. Your objection might be right if the cosmic maker's knowledge of material causes such as earth was an effect, but we hold that his knowledge is eternal. Therefore, the absence of a body does not entail the absence of the knowledge required. . . .

The challenger argues next that the class of objects in the reference class that are supposed to show correlation between "being a product" and "having a conscious maker" has no example of a God-like maker. Therefore, to infer a special God-like maker would cross the boundaries of legitimate inference. Vācaspatimiśra responds that in all inductive reasoning there is an element of inference to the best explanation that allows one to extend the correlations to a novel case that may well have special properties. This procedure relies on what is called pakṣa-dharmatā-bala, *"from being a property of the inferential subject," or what is entailed in a property actually qualifying a specific subject of inference. Knowledge of pervasion (*vyāpti *= entailment) is not all that makes inference work. Such knowledge together with knowing that the proved property qualifies* this particular *inferential subject allows us to infer something new—something about a current subject as a novel case—from the proved property as its qualifier. Specific details about what's inferred may be filled out according to what else we know about the particular subject. For example, an anthropologist infers that footprints found in a rock stratum are humanoid, on the grounds that the prints have properties that are reliable indicators of human feet. Then she fills out details of the specific humanoids in question, such as migratory patterns or likely diet, according to what would be required for such creatures to be in a position to leave such traces in that area. Vācaspatimiśra says below, "(the maker has to have knowledge of) the simultaneity of production of effects throughout immeasurable and unlimited space at every place and location, effects perceptible and imperceptible in animals and plants and the organic world as a whole and so on" [565.14–15]. In other words, now that we have proved that human bodies, mountains, and the like are indeed produced, we may infer a maker who is capable of all this. No ordinary agent will fit the bill, but only a God-like maker.*

Vācaspatimiśra [565.6–566.4]: Opponent: The property *being produced* entails *being preceded by a maker knowledgeable about the material cause, etc.*, but nothing more, as seen in examples such as pots. You may establish this much only for things such as earth. Where do you get the distinct property *having a maker with eternal knowledge that grasps all things*? For, it is not found in examples of things produced such as pots.

Response: From the property *being an action,* which holds for our perceptual experience of colors and so on, how do we get an inference proving the existence of sense organs? (The process is not direct.) For, we don't find that actions such as cutting prove that there are sense faculties. Rather, they prove the existence of things such as axes. But by force of *being a property of the inferential subject,* the inferential mark, *being an action,* does prove the existence of sense faculties, although, indeed, it is not found to belong to the property-possessing example. For, the fact that perception of color is an action means that it relies on an instrument that is capable of producing perceptual cognition. According to the principle of what's involved in *being a property of the inferential subject,* we are led to eliminate instruments such as axes, which do not have the proper character, and conclude that there are organs of sight and so on, although such things have not been known previously (in some other fashion).

The same holds here with the argument for God. If the maker's knowledge was not eternal (uncreated), and did not range over all things, there could not be what there is in fact: the simultaneous production of effects throughout immeasurable and unlimited space at every place and location, effects perceptible and imperceptible in animals and plants and the organic world as a whole and so on, from which we prove that the maker is God.

And such knowledge belonging to the Supreme Lord could not be produced by things that are themselves effects, created bodies and sense faculties like our own. We would have to conjure up yet another Lord to produce such a body that is capable of generating the knowledge in question, and this would entail an unavoidable difficulty, since before that second Lord we would need yet another to create *his* body, *ad infinitum*. It is better to propose a single, imperceptible being with eternal knowledge than innumerable imperceptible beings.

From this consideration alone, the proposal that there is an eternal body or eternal senses is also rebutted.

By this reasoning, what some say—

It may be that anything having the likes of
structure has some kind of intelligent cause.
But how from structure or the like could *a single*
cause be proved?

—is also set aside.

One who wishes to refute the omniscience of the maker could do so if fleshy eyes had the power to see atoms along with witnessing selves and the karma inhering in them. But there are no fleshy eyes with such capacity. Therefore, you would have to postulate many beings capable of perceiving such supersensible things who would be very different from us and our kind. It is better, for the sake of simplicity, to posit just one such being.

Vācaspatimiśra is claiming in effect that the argument for God involves inductive reasoning along with inference to the best explanation as well as an appeal to simplicity (lāghava)*—akin to what is sometimes called Ockham's razor—including avoiding the impossibility of an infinite regress. The argument is thus complex. But we may say that in a nutshell it is that a single bodiless creator with appropriate knowledge is the best explanation for the world as brought about.*

Below, another imagined opponent proposes that there are counterexamples to the proof, cases that illustrate production of structured effects without intelligent agency. If these stand, Vācaspatimiśra's prover, being a product, *would "deviate" from what he is trying to prove (see Chapter 9, "Debate," for more on inferential deviation). His response is that these sorts of cases are exactly what he is arguing about, and that they cannot, therefore, be used as counterexamples on pain of begging the question against him.*

Vācaspatimiśra [566.7–13]: Opponent: Your argument is beset by deviation, since we that without supervision the mind and senses produce cognition, without guidance, insentient milk flows of its own accord from old to young cow, and without conscious effort, trees flourish in the forest.

Reply: You cannot use these cases as counterexamples, as they are included within the inferential subject of our very proof and are thus currently under dispute. And you cannot claim that intelligent agency is to be denied in this case because it isn't observed, in the way that we deny that a rabbit has a horn on its head because we don't see one. Since the Lord is not fit to be apprehended by ordinary perception, proof by non-perception does not apply here. And if we are to think that in general non-perception of something that someone is trying to prove is enough to rebut the proof, then inference would be finished! Of course, we accept the evidence of non-perception regarding something like a rabbit's horn, since such a horn is in principle perceptible, like the horns of horned animals such as calves.

In Indian philosophy and logic, a "rabbit's horn"—an antler-like appendage on the forehead of a rabbit—is a stock example of something that doesn't exist and is universally known not to exist. Here, Vācaspatimiśra notes that we reject the existence of a rabbit's horn because we do not see one when we look at rabbits. Non-perception is enough to refute the existence of something perceptible. But, God is by nature imperceptible and could not be refuted by mere non-perception.

In the next passage, Vācaspatimiśra's imagined opponent continues to press the charge that his reasoning crosses the boundaries of legitimate inferential practice, charging this time that not all cases of being produced *correlate with* having an intelligent agent.

Vācaspatimiśra [566.14–20]: Opponent: It is false that the simple fact of *being produced* is naturally concomitant with *having an intelligent agent.* Rather, it is only a particular kind of *being produced.* When someone sees something that she has not personally witnessed being made, she still knows, upon consideration, that it has been made, by inference. This holds for things such as pots, whose existence or absence is known to conform to the existence or absence of an intelligent maker. But it does not hold for those things that have the unqualified property, *being produced,* such as organic bodies and earth, since these other things are not experienced as being associated with makers in the way you propose. Therefore, the general property, *being produced,* is tied to *having an intelligent maker* only because there is an additional condition (*upādhi*) that qualifies it. There is no natural relation of concomitance between the two but only one that is supervenient, that is, one that requires this special qualification. Therefore, *being produced* is not fit to establish your claim. If it were, there would be the unacceptable consequence that one could infer fire from the pale color of smoke—which is also found in lotuses and doves!—because it supervenes on the natural concomitance between smoke and fire.

> *An* upādhi, *or "additional condition," is not a counterexample but would entail a counterexample. While smoke is enough to infer fire, the reverse does not hold. The presence of fire is not sufficient for smoke, since something else must be present, namely, wet fuel. Thus, from knowledge of fire, we cannot infer smoke unless we can be sure that there is also wet fuel. A commonly cited counterexample entailed by the* upādhi *is a hot ball of iron, where it is thought there is fire (accounting for the heat) but not smoke because there is no wet fuel.*

Vācaspatimiśra [566.21–567.9]: Response: Here is our answer, which you should think about carefully. Consider the two options: Is the particular kind of *being produced* that you admit correlated (a) with intelligent agency in general, or (b) only with that intelligent agency previously experienced as connected to it? If the first, then yours is our position, precisely what is accepted by us who maintain that things like organic bodies and the earth have an intelligent maker as a cause. For, one cannot shamelessly claim that an effect and its cause are not correlated. Then, to consider the second option, if this particular kind of *being produced* is correlated only with things that have already been directly experienced to have intelligent makers, then people who have not witnessed something's being made would not be able to know it has a maker inferentially. Only that very cloth that has been experienced as conforming to the presence or absence of an intelligent maker could be inferred to be the product of intelligent agency, and not some other one in the market.

Opponent: Well, maybe. Then what we should say is that things of *the same kind* are perceived to correlate positively and negatively, although the conformity of some specific thing in question is not directly experienced. Being of the same kind, it would be similar.

Reply: Come now, this is not a stick with which you can threaten us, sir! Things such as pots, insofar as they are *produced*, correlate positively and negatively with *having a maker with intelligence*. Something else of the same kind, namely, things produced, such as organic bodies and the earth, would be similar, that is, have a maker with intelligence!

Opponent: Then what we should say is that things of the same kind as pots correlate with an intelligent maker in being produced.

Reply: That is clearly objectionable, since in that case palaces and the like could not be inferred to have had an intelligent maker on the basis of having been produced: they are not of the same kind as pots. We may accept that something not directly experienced as correlating positively and negatively with having an intelligent maker can be inferred to be so, but only so long as things of its same kind are seen so to correlate. But now how is it that things such as palaces that have been made can be considered to have intelligent makers whereas things such as organic bodies and the earth cannot? We may assume that in both cases there has been no direct experience of correlations. There is indeed no difference at all with respect to being of the relevant type (namely, everything that has been made, *kārya-jātīya*). . . .

*Dense discussion follows that considers God's standing with respect to the karma inhering in each individual self. The Lord must be able to "read" it and thus apportion justly one's lot in life, in particular one's future birth. Two standard relationships that exist in Nyāya metaphysics, conjunction (*saṃyoga*) and inherence (*samavāya*), appear problematic since God is said to be transcendent, untouched by* karma *whether good or bad. But he has to be related to it in some way or other in order to know and actualize it, according to Nyāya theory. Vācaspatimiśra suggests the relation* inherence-in-the-conjoined-conjunct. *As an example, a mother can know of a child's fever by kissing his forehead. Here, the mother and child's bodies are related by conjunction, by skin-to-skin* *contact. She then knows of her son's high temperature because of the warmth of his body. Warmth is a quality that inheres in the body of the son, which is itself in conjunction with the mother. She thus knows of his temperature through* inherence-in-the-conjoined-conjunct.

In the case of God's knowledge of individuals' karma, the following relation is suggested. God is in contact with the karma in individual selves by way of his contact with selves. The relation to it is even further displaced in that it occurs through contact with the atoms that make up the bodies that are conjoined with selves who are not liberated. Such a displaced relationship captures appropriately the distance between God and karma. Otherwise, it would seem that God would be stained by karma, contrary to the teaching of scripture (e.g., Bhagavad Gītā *4.14). Vācaspatimiśra makes room for distinct ways in which God may control on-going creation without being tainted. And in his view, as in Vedānta and most Buddhist schools too, while there are cycles of creation and destruction, the manifest world is strictly beginningless. Mainstream Hindu theodicy has it that God is never absolutely free to create a world without pain and suffering, as this would ignore selves' karma which he activates at the time of a new round of creation. It is thought that even at the time of a cosmic destruction (*pralaya*), karmic traces remain in seed form until the next creative cycle begins.*

In the following passage, Vācaspatimiśra's goal is not to offer a final, definitive account of the nature of God or his knowledge, but to argue that the impossibility of a theory that is in every detail worked out satisfactorily should not be cited as a reason to deny God's ongoing causal role. The example provided of a healer invokes a common idea that there are people who are able to remove poison by means of chanting mantras, thus not having to touch it directly.

Vācaspatimiśra [568.16–22]: . . . The Lord is capable of overseeing karmic merit and demerit which inhere in other selves owing to a connection he has with them. For the operative relationship is not direct. It need not be restricted to the two, conjunction and inherence, but could also be inherence-in-the-conjoined-conjunct. Atoms and other primitives have to be in contact with the (all-pervading) Lord. And selves are connected to atoms (by having bodies composed of atoms). Karmic merit and demerit inhere in selves. Alternatively, the relationship could be inherence-in-what-is-conjoined on the part of God and selves, the possibility of a beginningless conjunction being realized. Furthermore, God would take up karmic merit and demerit without incurring diminution of his own merit (*dharma*). Alternatively, he would control atoms, which are disposed to initiate their peculiar types of effect, like someone who knows how to extract poison that is set to produce its peculiar effect. By this, his connection with material causes that are conscious is also explained.

Vācaspatimiśra closes by suggesting that his proof is merely an extension of Uddyotakara's work. And he claims the proof is confirmed by leading accounts of God found in sacred testimony.

Vācaspatimiśra [568.22–569.15]: *Consciousness* is the prover provided by Uddyotakara through indirect indication. Reasons such as *being produced* should be understood as implied according to context.

Sacred tradition reinforces our argument:

> This is the Imperishable, Gargī, on whose order the
> heaven and earth remain separate.[4]
> The one God producing heaven and earth.[5]
> He reflected to himself: Let me, who am one,
> become many. Let me propagate.[6]

And so on. And there are traditional texts (*smṛti*) as well.

> The unknowing creature is not the Lord. Moving away from the self (*ātman*), impelled by the Lord, they go towards happiness or distress, towards heaven or hell.[7]

---

4 *Bṛhadāraṇyaka Upaniṣad* 3.8.9.

5 *Ṛg Veda* 10.81.3.

6 *Chāndogya Upaniṣad* 6.2.3.

7 *Mahābhārata* 3.20.28.

And the Veda reveals that the Lord's knowledge is eternal, without a cause.

> Without feet or hands, he is swift, he who comprehends. Without eyes, he sees. Without ears, he hears. He knows what is to be known, but no one knows him. They speak of him as the Great One, the Supreme Person.[8]

And so on. These very texts demonstrate that the Lord is bodiless.

I have elaborated only what was left out by Uddyotakara, the author of the *Vārttika*, and this is now done.

Suggestions for Further Reading

Gopikamohan Bhattacaryya, *Studies in Nyāya-Vaiśeṣika Theism*. Calcutta: Sanskrit College, 1961.

C. Bulcke, S. J., *The Theism of Nyāya-Vaiśeṣika: Its Origin and Early Development*. Delhi: Motilal Banarsidass, 1968.

Arindam Chakrabarti, "From the Fabric to the Weaver." In *Indian Philosophy of Religion*, ed. Roy W Perrett. Studies in Philosophy and Religion, Vol. 13. Dordrecht: Kluwer Academic Publishers, 1989.

George Chemparathy, *An Indian Rational Theology*. Vienna: Indologische Institut der Universität Wien, 1972.

Matthew R. Dasti, "Indian Rational Theology: Proof, Justification, and Epistemic Liberality in Nyāya's Argument for God." *Asian Philosophy* 21.1 (2011): 1–21.

Parimal G. Patil, *Against a Hindu God: Buddhist Philosophy of Religion in India*. New York: Columbia University Press, 2009.

John Vattanky, "Aspects of Early Nyāya Theism." *Journal of Indian Philosophy* 6 (1978): 393–404.

John Vattanky, *Gangeśa's Philosophy of God*. Madras: Adyar Library and Research Centre, 1984.

8 *Śvetāśvatara Upaniṣad* 3.19.

Study Questions

1. How do the commentators interpreting the theistic sūtras utilize the notion that God actuates human karma?
2. What are Uddyotakara's and Vācaspatimiśra's formal arguments for God's existence?
3. What views inform Nyāya's contention that things made of insentient material require a conscious agent to form them?
4. Why does Uddyotakara deny that God creates the universe as a kind of play or amusement?
5. Into which ontological category does God fit according to Nyāya? Why?
6. In his *Dialogues Concerning Natural Religion,* David Hume argues as follows:

   > If we see a house, Cleanthes, we conclude, with the greatest certainty, that it had an architect or builder because this is precisely that species of effect which we have experienced to proceed from that species of cause. But surely you will not affirm that the universe bears such a resemblance to a house that we can with the same certainty infer a similar cause, or that the analogy is here entire and perfect.

   Identify at least three specific instances where Uddyotakara's and/or Vācaspatimiśra's imagined challengers anticipate Hume's concern here. Do our commentators provide adequate responses?
7. Vācaspatimiśra argues that *being a property of the inferential subject* provides a basis to infer that God has unique properties that are unlike makers found within common experience. What is this principle of inference, what are other examples, and is it acceptable?
8. Why do Naiyāyikas claim that God's knowledge is eternal and uncaused?

Chapter 7

Word and Object

*The Nyāya concern with the meaning of words and sentences derives most directly from its endorsement of testimony as an irreducible knowledge source (*pramāṇa*; see* Nyāya-sūtra *1.1.7–8). Words and sentences are the vehicle of testimony. There is also an increasingly firm recognition that any kind of knowledge is verbalizable (*savikalpaka*) and thus capable of analysis through broadly linguistic categories. The Paniṇian tradition of grammar—which is the oldest in the world (from 500 BCE) and vast in scope—forms crucial background for Nyāya reflection on language, including its definitions of "word" and "sentence." Another important source for Nyāya's views of language is the Mīmāṃsā school known for its astute analyses of meaning. Nyāya authors follow the grammarians in their understanding of a word as a basic semantic unit with inflections indicating its place in a sentence (*Nyāya-sūtra *2.2.58), and they see the sentence as the vehicle for communication among persons. This contrasts with a religious and ritualist understanding of language found in Mīmāṃsā. Nyāya philosophers nevertheless learn a lot about verbal and sentential meaning from the theories and arguments developed in Mīmāṃsā subschools, despite their opposition to Mīmāṃsā on certain issues. The two schools also share realist sensibilities.*

Our focus in this chapter will be on issues of ontology as much as of language. The central question is: To what does a common noun such as "cow" refer? It is pretty much presupposed throughout that meaning is reference; the meaning of a term is the object or objects that it picks out. Still, we shall see that secondary meaning, which is not directly referential, is also admitted by our philosophers and in a different way from that of the rival Mīmāṃsā school.

Mīmāṃsā tends to favor the view that words generally refer to universals, *or at least repeatable shapes or forms. After all, Vedic meaning does not change from one recitation to the next. The Veda in fact has no origin: "Just like our recitation, just like now," says the famous Mīmāṃsā philosopher Kumārila (c. 700 CE). This is what is meant by the central Mīmāṃsā tenet that the Veda is eternal—"constant, continuous" is actually what the Sanskrit word "*nitya*" means; the Veda is constant, and one's recitation now is as it has always been throughout the incalculable past.*

A universal is a timeless entity, and so eternal in a different sense, but also constantly there to be referred to by words and sentences that have fixed *meaning. A universal is manifest in individual instances that are located in time and space. For example, cowhood, what it is to be a cow, is manifest in innumerable individual cows in various places and times. A similar theory is present not so much in Plato as in Aristotle, to make a quick Western comparison.*

Another voice that is represented in our passage below is that of a nominalist—possibly a grammarian, possibly a Buddhist—who views bare particulars (things bereft of universals or general properties) as the genuinely real. For the nominalist, general properties are mental fabrications. In the context of language, this thinker would hold that it is the individual that is the meaning of a common noun such as "cow."

Is, then, the main meaning of a word (a) the individual cow such as Bessie, (b) the cow shape, as in a clay cow or a cow-shaped pastry, or (c) cowhood, the universal? Nyāya holds that meaning is conventional, set by mandate, but once the conventions are set, there is nevertheless an invariable connection between a word and what it means. Otherwise, we would not be able to understand one another. Each of the three candidates exhibit this kind of necessity in that it's the word "cow" that has to be used in each case if one is to be understood.

Our stretch of sūtras, which occurs at the very end of Nyāya-sūtra *chapter two (2.2.58–69), is traditionally designated, "On the Examination of the Meaning of a Word."*

*In Sanskrit, the word here for "meaning" is "*artha,*" which has a wide semantic range, much like that of the word "object" in English. The object of a word is its referential meaning. We will therefore often use the phrase "meaning and object" to translate "*artha.*"*

Picking out an object is what a word does, and for Nyāya its meaning is the thing or things to which it refers. But we need to understand this with great care, as implied by the sūtra-maker Gautama, who opens by giving voice to various views.

Vātsyāyana [128.10–11]: The motivation for the next section is to get the right idea of the object meant by a word. And nouns are the words on which we shall focus in our inquiry. As an example, the word "cow" will be used. The next sūtra questions the word's meaning.

2.2.59: Since a word is used to refer to (a) an individual (*vyakti*), (b) a shape or form (*ākṛti*), and (c) a universal or class (*jāti*), there is doubt (sparking inquiry).

Vātsyāyana [128.13–129.2]: The linguistic reference mentioned here is a necessary connection between a word and its object. Necessarily, the individual, the shape, and the universal in question are spoken of by use of the word "cow." It is not known which among these is the object or meaning of the word, or whether all of them might be meant.

A word's object is ascertained by its capability for usage. Therefore:

2.2.60: (Opponent 1:) It's the individual, since the usage is for an individual in the case of the word "which" as well as with words for group, offering, possession, number, growth, reduction, and color, and in verbal compounds—uninterrupted succession, too.

Vātsyāyana [129.5–19]: Here the individual is said to be the meaning and object of the word. Why? Because it is the individual that is meant when the **word "which"** and the rest as mentioned in the sūtra are used. The word "**usage**" in the sūtra means verbal employment, use. "The cow *which* is standing," "The cow *which* is sitting"—in phrases like these the word "cow" does not denote a universal, because a universal is undifferentiated in its instances. The denotation must be directed towards an individual thing, because that is distinct from other things of the same class.

Furthermore, because of the differentiation shown in the expression, "a **group** of cows," it is individual things that are denoted, not the universal, which is undifferentiated. In the statement, "He gives a cow to the doctor," the **offering** is of something individual, not of a universal, because it's not possible to offer something that does not have a concrete form, and because a universal is not part of the "before" and "after" ceremonies when such offerings are made. **Possession** regards the ownership of property. "The cow belongs to Kaundinya," "The cow belongs to the *brāhmaṇa*"—in sentences such as these an individual thing is denoted such that it is possible to have different relations because of the differences among individuals. (And so on.) . . .

Next, this view is refuted.

2.2.61: (Opponent 2:) This is wrong, because there would be no way to ascertain the word's object and meaning.

Vātsyāyana [130.2–8]: It's wrong to hold that the individual is the word's object and meaning. Why? **Because there would be no way to ascertain it**. In the case of the word "**which**" and the other items mentioned, that which is distinguished or qualified is the meaning and object of the word "cow." It's a *cow* which stands, which sits (and not a horse or something else). Here it is not merely the unqualified individual substance that is referred to, unqualified by the universal (cowhood). What then? The referent is what is qualified by the universal. Therefore, the individual is not by itself the meaning and object of the word. This is the way to understand "**group**" and the other items mentioned above.

"If the individual is not the meaning of the word, how then is there usage directed to the individual?" (Opponent 2:) Even when something is not directly referred to, it can be understood on the basis of secondary usage (*upacāra*). For we do find that—

2.2.62: (Opponent 2 continued:) Even in the absence of what a word denotes, it can have meaning through secondary usage (*upacāra*, "transference"). For example, (a) a *brāhmaṇa*, (b) the "stands," (c) mats, (d) the king, (e) flour, (f) sandalwood paste, (g) the Gaṅgā (Ganges River), (h) cloth, (i) food, and (j) the person, through the relationships of (a) association (walking sticks with *brāhmaṇas*), (b) location (stands locating spectators), (c) purpose (grass collected to make mats), (d) comportment (names of gods used for the king), (e) measure (the measure for the flour measured), (f) container (the container of sandalwood paste specifying the sandalwood paste contained), (g) proximity (land bordering the Gaṅgā), (h) connection (the cloth's color for the cloth), (i) indispensable means (food for life as its means), and (j) importance (the dynasty for the founding person).

Vātsyāyana [130.12–131.2]: The claim made in the sūtra, **Even in the absence of what a word denotes, it can have meaning through secondary usage**, says that the very word whose primary designation is absent can still be used to designate something else. From **association**: "Feed the *stick*" denotes a *brāhmaṇa* because *brāhmaṇas* are associated with the walking sticks which they carry. From **location**: "The *stands* are shouting" picks out people located in the stands. From **purpose**: collected grasses being woven together to make mats can be referred to by saying, "A *mat* it is that he's making." From **comportment**: "The king is *Yama* (the lord of Death)," "The king is *Kubera* (the lord of Wealth)," since he conducts himself like those gods. From **measure**: flour having been measured out into ten-pound bags, one says, "That is a *ten-pounder*." From **container**: sandalwood paste having been put onto a balancing scale, one says, "This is *balance-scale* sandalwood paste." From **proximity**: one says, "The cows are roaming the *Gaṅgā*," designating land that borders the Gaṅgā. From **connection**: regarding a piece of cloth having the color black, one says, "The *black* (is what I want)." From **indispensable means**: "*food*" can mean life, as life requires food. From **importance**: "Such and such *person*" can mean the entire family. "*So and so*" can stand for the entire lineage, as they are important members of the lineage.

(Opponent 2 continued:) You ask how a word, which directly means a universal, can be used for an individual. It's **through secondary usage**; among the kinds mentioned in the sūtra, the move from the universal to the individual works through association or connection.

With the voice of Opponent 2, Vātsyāyana appears to have in mind a Mīmāṃsā subschool that uses a theory of reference to defend the eternity, or constancy, of the Veda. The most direct reference of words is to universals such as cowhood, and reference to individuals is indirect, a kind of secondary usage. The examples listed in the sūtra show different kinds of transference from a referent that is absent to something thus indirectly indicated. "The moon," says the poet indirectly indicating his beloved's face. In contemporary English, we speak of the president and his advisors in the phrase, "The White House has made its recommendation." The range of examples given in the sūtra shows that transference is not only possible but common in everyday speech.

Note that the transference to an individual from a directly denoted universal is said to occur by either association or connection as the relation underpinning the shift. Centuries later, Indian literary critics develop complex theories of metaphorical transference that are continuous with Vātsyāyana's remarks here.

*In the next passage, although no interlocutor is directly identified, it seems a distinct Mīmāṃsā subschool is made to voice a different theory: "form" or "shape" (*ākṛti*), not a universal, is what a noun means denotatively. Secondary usage would presumably still explain how individuals can be meant.*

Vātsyāyana [131.4]: (Opponent 3:) If indeed the meaning of the word "cow" is not the individual in sentences such as, "There is a cow," then let us say:

2.2.63: (Opponent 3:) It is form or shape (*ākṛti*) that is the primary meaning, because determination of what exists depends upon it.

Vātsyāyana [131.6–13]: (Opponent 3:) **Form or shape** is the word's object and meaning. Why? **Because determination**

of what exists depends upon it. Such form or shape amounts to a fixed arrangement of something's parts along with its sub-parts. When shape is grasped, what exists is determined, and we say, "That's a cow," "That's a horse." Without this being grasped, such instances of knowledge would not occur. The rule is: the thing that is properly denoted by a word is that which, through its being grasped, results in what exists being determined. That is its object and meaning.

Response: This view does not fly. There is a connection with the universal when something is spoken of as qualified by a universal, for example, "That's a *cow*." And it's not the arrangement of parts which is connected to the universal. "What is it connected to then?" To a thing, to an individual substance that *has* a fixed arrangement of parts. Therefore, it is not the form or shape itself that is the meaning and object of the word.

(Opponent 4:) Then let us say that it's the universal that is the word's object and meaning.

2.2.64: (Opponent 4:) It is the universal (*jāti*), because a clay cow, though endowed with individuality and shape, cannot be the subject of the consecrating ceremonies of washing, and so on.

Vātsyāyana [131.16–132.3]: (Opponent 4:) The **universal** is the meaning and object of the word. Why? **Because a clay cow, though endowed with individuality and shape, cannot be the subject of the consecrating ceremonies of washing, and so on.** "Wash the cow," "Bring the cow," "Donate a cow"—these would not be used for a cow made of clay. Why? Because a clay cow would not belong to the proper class; it lacks the appropriate universal. For in these cases it is a certain individual cow, also a shape, which the clay cow is not and does not have. That in the absence of which the idea (cow) does not arise, well, that is the word's object and meaning.

Under the current sūtra, Uddyotakara takes the opportunity to explain the universal as a fundamental item of Nyāya-Vaiśeṣika ontology (he explicitly mentions the Vaiśeṣika-sūtra*), and to answer objections from Buddhists and others* *who hold that there is no such thing. One mark of a genuine universal is that it pervades its loci: cowhood is in every bit of Bessie while she is alive. The universal is also indivisibly present in its instances: although Bessie has parts, her cowhood does not. And whereas recurrent application of an idea such as "cow" to multiple individuals is underpinned by a universal, some recurrent ideas are not. There is no such thing as a higher-order "universalhood" that inheres in all universals, for instance. Uddyotakara does not shy away from addressing this, which is perhaps the weakest plank in the Nyāya-Vaiśeṣika theory. Doing so, he precurses much work on the part of later Naiyāyikas to understand our unitary conceptions in cases where there are no universals. But we may ask whether he is not trying to have his cake (general ideas require universals as their objects) and eat it too (but not all general ideas are underpinned by universals). The nature of true universals and especially how they are identified remain important topics throughout the later centuries of Nyāya literature.*

Uddyotakara [303.19–304.19]: If you deny the existence of a universal that exists over and above the individual, you must then state what is the actual source of our common and recurrent conceptions, in the absence of a unitive universal. For, on our view, in the absence of a universal, we would fail to have common and recurrent conceptions.

Opponent: What if we did find some common and recurrent conceptions even in the absence of a universal? You yourself admit that this happens! For example, with respect to cowhood, horsehood, and pothood, you would say commonly and recurrently, "This is a universal," "This is a universal," and so on, with the idea of a universal arising over and over again. But you do not accept that there is something else, something over and above the universals themselves that unifies them. (That is, there is no higher-order *universalhood*.) Therefore, owing to such counterexamples, your thesis that the recurrent conception establishes a universal is false. You are trying to teach something equivocal (that recurrent conceptions are underpinned by universals but there are some that are not).

Reply: But we do not admit what you imply, namely, that in the case of cowhood, horsehood, and pothood the recurrent conception has no foundation at all. Therefore, you have only dodged the challenge to provide an alternative theory.

Opponent: I suppose, then, you are giving up the thesis of the *Vaiśeṣika-sūtra* (8.5) since you accept that there is a universal that inheres within universals. Your view is thus in contradiction with the sūtra: "There are no universals in universals, no individuators in individuators. . . ."

Reply: No. You misunderstand the sūtra. Here is what it means. The conception "substance" occurs with respect to a substance that has substancehood as a *qualifier*. But the same does not occur with regard to universals or individuators. The point of the sūtra is not, to repeat, that recurrent cognition has no basis at all.

Opponent: Then what's the basis?

Response: So, with respect to universals such as cowhood, are you are asking what is the basis for saying it is a universal? And why call it a universal? The answer is that a universal inheres in a plurality of instances. For example, cowhood inheres in a plurality; similarly, horsehood, and so on. It is because of the sameness of each universal's inherence in multiple instances that there is a common and recurrent conception with regard to cowhood and the rest.

Objection: Then would this be like what goes on with nouns like "cook" (where there is nothing other than cooking that unifies the instances of the recurrent conception)?

Reply: What you are implying is that as there are words such as "cook" where we do work with a common and recurrent conception without any *cookhood* universal, so there are common and recurrent conceptions with respect to cows and the like without anything like cowhood. If this is what you mean, you are wrong, because you misunderstand the meaning of the reason we gave for the difference. What we said was that conceptions of individuals would be accidental (were it not for the universal or some other underpinning). Our point is that there must be an origin to an idea of something distinct from what is picked out by an idea of a particular individual. This, however, does not commit us to the view that every common and recurrent conception derives from a universal. And this is precisely what is going on in the case of your example. The basis or means for use of the word "cook" or the like is what is predominantly meant, namely, the action of cooking. And the fact is that such predominance can be found even in the case of people who are not cooks. Thus you have not found a flaw in our view.

Now we return to Gautama's text and the next sūtra of the section concerned with the meaning of words. This is meant to refute the view that it is only the universal that is the word's object and meaning.

2.2.65: (Reply:) Wrong, because the universal is made manifest by the form or shape and the individual.

Vātsyāyana [132.6–9]: The manifestation of the universal depends on the form or shape and the individual. It is not the case that when the form and the individual are not grasped, the pure universal is grasped by itself. Therefore, the universal is not the object and meaning of the word.

Still, it is not possible that the word have no object or meaning. What, then, is it?

We are now given the answer representing Nyāya's position.

2.2.66: Nevertheless, the individual, the form or shape, and the universal together constitute the word's object and meaning.

Vātsyāyana [132.11–133.2]: The word "**nevertheless**" in the sūtra signals that there is a qualification. "What is it?" we may ask. It is that there is no rule about which of the three would be the meaning element that is predominant in a sentence. For, when one wants to talk about a distinct thing and in the manner of specificity, then it is the individual that is the predominant meaning and the universal and shape subordinate. But when one does not want to talk about distinctness or difference, but is speaking in the mode of generalization, then it is the universal that is the predominant meaning and the individual and shape subordinate. All this is richly illustrated in usages; not so in the case of the form or shape being predominant, which is nevertheless comparable.

How then do we know that the individual, the form or shape, and the universal are different? Because they have different characteristics. Among them, first of all:

2.2.67: The individual (*vyakti*) is the concrete form that supports particular qualities.

Vātsyāyana [133.4–6]: The word *vyakti*, "individual," derives from the verbal root "*añj*" and the prefix "*vi*," together which mean "to make manifest." A *vyakti* can be grasped by the sense faculties. Not every substance is a *vyakti*. In having concrete parts, it is a **concrete form**, a substance that supports, as the case may be, **particular qualities** such as touch, weight, density, fluidity, and disposition, for example, as well as dimension.

2.2.68: Form or shape (*ākṛti*) is so designated in being the sign of the universal.

Vātsyāyana [133.9–13]: Insofar as a universal and its signs are recognized, one would know the form or shape, *ākṛti*. And it is nothing more than the fixed arrangement of a thing's parts and sub-parts. The arrangements of fixed parts belonging to some entity signal a universal. For example, we infer that it is a cow over there because of its head, its feet. And given that there is a fixed arrangement of the parts of the entity, we recognize the universal, cowhood, for instance. If a universal were not made manifest by some form or shape, then we would not know it in such cognitions as "That's clay," "That's gold," "That's silver." We would lose the words' meanings.

2.2.69: The universal (*jāti*) has the character of producing an idea of things being the same.

Vātsyāyana [133.16–134.2]: The universal is that which produces a single idea for things that are the same but at distinct locations and that by which a bunch of things are not separated out and individuated. It is that object of a word that is the basis of recurrent, common notions. And that which underpins non-distinctness among a variety of things, or distinctness sometimes (between different kinds of things), is a specific universal.

A group of cows is unified by the universal cowhood that also serves to distinguish things, in that a group of horses and cows could be divided up into two groups because of the two universals, horsehood and cowhood.

Under sūtra 2.2.66 above, Uddyotakara and, following him, Vācaspatimiśra present long expositions of controversy with a rival Buddhist theory of meaning called apoha, *the "exclusion" theory of meaning. The Buddhist nominalist admits no universals or general properties but only particulars as the things to which words refer, including general terms such as "cow." In Uddyotakara's reading, it is as though this adversary has taken up Uddyotakara's challenge under 2.2.64 to provide an alternative theory. According to the Buddhist, in reference there is* exclusion *of the least salient possibilities, for example, rocks, horses, and people—all non-cows—from Bessie, Flossie, and so on when we call them cows. The debate is intricate and further details are beyond our purview. Suffice it to say that Vācaspatimiśra and Uddyotakara find numerous reasons for rejecting the* apoha *alternative, and agree with Mīmāṃsā and Vaiśeṣika about universals. They also fend off as best they can a variety of nominalist attacks. Much of their discussion resonates with an enduring debate in Western philosophy over the reality of universals and particulars.*

As the section we have now completed is concerned as much with ontology as philosophy of language, to close the chapter let us look at a few other sūtras, from Nyāya-sūtra *chapter one, which illustrate much about Nyāya positions on word reference and secondary meaning. The sūtras' main topic is specifically obfuscation by equivocation as employed in debate, usually illegitimately, unless the debate has mere victory as its goal as opposed to truth. But even though we should not equivocate when we are doing philosophy, and specifically should not obfuscate another's meaning by interpreting a word or statement in an unwanted meaning, we need to be able to detect equivocation in all of its varieties in case it is employed against us. According to Nyāya canons, if it is used, we have to point it out lest we commit the debate error and clincher* (nigraha-sthāna, *"point of defeat") known as "overlooking the censurable."*

1.2.12: Equivocation with words is construing a meaning other than that intended, when a speaker's reference to an object is not univocal.

Vātsyāyana [47.8–48.10]: Someone utters (*nava-kambalo 'yaṃ māṇavakaḥ*) "The boy has a new blanket / nine blankets." (The sentence could mean either "The boy has a *new* blanket" or "The boy has *nine* blankets," since "*nava*" means both "new" and "nine.") Here the intention is to mention the *new* blanket. But analysis of the compound ("*nava-kambala*") admits different resolutions, although the expression employing the compound is the same. Here a debater using (obfuscating) equivocation construes another, unwanted meaning different from the original speaker's intention, "That he has *nine* blankets is what you, sir, have just now pointed out." And having so construed the words, the obfuscator would refute the speaker by showing their failure to capture the fact, "He has one blanket. Why then do you claim that he has *nine* blankets?" This is **equivocation with words**, obfuscation that targets the homonym or the words in common.

The move can be refuted. When the same word has more than one meaning, a speaker's exact meaning depends on making explicit the one or the other as what is meant. The expression "*nava-kambala*" ("new blanket / nine blankets") could make reference to more than one thing or fact: "He has a new blanket," and "He has nine blankets." When there is such a usage, the obfuscator has the rendering, "That he has nine blankets is what you, sir, have referred to, and that does not accord with the fact (that he has only one blanket)." In the case of such alternative renderings of the reference, the exact meaning must be construed whereby something specific among possible exact meanings is understood, "This thing or fact has been referred to by the speaker." And in the example under discussion, there is no such thing or fact in the rendering of the obfuscating equivocator. Therefore, that is nothing but a false application of the principle.

Furthermore, employment of the rules about reference together with what is referred to is generally followed in the everyday world. This employment involves the relationship between words and objects: "This is the object meant by that referring expression," "This word refers to that object." Something of the same kind is referred to by a general word or expression; something particular is referred to by a specifying word or expression.

Moreover, such words employed for an object or fact rely on previous usages. One does not employ words that have not been employed previously. The employment has the purpose of invoking common ideas about an object or fact. And everyday discourse and activity flow from the idea of the thing that is spoken of.

In these matters, there are rules for usage of a general word or expression on account of the capacity of words to be employed in this way for objects and facts. With "Bring a goat to the village," "Get some ghee," "Feed a priest," we have general words and expressions used for individual things that are part of their meaning, because they have that capacity. Where commanding an activity that has an object (such as bringing a goat to a village) is in accord with the facts, there people proceed to act, although not with respect to the general meaning (to include all goats), because such commanding would not accord with the situation. The example of the general expression "*nava-kambala*" ("new-/nine-blanket") in this way accords with the facts when it is taken to mean that the person has a new blanket. One could proceed to act with respect to that object or fact, but not with the claim, "He has nine blankets." An attempt to refute another's statement through rendering an impossible meaning is not the fault of the original speaker.

Vācaspatimiśra [304.16–20]: At the time of fixing a convention between word and object or in the already existing usage of our elders, a particular word by itself does not make us know the particular object that, let us say, a current speaker wants to point out. Rather, the speaker makes the word designate the particular object or fact he wants to point out by employing a word's meaning in general aided by contextual factors. Therefore, blame need not attach to one who wants to make us know something in particular when words intended to pick out the particular fail to do that. Rather, the fault may lie with the habit of understanding words in their general meaning at the expense of the particular.

1.2.13: Equivocation with generality is rendering an unintended meaning through excessively generalizing a meaning that is possible.

Vātsyāyana [48.14–49.5]: In response to the utterance, "Well, yes, this priest is accomplished in both knowledge and character," someone says, "Accomplishment in knowledge and character is appropriate for a priest." One can generate a contradiction of the second statement through rendering an unintended meaning by means of an explanation of an alternative, "If accomplishment in knowledge and character is appropriate for a priest (*brāhmaṇa*), then it should occur with a *vrātya* (a *brāhmaṇa* who is delinquent in character). A *vrātya* is also a *brāhmaṇa*. Such a one too should be accomplished in knowledge and character." And whatever includes but goes beyond an intended meaning, that is an excessive generalization. For example, being a *brāhmaṇa* applies in some cases to people accomplished in knowledge and character; sometimes it applies to those who are not (for example, in the case of a *vrātya*). Equivocation based on such generalizing is **equivocation with generality**.

The move can be refuted. . . . For example, "In this field, rice could come up." That the rice would be seed-born is not denied nor is the idea intended, but an obfuscating equivocator could render the meaning as, "In this field, rice could come up *without seeds*." The intentional content associated with the original speech act is praising the field (for its capacity to grow rice). Such would be the way to repeat (or paraphrase) the statement about the field. Rice is not the subject of assertion. But of course it is from seed that rice is produced. That being the case, what is alleged is not intended. . . .

Relevant background information about the first example given is that a brāhmaṇa *priest is ideally a moral person and a scholar, but priesthood is a hereditary position and there are some brāhmaṇas who neglect their duties but are still referred to as "*brāhmaṇas.*" The equivocator ignores the multiple meanings of the general term, which refers both to priests and those who are born into a certain caste or class.*

1.2.14: Equivocation over secondary meaning is denial of the real meaning when a description designates something through imaginative use of its property.

Vātsyāyana [49.13–50.7]: **Property** as mentioned in the sūtra is proper usage of a denoting expression. **Imaginative use** of a description's property or denotation is the employment in a different sense from what is normally found elsewhere. Such a **description** as mentioned in the sūtra is one that **makes imaginative use of its property to designate**. For example, in the statement, "The stands are shouting," the real or primary meaning is negated. *People* situated in the stands are shouting, but not the stands. . . . The intentional content of this kind of equivocation hinges on a meaning transfer or secondary sense: thus it is called **equivocation over secondary meaning**. The secondary meaning is the correct meaning here. . . .

Here is how to answer this kind of obfuscating equivocation. When a speaker's usage is standard or well-known, both concurrence with and denial of the relation to the objects mentioned by him should be according to his intention, not imposed from another. It is well-known that a word may be used in a primary sense or a secondary, figurative sense. Both occur. As a speaker's intention is understood when his usage is standard or well-known, that's how the relation of word and object is to be taken, whether affirmed or denied, not willfully imposed. If a speaker uses a word in its primary sense, then, whether affirmed of denied, that's the way the things are to be taken, not some way willfully imposed. If there is a figurative usage, then the intention should be understood with the figurative meaning. But in cases where a speaker uses a word in a *figurative* sense, and an equivocator "refutes" what is said while construing the word in its *primary* sense, then the denial hinges on the equivocator's own imposition. The equivocator does not really refute the other, the original speaker.

Suggestions for Further Reading

Gopika Mohan Bhattacharya, "Śābdabodha As a Separate Type of *Pramāna*." *Journal of Indian Philosophy* 5.1–2 (December 1977): 73–84.

Arindam Chakrabarti and B. K. Matilal, eds., *Knowing from Words: Western and Indian Philosophical Analysis of Understanding and Testimony*. Dordrecht: Kluwar, 1994.

Kisor Kumar Chakrabarti, "The Nyāya-Vaiśeṣika Theory of Universals." *Journal of Indian Philosophy* 3 (1975): 363–82.

Raja Ram Dravid, *The Problem of Universals in Indian Philosophy*. Delhi: Motilal Banarsidass, 1972.

Jonardon Ganeri, *ARTHA Meaning: Testimony and the Theory of Meaning in Indian Philosophical Analysis*. New Delhi: Oxford University Press, 2006.

B. K. Matilal, *The Word and the World: India's Contribution to the Study of Language*. New Delhi: Oxford University Press, 1990.

Roy Perrett, ed., *Indian Philosophy: Logic and Philosophy of Language*. New York: Routledge, 2001.

K. K. Raja, *Indian Theories of Meaning*. Madras: Adyar Library and Research Centre, 1963.

Mark Siderits, *Indian Philosophy of Language. Dordrecht: Kluwar, 1991.*

Study Questions

1. What are the three candidates proposed for the meaning of a word as discussed in *Nyāya-sūtra* 2.59–66? Explain for each one the reason or reasons given that it cannot be the only meaning.

2. What is Nyāya's final answer to the question about the meaning of a common noun?

3. What is a universal? What are Nyāya's reasons for accepting universals as real?
4. Lay out one challenge to Nyāya's concept of a universal given in the selections, and explain Nyāya's response.
5. What does it mean to say that something's form or shape is a sign of a universal? Are these truly reliable indicators?
6. Explain the following and give an example of your own for each:

   Equivocation with words
   Equivocation with generality
   Equivocation with secondary meaning

Chapter 8

The Right and the Good

It is practically a genre requirement of classical sūtra texts to open by telling us what positive good comes from their study. The first two sūtras of the Nyāya-sūtra *proclaim that mastery of the system results in the austere goal of* apavarga, *commonly understood as "liberation,"* mukti *or* mokṣa. *The word is better translated "final beatitude," and the second sūtra tells us it is the supreme good. Liberation is spoken of as a major concern by several Indian schools. It is the chief concern of Vedānta, the prolific school that bases its philosophy on ancient Upaniṣads. But liberation is understood somewhat differently in each of the perhaps seventeen (or more) prominent Vedāntic subschools, as well as in philosophic and religious systems flying other banners. These include the Yoga philosophy of the* Yoga-sūtra. *Nyāya draws on a broad-based, roughly "Hindu" understanding of the ultimate goal of life connected to notions of* dharma, *"ethical and religious duty," to be carried out across multiple lifetimes. But it also ties its conception of the supreme good to its own distinct metaphysical positions on the nature of the self (*ātman*) in particular.*

Not all scholars agree with this understanding of Nyāya's relationship with Vedic culture, or at least with the most conservative strand of Hinduism known as Brāhminism. The great Nyāya scholar S. C. Vidyabhusana argues, prominently, that Gautama, the author of the sūtras, was opposed to Brāhminism. Vidyabhusana groups the sūtra-maker with the founders of Buddhism and Jainism as proclaiming an experiential goal opposed to the heaven-oriented, ritualist system of Brāhmaṇa priests. Vidyabhusana also cites opposition in early Brāhminical sources to "those addicted to reasoning," possibly targeting

Nyāya.[1] *Later, he speculates, Nyāya was integrated into various religious systems and brought into the mainstream of Vedic culture.*

Probably, as Vidyabhusana stresses, Gautama was indeed a yogin. One of his nicknames was apparently "Long Austerity" (dīrgha-tapas). *Our sūtra-maker clearly connects his understanding of a supreme good to yoga practice, as we shall see with sūtras near the end of the chapter. Promotion of intellectual understanding and philosophical method as internal to a yogic quest may be said to be Gautama's great contribution to yogic soteriology. This is just the opposite not only of the dogmatism of ritualists but also of the way that much of Buddhism and Vedānta distrust theoretical reasoning. Advaita, for example, refuses to take up the metaphysical task of explaining the world in relation to Brahman, holding that it is* anirvacanīya, *"impossible to explain." For Gautama, in contrast, correct understanding achieved by critical reasoning is an important part of the path to the supreme good.*

Thus it is no accident that the first topic mentioned in the first sūtra is pramāṇa *or knowledge source. As we have seen, Nyāya motivates epistemological refinement by connecting cognitive success with success in life and action. It is worth repeating Vātsyāyana under 2.1.20: "Motivation to seek righteousness, wealth, pleasure, and liberation, and to avoid what is opposed to them, proceeds through comprehensions of knowledge sources and their objects." The idea of success along these lines surfaces throughout Nyāya's epistemological program, including the rationale given for default trust in cognition and the role of doubt in triggering review in order to be able to act "unhesitatingly." In the first two sūtras, success in action and in cognition are understood in connection with "attainment of the supreme good."*

Now, whereas Nyāya's understanding of the good is tied tightly to its overall metaphysics, the same does not quite hold for the school's conception of "the right," of ethical values, dharma, *where there is much less integration with its particular metaphysical teachings than with* apavarga,

1 Vidyabhusana, pp. ii–xiv.

"final beatitude." Although there is a virtue ethics articulated in connection with yoga advocacy, the main connection with dharma *is in Nyāya's epistemology of testimony, as we shall see. So let us begin with "liberation" and the first two sūtras of the entire text. The second sūtra provides a formula for attaining the supreme good.*

1.1.1: Knowledge sources, objects of knowledge, doubt, motive, example, accepted position, inferential components, suppositional reasoning, certainty, debate for the truth, disputation, destructive debate, pseudo-provers, equivocation, misleading objections, and clinchers: from knowledge of these, there is attainment of the supreme good.

1.1.2: When pain, rebirth, activity, vice, and wrong understanding have been dispelled in reverse order, there is final beatitude (*apavarga*).

Vātsyāyana [6.9–8.3]: **Wrong understanding**, among the items mentioned, occurs in many ways with respect to objects that range from self (*ātman*) to **final beatitude**. There is, first of all, the wrong understanding, "There is no self"; then thinking, "This is pleasure," when something is rather a source of **pain**; thinking "This will last," when something is impermanent; "This provides safety," when something cannot do so; "This is nothing to be afraid of," when one should be afraid of it; "This is acceptable," when something should be rejected with disgust; and "This should not be renounced," when it should be. Other examples of wrong understanding include: "Karma is not caused by one's actions," and "There are no karmic consequences." "**Vices** do not perpetuate the cycle of birth and rebirth (*saṃsāra*)." "There is no **rebirth**, whether for the creature or the individual soul (*jīva*) or some pure being (*sattva*) or for a self (*ātman*), such that one having died would again come to be after death." "Rebirth is uncaused." "Cessation of rebirth is uncaused." "Rebirth has a beginning but it has no end." "Rebirth while caused is not caused by karma." "Rebirth does not involve a self (*ātman*) but rather the body, the sense organs, the mind, and consciousness in a stream that breaks up and comes together again." With regard to **final beatitude (*apavarga*)**, "It must be frightful, as there is no longer anything to do," and "Since final beatitude is disengagement from everything, much good would be lost." And "What intelligent person would be pleased at the prospect of such *apavarga* leading to the ending of all pleasure and no further experience?"

Under the influence of **wrong understanding**, one becomes attached to what is comfortable and averse to what is uncomfortable. **Vices**, including dishonesty, jealousy, resentment, and pride, result from attraction and repulsion.

Beset by such vices, one sets out to do bodily acts of violence, theft, and illicit sex. Through speech, one engages in lying, vulgarity, and incoherence. With one's mind, one indulges in treachery, desire to have another's wealth, and refusing to accept what is true. Such is sinful **activity** directed towards unrighteousness (*adharma*). Now there are good acts as well. There are bodily acts of charity, protection, and service, with the body. Through speech, truthfulness, agreeableness, affection, and self-study (in light of yogic texts). With one's mind, compassion, detachment, and faith. Such **activity** is directed towards righteousness (*dharma*).

Activity is instigated by righteousness (*dharma*) and unrighteousness (*adharma*). These are what is really meant by the word "**activity**" in the sūtra. For an example of this sort of usage, there is the phrase, "Food is verily the life-breath of the living being,"[2] as the life-breaths (*prāṇa*) are brought about by food. **Activity**, as understood here, causes rebirths that are despicable, honorable, and in-between; **rebirth** is the arising of body, sense organs, knowledge, and consciousness in assembly. When this occurs, there is **pain and suffering** (*duḥkha*). This is understood as what is "disagreeable," including affliction, physical pain, and sorrow.

All these features—beginning with **wrong understanding** and ending with **pain**—involve continuous, unbroken action within *saṃsāra*, "the cycle of birth and rebirth."

In contrast to all of this, when wrong understanding is dispelled by knowledge about the self and the rest, vice is unsupported and goes away. Vice now gone, the activity that it compels ceases. With activity ceasing, rebirth ends.

2 *Mahābhārata* 13.63.25.

With rebirth left behind, pain departs. And with pain completely removed, final *apavarga* occurs, the supreme good.

Now knowledge of the truth may be explained as understanding that is opposed to the wrong understandings mentioned above. First of all, "There is a self (*ātman*)." Then in this way, pain, the impermanent, which cannot offer protection, and the truly frightful, are to be understood as things to be avoided or rejected as the case may be. One further understands: "When one undertakes activity, there is karma in the sense of the results of action." "There are vices, and the round of birth and rebirth is caused by vices." "Rebirth is a reality, whether it be of the creature or the 'individual soul' (*jīva*) or some pure 'being' (*sattva*) or of a 'self' (*ātman*) that dies and having died comes to be again after death." "Rebirth, which has a cause, ceases, and that cessation has a cause." "Rebirth has no beginning, but it does have an end in final beatitude." "Rebirth, which is caused, is caused specifically by activity." "Rebirth does involve a self acting (and coursing) through the breaking up and coming together again of the stream of the body, the sense organs, the mind, and consciousness." "In final beatitude (*apavarga*), one at last finds spiritual peace; disengagement from everything, the cessation of everything, is what *apavarga* amounts to; an abundance of difficulties, matters dreadful, full of sin, waste away." And: "What intelligent person would *not* be pleased at the prospect of such an *apavarga* involving the cessation of all pain (*duḥkha*) and no awareness of any pain at all?" Therefore, as food that is a mixture of honey and poison is not to be taken, so pleasure that is shot through with pain is not to be sought.

Sūtra 1.1.2 charts a direct connection between right understanding and attainment of the highest good. There is a chain of dependencies such that if we remove misunderstanding, then suffering will be removed in due course in the form of final release, viewed as liberation from rebirth. Vātsyāyana says that misunderstanding regarding the deep self is to disbelieve in its existence or to take it to be identical with the non-self (the physical body). Acting on either of these bases, Uddyotakara elaborates, leads one to entanglement in karma and continued suffering, while knowledge of the deep self removes these misunderstandings and sets one on the path to liberation. However, such knowledge is not merely intellectual, as a passage in Nyāya-sūtra *chapter four brings out (see below). There has to be deep understanding of the deep self akin to yogic trance.*

In overview, Vātsyāyana's exposition of "final beatitude" underscores Nyāya's allegiance to a broad cultural and religious movement stemming from the middle of the first millennium BCE that gave rise to yoga as well as to Buddhism, Jainism, and the Upanishadic strain of Hindu thought. At least some participants in this movement seem to have been concerned with philosophy and argument as well as with mindfulness, meditation, and yogic practices. A few scholars, notably the Oxford don B. K. Matilal, considered Nyāya's soteriological theorizing mere lip-service to existing cultural ideals, and just how much is central to the Nyāya project may legitimately be debated, despite what we have seen from Vātsyāyana here. Nevertheless, for our purposes we need to keep in mind that philosophical inquiry is endorsed, because, as Nyāya philosophers tell us repeatedly, it leads to the attainment of our goals and purposes in general.

Finally, we should note that Vātsyāyana integrates a virtue ethics into the Nyāya soteriology. He lists interpersonal characteristics that are putatively also conducive to one's own best interest, including many that are mentioned in the Yoga-sūtra, *for example, "charity," "readiness to assist," "service," "truthfulness," "benevolence," "self-study," "compassion," "contentment," and "faith." These are organized according to a common assumption in classical Indian ethical literature that activities may be performed with one's body, speech, or mind. Vātsyāyana explains how vice and virtue manifest through the three outlets.*

Next, given the importance of "karma" in moral and religious life, we consider a couple of sūtras where Nyāya explains its functioning. Here, karma is understood not only as comprised of habits—good and bad dispositions to act—but also as a moral force in the universe. One's habits of action, emotion, and thought, have, as it were, moral coefficients, vectors contributing to an Unseen Force that shapes events and indeed objects, but not necessarily right away. This includes shaping the nature and situation of your physical body in your next incarnation, according to moral desert. Thus the theory of karma embraces two dimensions: (a) continuity of habits formed by repeated action, and (b) aggregating moral desert. And the exhaustion of one's karmic burden is said to be crucial to attaining "final beatitude."

3.2.66: As karma causes the construction of a body, it is also responsible for a body's connection with a self.

Vātsyāyana [213.2–7]: . . . (Without the causal influence of karma) every individual self would have a similar body as the locus of its pleasure, pain, and consciousness. What we find, however, is that each specific body is arranged in connection with an individual self: the karma that causes the making of a body is also responsible for a body's being connected with an individual self. For, karma fructifies as restricted to a specific self, which is its abode. The rule is that according to the self that houses certain karma, a body is produced that will serve as the seat of the experience that is specifically that self's. So karma is responsible for such an arrangement overall. In this way it is declared in the sūtra, **As karma causes the construction of a body, it is also responsible for a body's connection with a self**. We understand by the word "**connection**" the overall arrangement, such that a specific body is related to a specific self.

Here we see Nyāya part ways with the metaphysics of Sāṃkhya and Yoga over the conception of the self. Nyāya finds the self to be the direct locus of moral qualities such as karmic merit and demerit, along with desire, aversion, knowledge, and the rest. Sāṃkhya/Yoga, the most radically dualistic tradition in India, introduces an intermediate subtle body that possesses these traits. This allows the self to remain pure and untouched, not affected by karma directly. Nyāya argues that individual selves must themselves bear karmic traces or else we have no way to explain why any specific individual is tethered to a certain body and a certain set of experiences dictated by her past moral decisions and action.

3.2.67: Accordingly, lack of universality among beings is explained.

Vātsyāyana [213.12–20]: . . . Question: What, first of all, is meant by "**universality**" in the sūtra?

Answer: If a single individual self had such and such a body, then every other self would have the same—this would be **universality**. **Lack of universality** amounts to one self being one way and another self being another way. Such distinctness is exclusionary, specific. And it is a matter of common experience that there are these distinctions of life: one is of noble descent and another of ignoble; one glorified, another criticized; one suffers one malady after another, another is never ill; one has all her limbs intact, another is maimed; one person is afflicted by recurring pain after pain, another is all the time happy; one is endowed with excellent traits of character, another just the opposite; one is praiseworthy, another is blameworthy; one clever, another dull. And there are of course subtler differences, immeasurably many. This is what we mean by distinctions of life. They become possible through differences of karma governed by the laws that tie it to individual selves. For, if there were no such differences in karma as tied to selves, then because there would be no karmic accretions associated with selves—who, moreover, would all be alike—the elements of earth and the rest would produce the same body for each self. For they lack a cause or reason to generate diversity in themselves. This is the difficulty. Life as we know it would not occur. Therefore, the making of a body is not without karma as a causal influence.

Uddyotakara [418.15–419.2]: What, then, is this **universality**? It is explained as what would obtain if a single self's having a body meant that every self would have that same body. **Lack of universality** is explained as one self being one way and another self another way. That the difference is exclusionary is a matter of common experience. Living things have bodily differences that are multitudinous. And this would not be in the order of things if material elements worked alone, independently of the influence of karma, when bodies are produced. But it *is* in the order of things that bodies are different according to differences in karma.

And it is possible that a self can be separated from the body, because it is possible that karmic influence be exhausted. A body is produced from two natures, one visible, the other invisible. Of the two, the invisible is designated *karma*. It can be completely exhausted through the experience it generates. And when karma is completely exhausted, then, although there are in place all the necessary material elements, they do not produce a body. Thus it is possible that there be a final beatitude (*apavarga*). If the material elements worked alone, independently of the influence of karma, then how could it be that those being liberated would ever find final beatitude by means of the complete exhaustion of what binds them? For there is no interruption of the causal power of the material elements.

Above, we have seen that (a) karma inheres in individual selves, and (b) bodies are generated in accordance with a self's karmic history. The theory of karma provides individuals with motivation to be moral, in that being moral secures better future embodiments as well as the possibility of final beatitude. The theory tells us why it is in our own best interest to act morally. But what is moral action? And how do we know what is morally right? Here Nyāya turns to its epistemology of testimony. Nyāya-sūtra *1.1.7 defines testimony as the statement of an* āpta, *an "expert," and Vātsyāyana defines an* āpta *as one who knows the truth and wants to communicate it faithfully. The contents of morality are given to us through reliable testimony by experts who exemplify the teachings they give. There is an element of circularity here, but arguably, this is not vicious but rather self-subsumptive or self-exemplifying.*

Immediately below, we take up sūtra 4.1.62. Here, our commentators explain that we learn the canons of ethics from our teachers, who learn them from their teachers, back to a seer or divine being whose teaching is codified in a sacred text such as the Veda or didactic texts such as the Purāṇas or Dharma-śāstras. Heading off the criticism that there are too many authoritative texts with different if not contradictory messages, Vātsyāyana says that sacred testimony is divided according to topic and is concordant overall. Vācaspatimiśra elaborates that even moral preceptors such as the author of the Mahābhārata *(the* Great Indian Epic*), who base their teachings upon their own experience, still concur with what's in the Veda.*

4.1.62: Karmic results mentioned do not occur for everyone, because it is impossible for some (for example) to carry out the rites that end with a collection of the sacrificial vessels.

Uddyotakara [467.2–5]: The reason is that renunciants, people whose desires and cravings have ceased, do not undertake **the rites that end with a collection of the sacrificial vessels.** And if the injunctions to perform those rites included every Brāhmaṇa without exception, then the unfortunate consequence would be that everyone should perform the rites that end with a collection of sacrificial vessels. The rest is clear in Vātsyāyana's *Commentary*.

Vātsyāyana argues that certain secondary scriptures are indeed pramāṇas *for moral knowledge, in that the Veda itself, which is the ultimate knowledge source for sacrificial duties, attests to this in its portion called Brāhmaṇa.*

Vātsyāyana [253.16–254.8]: . . . To hold that there is a single life-stage (and thus moral rules) applicable to everyone in every situation is unsupportable, because the view that there are four life-stages is asserted in "histories" (*itihāsa*, such as the *Mahābhārata*), Purāṇas, and Dharma-śastras.

Opponent: Those are not knowledge sources for morality.

Answer: You are wrong. That they are knowledge sources may be ascertained through another knowledge source. That traditional histories and Purāṇas are knowledge sources is ascertained through the portion of the Veda which instructs us on ritual. And this is itself a knowledge source. . . . And if Dharma-śastras were not sources of (moral) knowledge, the untenable consequence would be that there would be a disruption in the conventional practices of living things. The world we know would implode.

Furthermore, that these are not knowledge sources is unsupportable, because the seers (responsible for some texts) and the transmitters (responsible for others) are the same persons. Just those who are the mystic seers responsible for the Mantras and Brāhmana texts within Vedic literature are the very ones, moreover, who have recounted and proclaimed the histories and Purāṇas and the Dharma-śastras as well.

Furthermore, knowledge-source status varies according to topic, because the texts are organized according to topical differences. Mantras and Brāhmaṇas have their topics; histories, Purāṇas, and Dharma-śastras have others. The topic of otherworldly ritual sacrifice belongs to Mantras and Brāhmaṇas, whereas how this world generally works is the topic of histories and Purāṇas. The arrangement of people's conventional practices is the province of Dharma-śastras. It is not that one among these determines everything. Therefore, these function as knowledge sources according to topic, just as the individual sense organs are authoritative with respect to their own proper content, and so on.

Note that while members of the priestly and intellectual class in India are called Braḥmaṇas, *this is also the name for a portion of the Veda that is centered on the practice of sacrificial rites, as mentioned immediately above.*

In the next selection, it is crucial to know that the word "veda" *is not only the name of a collection of sacred texts but also of knowledge in general, or wisdom, or spiritual experience. Vācaspatimiśra uses the word in its broadest and best connotation when he says below that self (*ātman*) is* veda.

Vācaspatimiśra [601.1–10]: . . . If the Dharma-śastras were not *pramāṇas,* all the conventions and practices mentioned above would not be possible. And although the author of the *Mahābhārata* and others like him are endowed with knowledge of *dharma* as well as dispassion and the yogic perfection of control, giving us their teachings based on their own experience, their teachings are nonetheless grounded in the Veda. That is to say, epic histories (such as the *Mahābhārata*), Purāṇas, and so on are grounded in the Veda. This is the reasonable view. For it is said, "The Veda as a whole constitutes the foundation of *dharma,* and those who know the Veda find it in the moral teachings of Smṛti ('tradition' or 'sacred memory' comprised of histories such as the *Mahābhārata,* Purāṇas, and Dharma-śāstras). Whatever is dharmic for whomever as proclaimed by Manu (in a Dharma-śāstra by that name), all that is mentioned in the Veda. For the Veda consists of knowledge of everything."[3] And there are similar statements, indeed a plethora of statements in what a person says everyday about herself, to the effect that it is the self that is the knower. The self is *veda* ("spiritual knowledge").

Objection: Why then should we think that our current topic is within the province of the histories and the rest?

Reply: Nothing ever is said by the Veda in opposition to what is known by perception (and a similar principle holds here, that the Veda does not contradict other *pramāṇas,* and thus a dharmic teaching may be learned outside of the explicit statements of the Veda). We come to this conclusion because certain topics are not mentioned in the Veda (and thus there is room for other authorities). In our current time, some people claim that a putative fact or value that we do not accept comes from the author of the Veda. And although its status may have been settled already in the past, we deny or refute it again for the purpose of firming up our views. And this is what is going on with my predecessors in their talk about the division of texts by topic.

Next, we move from general concerns about dharma and the ways we learn about it to yogic practice, which is said to secure the supreme personal good, final beatitude. We focus on a stretch of sūtras at the end of Nyāya-sūtra *chapter four, which begins by advocating practices spelled out in yogic texts such as the* Yoga-sūtra. *The sūtras that follow seem to change topics away from yoga to matters of debate and discussion. However, we suggest that one could read them rather as extending the range of yoga practice to include certain kinds of philosophical reflection and debate. In any case, learning correct procedure in debate and engaging in debate for the truth* (vāda)*, like the more familiar yoga practices, are said to lead to "final beatitude,"* apavarga.

3 Anantalal Thakur, editor of Vācaspatimiśra's long text, identifies quotations whenever he can. This one is not identified. Our best guess is that its source is a Mīmāṃsaka.

4.2.46: For the purpose of attaining *apavarga*, there should be self-purification by means of yogic restraints (*yama*) and observances (*niyama*) and by psychological instructions and methods taught in yoga.

Vātsyāyana [280.4–8]: For the purpose of attaining to *apavarga*, "final beatitude," **self-purification** is to be done **by means of yogic restraints (*yama*) and observances (*niyama*)**. The restraints are virtuous equally for those of different stations of life. The observances, in contrast, vary with life circumstances. In all cases, self-purification removes unrighteousness and increases virtue. **Psychological instructions** are to be studied according to yoga science (*śāstra*). They include asceticism, breath-control, sensory withdrawal, meditational practice (*dhāraṇā*), and meditation proper (*dhyāna*). And the practice of sensory withdrawal (*pratyāhāra*) is for the purpose of removing attraction and aversion. The **methods** mentioned in the sūtra, however, are rules about yogic practice more generally.

*From this passage, we see that Nyāya embraces a yogic ethics: leading a virtuous life makes one fit for yogic accomplishment, including "final beatitude." This thesis is implicit throughout the foundational Nyāya work of Gautama and Vātsyāyana if not with some later Naiyāyikas of so-called New Nyāya, who often write as philosophical technicians. An implicit yogic ethics is also common in many schools of classical philosophy, although details vary from school to school. Here we are told that practicing yogic restraints contributes to virtue (*dharma*) whatever one's stage of life. In other words, they are universal standards, as Manu, for example, also says. They are not spelled out by Vātsyāyana, but Vācaspatimiśra (636.13) confirms that the five ethical principles that comprise the first limb of the* aṣṭāṅga-yoga *of the* Yoga-sūtra *are precisely what are meant: non-injury, truth-telling, refraining from stealing, sexual restraint, and non-possessiveness.*

It is interesting that the practice of pratyāhāra, *"sensory withdrawal," is highlighted by Vātsyāyana because, although empiricist, Nyāya's theory of concept formation is thoroughly realist, as we have seen. We form the concept of cowhood through direct experience of individual cows, Bessie and Flossie and Śābalya. A verbalizable perception of a cow has its intentionality directed towards the real cow, not towards mental intermediaries such as sense-data, what some would call sensory objects proper such as sounds, colors, and shapes. Here with* pratyāhāra, *we see the idea that it is possible to turn away from the external world and direct our attention inward by redirecting the* manas *("mind") towards the self. This is one of the roots of Nyāya's doctrine of apperception,* anuvyavasāya, *where the mind or* manas *takes cognition, a mental state, as its own object. Thus the immediate object of experience would be, for instance, a particular sensory quality. And proper sensory objects, sounds, and so on would be in focus as opposed to, for instance, the drum making them. This is an immensely important concept for moves made by later Naiyāyikas in philosophy of mind. And its soteriological importance for Nyāya and other schools—including, to be sure, Buddhist traditions—probably cannot be overemphasized, since it is crucial to meditation and, as Vātsyāyana says, control of desire.*

As a final topic for this chapter, let us look again at the philosophic method called nyāya *and its connection to yoga practices. We see that the last two sūtras of the chapter, 4.2.50 and 51, depart dramatically from the themes not only of the proximate set of sūtras on yoga but also from all the themes of the second "lesson" of the fourth chapter, which centers on soteriology (see Appendix A). The topic of 4.2.50 and 51 is debate, especially the differences among its three major kinds. At first blush, this seems out of place. But our contention is that this is not strange if we look upon debate—and specifically the procedures called* nyāya*—as contributing to the goals of yoga, or, even more significantly, as forms of yogic practice. The intervening three sūtras, 4.2.47–49—between the section explicitly on yoga and the two sūtras on debate—concern the importance of learning systematic teachings (*śāstra*). These are perhaps, as Vātsyāyana suggests, teachings about the self in the Upaniṣads, but also perhaps yoga-śāstra, which is mentioned in the immediately preceding sūtra, 4.2.46. These three sūtras in any case highlight the intellectual dimension of the path towards final beatitude. The* *context supports the idea that acquiring an intellectual understanding of the difference between the self* (ātman) *and the body and so on is a form of yoga. Such a reading seems entirely consistent with the way in which removing misconception is said to be an aid to ultimate beatitude according to the commentaries on* Nyāya-sūtra *1.1.2 (see again the beginning of this chapter). Thus yoga would include not only debate for the truth,* vāda, *which is guided by* nyāya*—roughly philosophic or critical method—but also other forms of debate where it is especially important to be able to identify fallacies. Fallacies are of course the primary topic of* Nyāya-sūtra *chapter five. If this reading is correct, then several strands of Gautama's teaching are tied together through the idea of yoga practice.*

4.2.47: For the purpose of attaining *apavarga*, there should be repeated study of that science as well as discussion with those who know it.

Vātsyāyana [280.11–16]: According to context, the words, "**For the purpose of attaining *apavarga*,**" should be carried over from the previous sūtra. . . . The word "**science**" (*śāstra*) in the sūtra means knowledge of the self, that is to say, the science concerning the self. **Study** of it consists of learning and memorization. The word "**repeated**" in the sūtra means that one should engage continually in actions of learning, listening, and reflection.[4] The words "**as well as discussion with those who know it**" are directed to the purpose of bringing that wisdom to maturation. Such maturation, in turn, destroys doubt, making one know things not known previously, as well as giving one full command of things already understood. The word "**discussion**" means conversation or debate aimed at consensus.

The phrase "**as well as discussion with those who know it**" is not entirely obvious. To clarify, the sūtra-maker says:

4.2.48: The one who knows the science of the self should be admitted into the discussion along with pupils, teachers,

4 This echoes a famous verse from the *Bṛhadāraṇyaka Upaniṣad* (2.4.5): "The self (*ātman*) is to be learned from hearing about it, it is to be reflected upon, and it is to be made immediate in meditation."

and colleagues, those well-wishers who are distinguished by their seeking the supreme good.

Vātsyāyana [281.3–5]: Just reading the words of the sūtra is sufficient to get the correct sense. And if one should worry that the bandying about of theses and countertheses would be offensive to one's interlocutor, the sūtra-maker advises:

4.2.49: Alternatively, people who have no countertheses of their own are also to be admitted, to further the purpose of the discussion, if they seek the truth and the supreme good.

Vātsyāyana [281.7–13]: The words, "**are to be admitted,**" have to be supplied. Wanting to acquire knowledge and wisdom from the other, one can make known one's desire to know the truth without advancing a position of one's own, in order to correct and certify one's views overall as well as opponents' philosophies that are mutually contradictory.

And there are some who transgress the method of philosophy (*nyāya*) out of passionate attachment to their own views. Concerning them, the sūtra-maker says:

4.2.50: To protect truth that has been ascertained, disputation (*jalpa*) and destructive debate (*vitaṇḍā*) may be employed, in the way one would protect seeds and sprouts by covering them with thorns and branches.

Vātsyāyana [281.16–282.2]: This would be appropriate for those who have not yet achieved knowledge of the truth (of the self's distinction from the body), whose flaws remain undiminished, but who are working towards the goal nevertheless. And when an opponent would malign or demean the truth out of indifference to real knowledge or for any other reason, then one should engage him in:

4.2.51: Disputation by attacking through those two (*jalpa* and *vitaṇḍā*).

Vātsyāyana [282.4–5]: The word in the sūtra, "**attacking,**" means to engage with a desire to prevail, not with a desire to ascertain knowledge of the truth. All this should be done for the purpose of protecting real knowledge, not for gain, honor, or renown.

Vācaspatimiśra [638.15–639.4]: And the good, genuine debater opposes a certain kind of person. The sort of person who is to be opposed is anyone who has set out to undermine teachings about the Veda, Brāhmaṇas, an afterlife, and the like, in front of powerful people on whom many depend, because of pride in a bad philosophy to which he is accustomed, or pride in what he takes to be knowledge but is in fact false, becoming crafty and clever for no good end, or from utter indifference to knowledge of reality, or from seeking wealth, honor, or renown. The debater concerned for the truth, who cannot see clearly a legitimate way to refute him, should resort to disputation, *jalpa,* and destructive debate, *vitaṇḍā,* with a desire to prevail, to vanquish such an opponent by attacking, through use of disputation and destructive debate. In this way, one would dispute for the truth. The purpose would be to protect real knowledge.

We wish to avoid a collapse of righteousness (*dharma*) because of misleading views on the part of powerful people and of their numerous dependents who follow them in their conduct. This too gives purpose to the employment of disputation and destructive debate. But we see that the purpose should not be for wealth, renown, or the like. For, a true *muni,* a truly wise person, acts for the welfare of others, being supremely compassionate. Such a person does not teach a way to deceive the other for some specified end.

Suggestions for Further Reading

Wilhelm Halbfass, "Karma, *apurva,* and 'Natural' Causes." In *Karma and Rebirth in Classical Indian Traditions,* ed. Wendy Doniger O'Flaherty, pp. 268–302. Berkeley: University of California Press, 1980.

M. Hiriyanna, *Indian Conception of Values*. Mysore: Kavyalaya Publishers, 1975.

Roy Perrett, *Hindu Ethics: A Philosophical Study*. Honolulu: University of Hawaii Press, 1998.

Stephen Phillips, *Yoga, Karma, and Rebirth: A Brief History and Philosophy*. New York: Columbia University Press, 2009.

Karl H. Potter, "The Karma Theory and Its Interpretation in Some Indian Philosophical Systems." In *Karma and Rebirth in Classical Indian Traditions*, ed. Wendy Doniger O'Flaherty, 241–67. Berkeley: University of California Press, 1980.

Rajendra Prasad, *Karma, Causation, and Retributive Morality: Conceptual Essays in Ethics and Metaethics*. New Delhi: Indian Council of Philosophical Research in association with Munshiram Manoharlal Publishers, 1989.

Chakravarthi Ram-Prasad, *Knowledge and Liberation in Classical Indian Thought*. London: Palgrave MacMillan, 2001.

S. C. Vidyabhusana, *The Nyāya Sūtras of Gotama*. Originally published 1913. (Accessed February 21, 2016.) https://archive.org/details/TheNyayaSutrasOfGotama.

Study Questions

1. Explain in detail the four steps that Gautama says lead to suffering, beginning with error, in *Nyāya-sūtra* 1.1.2. Explain the process by which knowledge of the truth is supposed to lead to freedom from suffering.

2. Vātsyāyana argues that all four of the classic Hindu goals of life require knowledge produced by a *pramāṇa*: pleasure, wealth, virtue, and final beatitude. Based on your understanding of Nyāya, suggest the kind of knowledge one would need for each goal. Provide examples of the connection between the knowledge and the goal (pleasure and the rest) from your own experience or from everyday life in classical India as best you can imagine it (excluding or extending the notion of "final beatitude," if you wish).

3. Give three examples of the kinds of misunderstandings that cause suffering according to Vātsyāyana, along with the kinds of knowledge that would correct them.

4. How does Nyāya argue that karma is directly connected to individual selves? Why is this important for Nyāya?
5. Nyāya argues that we learn about *dharma,* or proper conduct and righteousness, from authoritative persons and texts. Do you agree in general that people's primary knowledge source for ethics is testimony? Why or why not?
6. Explain the connection between critical reasoning and yoga practice as discussed in this chapter.
7. What are the three major kinds of debate according to Gautama and his commentators? In what contexts are disputation (*jalpa*) and destructive debate (*vitaṇḍā*) acceptable even to those who seek the truth? What does each commentator say? Do you agree or not?

Chapter 9

Debate

From the Nyāya-sūtra's *very first sūtra through the end of its last chapter, debate categories and tools are examined including delineation of fallacies. Three types of debates are identified in the first sūtra: (1) debate for the truth, (2) debate for victory with a commitment to a thesis, and (3) debate for victory without a commitment, proceeding solely by attacking. The first is distinguished from the latter two in that while theses are put forth and opposed theses are attacked, one is unattached and happy to follow the argument where it may lead. We will refer to the three kinds as "debate for the truth," "disputation," and "destructive debate," respectively. The main point of the distinction seems to be to advocate the first, called* vāda, *as the proper context for doing philosophy. The distinction serves as well to denigrate the third kind in particular, destructive debate, called* vitaṇḍā, *which was practiced by skeptics associated with Mādhyamika Buddhism in the early period and later with the materialist Cārvāka school and certain Vedāntins. Indeed, in the passage below, under sūtra 1.1.1, Vātsyāyana takes the opportunity to denigrate the purely destructive reasoner, the skeptic who pretends he has nothing to advance or defend.*

Vātsyāyana [3.15–4.1]: Among the items mentioned in the first sūtra, **debate for the truth,** ***vāda,*** and **disputation,** ***jalpa,*** proceed from the motive to advance or defend a thesis. **Destructive debate,** ***vitaṇḍā,*** in contrast, requires examination. A destructive skeptic proceeds by **destructive debate**. If such a person entered a debate with a motive, he would be committed to a thesis as an accepted doctrine (*siddhānta*), and would abandon his skepticism. If he did not advance a thesis, he would not really "enter debate," as a layperson or as an expert.

Should one object that a skeptic's motive would be to refute someone else's thesis, that too is akin to what has been pointed out already (that is, one would then cease to be a skeptic in having something to promote or defend). To make something known, indeed to know something, to use an instrument of knowledge, and to refer to that which is made known—all this amounts to entering into debate (with a motive to advance, defend, or investigate some thesis or topic). If he does this, he is no longer engaging in destructive debate.

Should one claim that such a person does not "enter into debate," then the claim that one is motivated to refute somebody else's thesis would not make sense. **Destructive debate** is, then, a collection of statements void of intent to establish anything. Entering a debate about a designated object or topic requires that one has a thesis to be promoted and made accepted. One may say that the person would not "enter into debate." But if he has nothing to prove, his words would be mere prattle and pointless. So, for us who do not want to prattle, destructive debate holds no interest.

At the beginning of the second "daily lesson" of the Nyāya-sūtra's *first chapter (1.2.1–3), we are treated to definitions of the three debate types. Vātsyāyana then explains that when the goal of debate or discussion is to discover the truth, some of the tactics and methods for winning a hostile debate are irrelevant. These include equivocation, misleading objections, and clinchers (opponent's violations of the rules of debate). Please see Chapter 7, "Word and Object," for a discussion of equivocation. Misleading objections and clinchers are discussed at the end of this chapter.*

Vātsyāyana [39.4]: Three kinds of debate are: *vāda,* debate for the truth, *jalpa,* disputation, and *vitaṇḍā,* destructive debate. Among these:

1.2.1: Employing the five components of a formal demonstration, taking up theses and countertheses, debate for the truth (*vāda*) is a matter of proving and refuting by

means of knowledge sources and suppositional reasoning, without contradicting accepted positions.

Vātsyāyana [39.7–40.10]: Conflict results from two opposed properties—expressed by a thesis and a counterthesis—that are put forth with respect to a single topic or locus. For example, "There is a self (*ātman*)," and "There is no self." Two opposed properties or natures, which belong to *different* topics or loci, do not themselves result in a thesis and counterthesis. For example, "The self is permanent," and "Cognition is impermanent."

Taking up is a matter of (provisionally) accepting in an orderly arrangement the theses proposed. ***Vāda*, debate for the truth**, amounts to such **taking up theses and countertheses**. Its distinguishing feature is its use of **knowledge sources and suppositional reasoning**, to prove and refute; that is, knowledge sources and suppositional reasoning are used to prove, and knowledge sources and suppositional reasoning are used to refute. By the several sources along with suppositional reasoning, actual proving and actual refuting are achieved concerning any topic whatsoever.

Proving is establishing. **Refuting** is dismissing. Even though both of these, proving and refuting, may work interconnectedly and interrelatedly on both thesis and counterthesis, a supporter of the one view will desist at a point, dropping the view, inasmuch as the other becomes established. The view dropped has been refuted and dismissed. The view established is proved.

Clinchers or technical grounds for victory, *nigrahasthāna*, may be used in disputation, but they are normally precluded from debate for the truth. Still, the expression "**without contradicting established positions**" is used in the sūtra for the purpose of allowing some of them in certain contexts even though they are generally precluded from *vāda*. . . .

While knowledge sources and suppositional reasoning are included within the formal components of a debate (thesis, reason, illustration, etc.), **knowledge sources and suppositional reasoning** are mentioned separately in this sūtra in order to make clear the interconnectedness of proving and refuting. Otherwise, even two diametrically opposed views put forth with reasons purporting to prove each view's truth (but without effort to show the other's falsehood) could be a matter of *vāda*. Furthermore, we have already seen (in discussion of sūtra 1.1.41) that knowledge sources may make something known without the use of components of a formal demonstration.

Another reason why knowledge sources and suppositional reasoning are mentioned separately is that in whatever manner proving and refuting occur in *vāda* to make something known, they may also be used in *jalpa*, disputation. One should not think that *jalpa* excludes use of the clinchers that are allowed in *vāda*, since it is stated in the next sūtra that ***jalpa*, disputation, consists in** use of the further items listed in the first sūtra, **equivocation, misleading objections, and clinchers**. The idea that in *jalpa* one proceeds to prove or to refute only by means of equivocation, misleading objection, and clinching is wrong. Proving and refuting by means of knowledge sources and suppositional reasoning is not restricted to *vāda*.

1.2.2: Disputation (*jalpa*) includes what has already been explained for *vāda*, but also proving and refuting by means of equivocation, misleading objections, and clinchers.

Vātsyāyana [40.14–41.14]: Use of the words "**has already been explained**" has to do with taking up theses and countertheses as a matter of **proving and refuting by means of knowledge sources and suppositional reasoning without contradicting established positions**. Here the words "**proving and refuting by means of equivocation, misleading objections, and clinchers**" amount to saying actual proving and refuting are achieved with respect to some topic by means of equivocation, misleading objections, and clinchers—in this way disputation is characterized.

Objection: Nothing whatsoever is proved by means of equivocation, misleading objections, and clinchers. Tradition teaches us that according to general and specific accounts these tactics are only for the purpose of refutation. . . .

Answer: Because the three—equivocation, misleading objections, and clinchers—help to protect one's own view from attack, they are auxiliaries to the knowledge sources. Within one's own system, they do not prove anything. Equivocation, misleading objections, and clinchers operate as auxiliaries with whatever has been proved by the knowledge sources, because they protect one's own view. For, what is employed in contradiction to an opponent's counterthesis protects one's own view. . . . Moreover, whichever of these works with the knowledge sources to find fault with a counterthesis would then help to rule out an attempt at refutation on the part of the opponent. Thus they become auxiliaries.

Endorsement of equivocation and the others as auxiliaries in disputation does not amount to accepting them as proving anything within one's own system. But for refutation, they may well be used on their own on occasion.

1.2.3: That becomes destructive debate (*vitaṇḍā*) when there is no effort to establish a counterthesis.

Vātsyāyana [41.17–42.3]: The word "**That**" means disputation, which comes to be destructive debate, *vitaṇḍā*. What is the differentiating mark or special feature of destructive debate? It is lack of effort to establish one's own counterthesis. If there are two opposed properties attributed to the same locus or topic, they would be expressed by a thesis and a counterthesis—this has already been explained. Destructive debate is thought to be employed when there is only refutation of the other's thesis; one does not try to establish which of the two is to be preferred.

Objection: Then let destructive debate be defined simply as *jalpa* that is bereft of one's own counterthesis. (Why add the words "**effort to establish**"?)

Answer: Statements that have the characteristic of targeting an opponent's counterthesis in the attempt to refute it are the province of destructive skeptics. But while this does involve an effort to establish something, one does not put forth one's own proposition regarding any property to be proved whatsoever. Therefore, let the definition stand as given.

As mentioned, when Vātsyāyana talks here of destructive debate, vitaṇḍā, *he probably has Nāgārjuna's Mādhyamika school of Mahāyāna Buddhism in mind or its Prasaṅgika subschool.*

Debate—and, to extend the idea, collective inquiry—proceeds by the presentation and examination of inferences expressed according to formal practices meant to lead the hearer, opponent, or referee to arrive at the conclusion. This takes the form of the famous Nyāya syllogism, a statement form with components or "parts" (avayava) *that were alluded to in the discussion of* vāda *above. The following is a stock argument showing the five components:*

1. *The mountain is fiery,*
2. *Since it is smoky.*
3. *Whatever is smoky is fiery, like a fiery kitchen hearth.*
4. *The smoky mountain falls under the "whatever" of the general rule.*
5. *Therefore, the mountain is fiery.*

The five components are

1. *The "thesis to be proved,"* pratijñā*: "The inferential subject possesses the property to be proved":* a *is* S.
2. *The "reason,"* hetu*: "Since it possesses the prover":* a *is H.*
3. *The "illustration,"* udāharaṇa*, the statement of the general rule, "pervasion,"* vyāpti*: "Whatever possesses the prover possesses the property to be proved too," as shown by smoke and fire in a kitchen hearth: every H is also S.*
4. *The "application,"* upanaya*:* a*-as-H falls under the rule in part 3.*
5. *The "conclusion,"* nigamana*: same as part one, except now proved:* a *is S, or, it is known that* a *is S.*

The five steps are to be construed as a single statement governed by grammatical and semantic rules, designed to generate inferential knowledge in another person. The idea is that the five-membered form is an ideal ordering corresponding to requirements of syntactic binding and semantic appropriateness for provoking inferential knowledge in someone else. This requires a statement that provides the inferential terms—inferential subject (a), prover (H), property to be proved (S)—in the proper relationship. Now, although there are in Nyāya two kinds of inference, "inference for oneself" and "inference for another," they are thought of as essentially the same in principle. Inference for another is thought of as linguistically an ideal reconstruction of an inference for oneself.

Vātsyāyana devotes his commentary on the first sūtra of the section that spells out all the inferential "components" to arguing against a ten-part statement form. Under the sūtras to follow, he explains the five components.

1.1.32: The proposition (*pratijñā*), reason (*hetu*), illustration (*udāharaṇa*), application (*upanaya*), and conclusion (*nigamana*) are the inferential components, *avayava*.

Vātsyāyana [31.1–4]: . . . Desire to know and the others (on your list of ten components to the statement form) are indeed appropriate in the right context, because they are useful when the goal is to find something out. But the **proposition** and the rest are portions of an inferential statement that would establish something for another person, **inferential components, *avayava*,** because they are the means to accomplish the purpose of a formal demonstration.[1]

But of these so classified, we have the following.

1.1.33: The proposition (*pratijñā*) mentions the property to be proved (*sādhya*).

Vātsyāyana [31.6–7]: The **proposition (*pratijñā*)** is a summary statement that asserts a property as belonging to a property-bearer, that is, to something that is qualified by a qualifier. It **mentions the property to be proved**. For example, "Sound is impermanent."

In the example given by Vātsyāyana, the impermanence of sound is what is to be proved. In the next series of sūtras, the illustration is a case that exemplifies a general rule that underpins the inference.

---

1 Thakur lists an alternative reading from one of his manuscripts that we have adopted since it fits better in context than the one he decided upon, i.e., "*artha-sādhaka-bhāvāt*" instead of "*tattva-artha-sādhaka-bhāvāt*."

1.1.34: The reason (*hetu*) establishes a property to be proved from similarity with a supporting illustration.

Vātsyāyana [31.10–14]: The reason (*hetu*) is an assertion that establishes the **property to be proved** by commonality with an illustration. Taking a prover property and connecting it both to a property to be proved and to a supporting illustration, the **reason** is a statement that expresses a prover. For example, "Sound is impermanent *since it is a property that is produced*." (This presupposes) that the property of being produced has been perceived as belonging to things that are impermanent.

Question: Is just this much a suitable definition of a reason as a part of an inferential statement?

Answer: No.

Question: What then?

1.1.35: Likewise from dissimilarity.

Vātsyāyana [32.1–2]: And **from dissimilarity** that is illustrated, that is, a reason proves a property to be proved. How? With respect to the inference, "Sound is impermanent, *since* it is a property that is produced," it has been perceived that the property of not being produced belongs to things that are permanent, such as a self.

In contemporary propositional logic, this would be expressed as a logical equivalence: the contraposition, "If something is produced, it is impermanent," is logically equivalent to, "If something is permanent, it is not produced." But here the point has more to do with negative correlations. When arguing that H instances are also S instances, one would cite as negative examples things that are not-S and not-H.

1.1.36: The illustration (*udāharaṇa*) is an example of the property to be proved. It is used because of its similarity with other occurrences of the property to be proved.

Vātsyāyana [32.5–17]: "**Similarity**" is to be the same property as the property to be proved. **Because of its similarity**—for this reason—the **example** is an **occurrence of the property to be proved**. . . .

For whatever case—for example, the occurrence of the property *impermanence* belonging to the thing to be proved *since* that thing has the property *having been produced*—it would be **because of its similarity with other occurrences of the property to be proved** that it is an example (*dṛṣṭānta*). Since the thing under discussion has the property of having been produced, we would have something that has that property to be proved (*impermanence*) **because of its similarity with other occurrences of the property to be proved**. This is an **illustration**, just as defined. A substance such as a dish or the like, which has the property *having been produced*, is *impermanent*—this has been perceived. Wherever something has been produced, the thing has the property of *having been produced*. And something does not come to be as (somehow) already existing; similarly it loses itself; it is (eventually) destroyed—it is therefore impermanent. In this way, the property *having been produced* is the prover; *impermanence* is the property to be proved. . . .

1.1.37: Or, because of the opposite of that, there is the opposite (that is, an instance of something that lacks the property to be proved).

Vātsyāyana [33.3–14]: . . . And because of dissimilarity, something lacks the subject's property to be proved. Thus, it too is an example that serves as an illustration. "Sound is impermanent, *since* it has the property of having been produced. Whatever does not have the property of having been produced is permanent, such as a self." Things such as selves serve as examples of items that lack the subject's property to be proved (impermanence), because of their exclusion from things that are similar to that which is to be proved. That is, they do not have the property, *having been produced*. This property of *impermanence*, which we are trying to establish as belonging to sound, is not there in a self. Here things such as selves are examples because they lack the property *having been produced*. Someone seeing that *impermanence* is not present infers the opposite for sound: "*Since* the property *having been produced* is present, sound is *impermanent*." . . .

With regard to the example as discussed previously, whatever two properties a person perceives to be related as property to be proved (*impermanence*) and prover (*being produced*), she infers that the relationship between them holds also in a current instance of something to be proved. With regard to the example as discussed, because the absence of one of whatever two properties makes the person experience the absence of the other, she infers (rightly) the presence of the one from the presence of the other of the two properties in an instance of something to be proved.

This would not be possible if we were dealing with (fallacies, specifically) "pseudo-provers," *hetv-ābhāsa*. Thus pseudo-provers are not genuine provers.

The (epistemic) potentiality of the reason and the illustration is an extremely subtle matter understood with painstaking effort. It is to be known by the learned.

1.1.38: On the basis of the illustration, the application (*upanaya*) resolves the thing to be known as so or not so.

Vātsyāyana [34.1–8]: "**On the basis of the illustration**" means "depending on the illustration," or "by force of the illustration." "By force of" means "according to its power." When the illustration employs similarity, something such as a dish that has the property *having been produced* is found to be *impermanent*, and sound **as so** would be sound that has the property *having been produced* (and thus would also be impermanent). This is an example of **resolving the thing to be known**, for example, resolving that sound is impermanent based on its having the property of having been produced. . . .

Even though provers, of which there are two types (positive and negative), and illustrations, which also come in two types (the similar and the dissimilar), make the application occur in two ways, the conclusion is the same for each:

1.1.39: Restatement of the proposition after assertion of the reason is the conclusion (*nigamana*).

Vātsyāyana [34.10–35.21]: Whether one employs "similarity" or "dissimilarity," one resolves the thing to be known according to the illustration. After that, there is **the conclusion (*nigamana*)**, (for example) "Since it has the property of having been produced, sound is impermanent." The etymological analysis of the word "conclusion" (*nigamana*) is: "They are brought together by this," in that the conclusion brings together the proposition, the reason, the illustration, and the application to make a unified case. "They are brought together" means "They are made efficacious," "They are bound together."

Of the two (similarity and dissimilarity), to take up, first of all, the employment of similarity: with that kind of reason we have the statement, "Sound is impermanent," as the proposition. "Since it has the property of having been produced" is the reason. Mentioning something that has the property of having been produced, such as a dish, which is impermanent, is the illustration: "It (the dish, known to have been produced) is impermanent." The application is, "And so is sound in having the property of having been produced." After that, the conclusion, "Because it has the property of having been produced, sound is impermanent."

With employment of dissimilarity too: "Sound is impermanent" (proposition); "Since it has the property of having been produced" (reason); "Something such as a self (*ātman*) that has the property of not having been produced is found to be permanent" (illustration); "And sound is not so, that is, does not have the property of not having been produced" (application). What then? "It has the property of having been produced." After that, we have "Since it has the property of having been produced, sound is impermanent" (as the conclusion). . . .

The interrelationship of one component to another is essential. If there were no proposition, the reason and the rest would be unfounded and could not do their job. If the reason were absent, then what could be demonstrated by the inferential method? And if the illustration with respect to what is to be proved is absent, what could be resolved? And what would the conclusion show in restating the proposition? If there were no illustration, how could one appropriate similarity or dissimilarity to establish the property to be proved? And the resolving would proceed by force of what?

And without the application, the prover would not be applied to the property to be proved and could not establish the claim. And in the absence of a conclusion, who would be brought to understand a claim, "It is so," since the proposition and the other components would not be related?

Next, the purpose of each of the components. The point of the proposition is to propose a relationship between a property to be proved (fieriness) and the property-bearing subject (the mountain) of the inference ("The mountain is fiery"). The point of the reason is to state that the property to be proved is established by means of illustration of one and the same property (smokiness) in a similar case or of its absence in a dissimilar case. The point of the illustration is to point to two properties in the relationship of prover and property to be proved in a single location (smokiness and fieriness together). The point of the application is to make clear that the prover property is co-located with the property to be proved (in the inferential subject). The point of the conclusion is—once the relation of prover and property to be proved has been spelled out as involving the two properties mentioned in the illustration—to reject the unacceptable consequence of disregarding what has been proved.

And if by either the method of similarity or dissimilarity the reason and the illustration are perfectly correct, then in no way can we be defeated by misleading objections (*jāti*) or clinchers (*nigraha-sthāna*, "point of defeat") raised against us. The tricky debater may try to find fault with the illustration, which puts forth an inseparable relationship between the prover and the property to be proved. For, if the relationship between the prover and the property to be proved has genuinely been determined as known through an example (*dṛṣṭānta*), then citing a property as a prover property in the reason statement is not merely a matter of similarity or dissimilarity (but a stronger tie).

It is commonplace in debate and reasoning that some reasons are faulty. In Nyāya's terms, bad reasons are not reasons at all, and are commonly called ahetu, *"non-reasons." Yet there are some that mislead us, and seem often to be employed by our opponents and others in debate. To be on guard, we therefore study fallacies in general. In the context of formal inference, Gautama identifies five kinds of common fallacy, called here "pseudo-provers"* (hetv-ābhāsa). *They are called "pseudo-provers" because they often fool us by their resemblance to the genuine variety, good provers making for good arguments. And it is specifically the Nyāya syllogism that they imitate. Later we are treated to fallacies more broadly conceived. Five specific fallacies are discussed in the* Nyāya-sūtra, *but our commentators note (under sūtra 1.2.4) that many more exist that are not mentioned here.*

Four of these "pseudo-provers" are included in the next stretch of text: (1) the deviant, (2) the contradictory, (3) the inconclusive, and (4) the unproven prover. A fifth, the mistimed, is dropped by later Nyāya philosophers, usually in favor of (5) the defeated in advance (when someone tries to prove something that contradicts the settled findings of other knowledge sources). Uddyotakara introduces it under sūtra 1.2.9 through a creative interpretation of the word "mistimed."

The examples below are drawn from ancient Indian controversies in metaphysics. Regarding the temporal nature of sound, some philosophers argued that the sounds we hear with our ears are only manifestations of underlying eternal sound patterns. On such views, sound itself is strictly speaking eternal, and the things that we hear in ordinary life are temporary manifestations of this underlying reality. Nyāya opposes this view, but its concern is not to argue the case but to use the existing debate to provide illustrations of some of the fallacies.

Vātsyāyana [42.7]: Because they do not meet the definition of a prover (that is, they do not lead to knowledge), there are some things that are not provers but appear to so be because of commonality with the real thing. They are as follows.

1.2.4: The pseudo-provers (*hetv-ābhāsa*) are the deviant, the contradictory, the inconclusive, the unproven prover, and the mistimed.

Uddyotakara [155.16–156.6]: "What is the similarity between genuine provers and the non-provers mentioned here, such that they *appear* to be provers?" The similarity is that they are put forth after a proposition. Just as provers are employed after the proposition, so too are these pseudo-provers. This is the similarity. Alternatively, one could say that the similarity is that they conform to *some* of the features of a genuine prover. A genuine prover has three features . . . the difference between the genuine prover and the imitator is that the real thing is probative and the other is not. "Why?" Because the real thing has all of the features of a genuine prover, while the imitator has only some.

The "three features of a real prover"—first articulated by the Buddhist Dignāga and mentioned here by Uddyotakara—are that it (1) must exist as a property of subject of the inference (to use our stock example, the hill in question must be smoky); (2) it must be co-located with the property to be proved in at least one example (a fiery kitchen hearth has both smoke and fire); and (3) it does not exist where the property to be proved is absent (there are no known cases of smoke without fire). Pseudo-provers are similar to genuine ones in that they have some of the above features but not all three.

1.2.5: The deviant is the non-exclusive prover.

Vātsyāyana [42.13–43.8]: Deviation amounts to not being set in a single type of thing. Something that operates with deviation is called deviant. It is on display in the following:

Sound is permanent,
Since it lacks tactile qualities.
A pot, which is something tactile, is known to be impermanent.
Furthermore, sound is not like that, it is not something with tactile qualities. What then? It lacks tactile qualities.
Therefore, since it lacks tactile qualities, sound is permanent.

We find that the two properties given with the example, namely, *having tactile qualities* and *impermanence*, are not related as property to be proved and prover. An atom has a tactile quality while it is also permanent. And other permanent things such as a self (*ātman*) lack tactile qualities. . . . Thus the alleged prover *deviates* from *being permanent* (some things that lack tactile qualities are impermanent). An instance of occurrent cognition is something that lacks tactile qualities but is also impermanent.

Although there are in this way two kinds of example (positive and negative), there is no appropriate relationship between the property to be proved and the prover, because of deviation. Thus, there is no genuine prover because the definition of a prover is not satisfied.

In the example given, *permanence* demarks one distinct group of objects. *Impermanence* demarks another. A (legitimate) prover that is included in the one but not the other is said to be exclusive, *ekāntika*; if it is not, then it is (fallacious and) **non-exclusive**, because it is included on both sides (H and S; H and ¬S).

A straightforward way to capture in English the nature of the deviant is to say that it amounts to a counterexample, an exception to the claim that the alleged prover guarantees that the thing to be proved must also be present. To cite a simple case: if person A were to claim that all dogs are mean, and therefore Fido must be mean, person B could refute A by mentioning a dog known to be quite gentle, for example, Lassie. This would show that A's alleged prover is deviant, since being a dog *does not guarantee* being mean.

Under the next sūtra, discussing the contradictory, *Vātsyāyana uses an example apparently drawn from Sāṃkhya, which holds that everything except the self is a modification of primordial matter. The fallacy here involves internal contradiction, asserting something that contradicts one's own previously attested views. But the passage may also be read as a further attack on Saṃkhya's view of causation. Sāṃkhya holds that existing things are permanent and only undergo modifications. Nyāya argues that modifications themselves must be impermanent, and that the very idea of* modifications *contradicts Sāṃkhya's stated view. See the end of Chapter 5, "Substance and Causation," for more on the Sāṃkhya notion that an effect lies latent, "unmanifest" in its cause.*

1.2.6: Once one has accepted a position as established, the contradictory (*viruddha*) is a pseudo-prover that contradicts it.

Vātsyāyana [43.11–44.2]: The words "**that contradicts it**" are to be analyzed as derivative from the verbal root "*rudh*" plus prefix "*vi-*" in the active voice implying an agent who contradicts a position that was already accepted, that is, **a position as established**.

For example, "A modification of primordial matter can cease to be manifest." This commits the fallacy of being contradictory, because it rejects the idea of permanence. A modification that is yet permanent is not possible. One also cannot say without contradiction, "Even though the modification has disappeared, it remains," because to assert permanence is to deny destruction. . . .

The next fallacy is called the inconclusive, "prakaraṇa-sama." *A* prakaraṇa *is a topic for inquiry, such as, "Is there an enduring self?" This pseudo-prover fails to settle the issue and thus controversy continues. The fallacy is akin to "proof by selective reasoning" in contemporary informal logic. Vātsyāyana imagines a debater appealing to certain features of sound to make her case, while ignoring other salient features. What is lacking is an appropriately clear and definitive prover property that would definitely settle the case.*

In later Nyāya, "counterinference" takes the place of this fallacy on lists of the most important five. Counter-inference, sat-pratipakṣa, *is rather precisely defined: It is a supposed prover H that qualifies* a *and would prove that* a *is S on the basis of the rule that all things H are things S. But it is only a pseudo-prover in that it is faced with a counter-prover F that also qualifies* a *and would prove that* a *is not S on the basis of the rule that all things F are not things S. In other words, there is evidence that some topic or thing has an inferred property S, while at the same time there is distinct evidence that it does not have the S: the property or claim then remains controversial. Thus, until the issue can be resolved, an argument that is beset by a counterinference remains dubious. To use a simple example: "He is a Yankees fan, since he is wearing a Yankees cap" may be countered by the inference, "He is not a Yankees fan, since he has a Red Sox bumper sticker on his car."*

1.2.7: The inconclusive is a pseudo-prover that is put forward to generate certainty but allows concern about a topic of controversy to continue.

Vātsyāyana [44.6–17]: A **topic of controversy** (*prakaraṇa*) occurs when there is a thesis and a counterthesis subject to deliberation, neither known for sure. **Concern** about such a topic takes the form of examination through deliberation, etc., when one is not yet certain. There remains desire to know, sparking use of critical examination to achieve certainty, because both sides of the disputed issue are equal in terms of supporting evidence. The **inconclusive** is when a reason does not settle the controversy. It does not provide certainty. For example, there is the following argument:

Sound is impermanent
Since we do not find the property of eternality within it.
Things such as dishes are not experienced as having the property of permanence, and are thus known to be impermanent.

Now, when a property used as a prover generates doubt (because it could be used in support of either S or ¬S), that is not this fallacy of the **inconclusive**, but rather the **deviant**, which is itself doubtful (discussed in sūtra 1.2.5 above). But where deliberation is dependent on detail still to be uncovered and where there is also no awareness of doubt-resolving detail for either of the two sides, there the controversy continues on. For example, sound (considered as a type of thing) is not experienced as having permanence as its nature or property, nor as having impermanence. Such lack of awareness concerning details that would favor one of two views allows **concern about a topic of controversy** to continue. How so? That it does can be seen in contrast to the opposite situation, where controversy ceases.

If the nature or property of permanence were found in sound, then there would be no controversy. Alternatively, if the nature or property of impermanence were found, controversy would likewise cease. This fallacious prover motivates both of two opposed views, and makes the situation unripe for certainty about either.

The next fallacy is called sādhya-sama, *"the unproved prover." It is akin to "unwarranted premise" in informal logic. No premise used in support of a conclusion should be as dubious as the conclusion itself. This is precisely the fallacy of* sādhya-sama *in the* Nyāya-sūtra. *In the example below, someone argues that shadow is a substance, since movement is found only in substances. The prover is itself unproved, however, because it is not yet settled that shadows actually move on their own. The experience of a shadow's moving may rather be due to the movement of something that is obstructing light. That a shadow itself possesses movement is unwarranted.*

1.2.8: The unproved is a pseudo-prover that is as non-definitive as the property to be proved, because it itself remains to be proved.

Vātsyāyana [45.3–8]: Consider that one is trying to prove that a shadow is a substance (*being a substance* is the property to be proved and the proposition to be proved is, "A shadow is a substance"). The statement of the reason is "*since it possesses movement.*" That prover is as **non-definitive** as the property to be proved (do shadows really move?): it is an **unproved** prover. It too remains to be known, as the property to be proved remains to be known as qualifying the inferential subject, here shadows.

What is to be proved, first of all, is as follows: (a) Does a shadow move, like a person or any other substance? Or (b) is the experience of its movement due to a continuum of light that is present while being continually obstructed by some substance that is moving? Is it the part of light that is obstructed by a substance that is verily moving, such that just by its absence the apparent movement of the shadow is grasped in some vague way?

The next passage, which is from Uddyotakara, inaugurates a transition to a later Naiyāyika focus on the "defeated in advance" as the fifth type of pseudo-prover, making the starting-team list of five given in Nyāya-sūtra *1.2.4. above. Uddyotakara provides a distinct reading of the fallacy called the "mistimed" to introduce the idea that certain arguments may be patently rejected when they contradict what we already know. In the stock example, should someone try to prove that fire is cold, the conclusion may be rejected immediately, because we already know through sense perception that fire is hot. In Vātsyāyana's reading, in contrast, the "mistimed" is a somewhat odd pseudo-prover, occurring when an arguer puts forth a prover that would be appropriate at certain times but not in the direct context of his making an argument. Other theorists, represented below by imagined objectors, apparently took it to be a violation in the proper ordering of the inferential components in a presentation of an inference. Uddyotakara interprets the fallacy in a different way, making us aware that arguments are sometimes undermined by counterevidence and not necessarily by failures internal to the argument itself. His reading of the fallacy also helps to crystalize the idea emphasized in later treatises that there is a difference between logical errors involving inadequate provers, and speaker errors involving the violation of procedure and custom in formal debate.*

Uddyotakara [168.10–14, under sūtra 1.2.9 on the pseudo-prover called the "mistimed"]: Objection: The mistimed is not a pseudo-prover (*hetv-ābhāsa*) but rather a clincher (*nigraha-sthāna*), a point of defeat, because the prover is mentioned *after* the thesis in question has been leveled, defeated.

Response: . . . Tell us *by what* has the thesis been leveled. (It has been defeated by previous certified knowledge: you cannot prove that fire is cold.)

Objection: It has been leveled by failure to mention the prover (at the right time, and so we do have a clincher, not a pseudo-prover).

Response: If it has been leveled by failure to mention the prover, then why would the prover be ineffective?

Objection: Its ineffectiveness amounts to its being mentioned afterwards.

Response: Then it would not be ineffective, that is, not just because it happens to be mentioned later. That would be rather a fault of the speaker, not a logical flaw (whereas with a pseudo-prover we do have a logical flaw).

In summary, four of the five mentioned pseudo-provers or fallacies are as follows:

***The deviant**: A pseudo-prover is not "pervaded by" the property to be proved. All H is not S. There are available counterexamples. For example, "That is a dog, so it must be mean." Since there are cases of dogs that are not mean,* being a dog *does not guarantee* being mean.

***The contradictory**: A pseudo-prover is opposed to one's own accepted position. For example, "There are no single entities, since everything we see is made up from clusters of atoms." Since the arguer admits the existence of atoms, she contradicts her thesis that there are no single entities.*

***The inconclusive**: A pseudo-prover appeals to vague or selective features of something that don't effectively speak to the debate at hand. For example, "I say that Frank likes the Red Sox since he never roots for the Yankees." That Frank never roots for the Yankees does not decide the question of his rooting for the Red Sox, which remains open.*

***The unproved**: A pseudo-prover itself requires evidence as much as what it is meant to prove. For example, "President Obama is a pacifist, since he is a Buddhist." The president's being a Buddhist is not itself established, and it is thus incapable of proving that he is a pacifist.*

*The fifth prover, the **mistimed**, is replaced on later lists by the "**defeated** (in advance),"* bādhita. *The stock classical example is, "Fire is cold,* since *it is a substance." We know in advance that fire is not cold, and the claim is thus rejected because it contradicts secure knowledge.*

Our final passages focus on other sorts of faulty reasoning, and are from a section traditionally entitled, "On the general definition of defects in reasoning due to human frailties." These defects come in two sorts. The first, jāti, *"misleading objections," are for the most part fallacies targeting inductive generalization. Twenty-four are spelled out and analyzed in* Nyāya-sūtra *chapter five. In the interests of space, we will focus only on their general definition. They are not really fallacies so much as conundra concerning induction and inference. Responding to them often requires obtuse digressions into faulty metaphysical assumptions on the part of interlocutors. In contrast, the other sort, clinchers, or "points of defeat,"* nigraha-sthāna, *are more properly faults due to human error. Gautama includes even the pseudo-provers discussed above within the larger category of clinchers, since, as Uddyotakara points out, it is the disputant who puts a bad reason forth. Possibly the traditional title of the section could be given a slightly different rendering in the light of the actual variety of* jāti *and* nigraha-sthāna *spelled out in chapter five: "On the general definition of defects due to human, linguistic, and logical error." After a look at* jātis, *we will close by looking at a list of clinchers presented in* Nyāya-sūtra *chapter five.* Chala, *equivocation, is a topic that naturally fits within debate theory, and is thus often grouped with misleading objections and clinchers. But we have included it in Chapter 7, "Word and Object," owing to its helpfulness in understanding Nyāya's theory of meaning.*

1.2.18: Objections based on superficial similarities or dissimilarities are "misleading objections," *jāti*.

Vātsyāyana [51.11–14]: A *reductio* objection that is commonly employed against a (good) reason or prover is called a misleading objection, *jāti*. And it is a pseudo-*reductio* that purports to refute or find fault by way of **similarities or dissimilarities** . . . , that is, to find fault with something fallaciously. . . .

Jātis *are sophistical responses to arguments that try to confute them by drawing out irrelevant connections and parallels.* Nyāya-sūtra *5.1.1 lists twenty-four types of* jāti. *What they all share is an appeal to superficial or misleading similarities or differences that are irrelevant to the genuine correlations that would underpin legitimate inferences. For example, should someone argue, "Rob would make a good teacher, since he is an excellent communicator," an objection based on superficial similarity would be: "No, he'd be a bad teacher, since he is tall, just like Mike, who is tall and a bad teacher." Here, "being tall" is irrelevant to the question of being a good teacher, even if it is true that Mike is both tall and a bad teacher. What is central to note here is that there exist a variety of dialectical tricks that appeal to superficial connections of which one must be wary. By definition, these tricks are deceptive. Uddyotakara thus notes under sūtra 5.1.1 [498.16–17]: "When it is said that a* jāti *neutralizes an opposing view, it is not meant that one who puts forth the original argument and the respondent are on equal footing. A* jāti *is a false response, and one who puts a* jāti *forth speaks falsely, while the opposing debater is not necessarily speaking falsely."*

1.2.19: And distorted understanding and failure to understand, and so on, are clinchers, *nigraha-sthāna*.

Vātsyāyana [52.3–8]: **Distorted understanding** is either simply wrong understanding or contemptible understanding. A debater with a distorted understanding gets defeated. To be defeated in this way amounts to facing a clincher. But **failure to understand** amounts to a debater's failure to engage in a debate on a topic already introduced. Or, it is not trying to contend with a position maintained by an opponent, or not trying to answer an objection.

The fact that the words in the sūtra ("distorted understanding" and "failure to understand") are not in compound indicates that these two are not the only clinchers.

Are misleading objections, *jāti,* and clinchers, *nigraha-sthāna,* of one kind, like the example (*dṛṣṭānta*), or, like the accepted position (*siddhānta*), do they admit of multiple varieties? To answer, the sūtra-maker says:

1.2.20: There are many kinds of misleading objection, *jāti,* and clincher, *nigraha-sthāna,* because of the many ways they are construed by objectors.

Vātsyāyana [52.10–15]: **Because of the many ways they are construed by objectors**—to include objections based on similarities and dissimilarities. There are many kinds of misleading objection. And there are many kinds of clincher, because of **the many ways they are construed** that amount to distorted understanding or failure to understand. Imagining in many ways is construing variously. Or, it amounts to construals of different types.

Of the two, five mentioned (in *Nyāya-sūtra* chapter five)... are clinchers of the failure-to-understand variety. The rest hinge on distorted understanding.

We close now by providing the Nyāya-sūtra's *list of clinchers, "points of defeat," in 5.2.1. Most of these may be captured in the major headings of (i) epistemic flaws, (ii) violations of pragmatic principles, or (iii) procedural errors.*

5.2.1: (A) Violating the proposition, (B) changing the proposition, (C) contradicting the proposition, (D) retracting the proposition, (E) changing the prover, (F) irrelevance, (G) nonsense, (H) unintelligibility, (I) incoherent speech, (J) the misarranged, (K) incompleteness, (L) superfluity, (M) repetition, (N) failure to register, (O) failure to respond, (P) distraction, (Q) evasion, (R) *tu quoque* (two wrongs don't make a right), (S) overlooking the censurable, (T) censuring the uncensurable, (U) incoherence with accepted views, and (V) advancing a pseudo-prover are clinchers (*nigraha-sthāna*).

"Clinchers" are established ways in which one may lose an argument. The list should remind us that the Nyāya-sūtra *was produced at a time when logic, epistemology, and debate theory were intertwined. In the Nyāya project, the goal is both to know the truth and, when called upon, to defend it publicly. Through the type of debate called* vāda, *one would advance the causes of knowledge and philosophy. But given hostile intellectual adversaries, recognized standards of formal dialectics are useful and necessary. One needs training to recognize the fallacious arguments of opponents, as well as to be on guard against bad reasoning on one's own part.*

Each of the clinchers presented would merit a dissertation if we considered their history in the literature, as they are used to combat opponents' arguments in treatises throughout the centuries. This is true of Nyāya composition but also, indeed, of all the classical schools. Fortunately, it is easy to find contemporary examples that do not require much contextualization. These errors are descriptively labeled, for the most part wearing their nature on their sleeves.

We offer a few examples and glosses, some classical and others contemporary, leaving it to the reader to fill in the rest. (A) Trying to prove that everything is momentary, one "violates the proposition" in admitting a counterinstance of something momentary. (B) Trying to prove that everything is momentary, one "changes the proposition" by trying to prove instead that everything is mind alone (a kind of topic switching). (C) Trying to prove that substances are distinct from qualities, one offers as a reason that only qualities can be perceived, thus "contradicting the proposition" (the reason being in favor of the opposite, that substances are not distinct from qualities). (F) One commits "irrelevance" by proffering a reason that does not bear on the proposition to be proved, for example, "Emeralds are green, since swans are white." (G) "Nonsense" occurs when phonemes are used that are not words. (H) "Unintelligibility" is said to occur when after repeating an argument three times a debater is not understood by the opponent, the judge, or the audience. (I) "Incoherent speech" is a flaw of sentences, not words, occurring when there is a failure of syntactic connection or semantic fittingness, for example, "The gardener is wetting the plants with fire." (J) The "misarranged" is a formal proof that puts the premises in the wrong order. (K) "Incompleteness" applies to proofs that leave out a step or component. (N) "Failure to register" is a flaw of a debater who fails to understand the opponent's position and argument. (O) "Failure to respond" occurs when a debater is left speechless, not knowing how to answer. (U) "Incoherence with accepted views" (apasiddhānta) *targets a proposition to be proved or a reason that fails to fit in with established background beliefs, for example, trying to prove that atoms lack color for the reason that they are invisible, when it is held (on the basis of other, in this case, Vaiśeṣika arguments) that atoms have color (since otherwise things made of atoms would be colorless). And finally (V) the "pseudo-provers" already reviewed: no debater should base an argument on a reason that is known to be "pseudo-" in any of the five types, as Gautama has explained them.*

Suggested Readings

Jonardon Ganeri, ed., *Indian Logic: A Primer*. Richmond, Surrey, Great Britain: Curzon, 2001.

Pradeep P. Ghokale, *Inference and Fallacies Discussed in Ancient Indian Logic (with special reference to Nyāya and Buddhism)*. Bibliotheca Indo-Buddhica Series, ed. Sunil Gupta. Delhi: Sri Satguru Publications, 1992.

B. K. Matilal, *The Character of Logic in India*. SUNY Series in Indian Thought. Albany: State University of New York Press, 1998.

Raghavendra Pandya, *Major Hetvābhāsas: A Formal Analysis*. Delhi: Eastern Book Linkers, 1984.

Stephen Phillips, "Fallacies and Defeaters in Early Navya Nyāya." In *Indian Epistemology and Metaphysics*, ed. Joerg Tuske. London: Bloomsbury Academic, 2017.

Ernst Prets, "Futile and False Rejoinders, Sophistical Arguments, and Early Indian Logic." *Journal of Indian Philosophy* 29 (2001): 545–58.

Ernst Prets, "Parley, Reason, and Rejoinder." *Journal of Indian Philosophy* 31 (2003): 271–83.

Ester Solomon, *Indian Dialectics*. 2 vols. Ahmedabad: Gujarat Vidya Sabha, 1976.

Alberto Todeschini, "Twenty-two Ways to Lose a Debate: A Gricean Look at the *Nyāyasūtra's* Points of Defeat," *Journal of Indian Philosophy* 38 (2010): 49–74.

Study Questions

1. Define the three major kinds of debate according to Nyāya. Which is the most reputable? Why? What utility do the other kinds have according to Nyāya? Do you agree with the commentators on this point? Why or why not?

2. List and define in order Nyāya's five "components" of a formal inference. Give your own example of an inference using these.
3. What are the first four of the "pseudo-provers" of Gautama? Explain and provide an example of your own for each.
4. What is a *jāti*? Why should we be on guard for them within debate and argument?
5. Select three "clinchers," and given your understanding of debate according to Nyāya, explain why in each case if one were caught committing the fallacy one would lose.

Appendix A

Outline of the *Nyāya-sūtra*

There are five chapters of the *Nyāya-sūtra,* and each has two subdivisions called "daily lessons." Traditionally, editors of the *Nyāya-sūtra* have grouped individual sūtras into sections according to topic (*prakaraṇa*). In this outline we generally follow the divisions and titles given in Sanskrit in Anantalal Thakur's volumes, although we have added a few and combined some into larger groupings. Corresponding placements here in our volume appear in parentheses.

Chapter One: Central Topics

First daily lesson

1.1.1–2: Sixteen topics of Nyāya and the goals of inquiry (see Chapter 8 of this volume)

1.1.3–8: Knowledge sources (Chapter 1)

1.1.9–22: Objects of knowledge (Chapters 4 and 5)

1.1.23–41: Formal inquiry and argument

- **1.1.23–31:** Preliminaries to inquiry (Chapters 2 and 9)
- **1.1.32–39**: Components of an "inference for others" (Chapter 9)
- **1.1.40–41**: Supplements to inquiry: suppositional reasoning (Chapter 2)

Second daily lesson

1.2.1–20: Debate

- **1.2.1–1.2.3**: Kinds of debate (Chapter 7)
- **1.2.4–9**: Pseudo-provers (Chapter 9)
- **1.2.10–17**: Equivocation (Chapter 7)
- **1.2.18–20**: Misleading similarities (to a good proof) and clinchers (Chapter 9)

Chapter Two: Doubt and Knowledge Sources

First daily lesson

2.1.1–7: Doubt (Chapter 2)

2.1.8–20: The status of *pramāṇas* in general (Chapter 2)

2.1.21–36: Perception

- **2.1.21–30**: Defense of the definition of perception
- **2.1.31–32:** Is perception a form of inference?
- **2.1.33–36**: Is there a composite whole? (Chapter 5)

2.1.37–43: Inference

- **2.1.37–38:** Defense of the validity of inference
- **2.1.39–43:** Can inference make something known past, present, or future?

2.1.44–48: Analogy

2.1.49–56: Testimony in general

2.1.57–68: Sacred testimony

Second daily lesson

2.2.1–12: How many irreducible *pramāṇa* types?

2.2.13–69: Sounds, letters, and words

- **2.2.13–39:** The impermanence of sounds
- **2.2.40–57:** Letters
- **2.2.58–69:** Meaning and reference of a word (Chapter 7)

Chapter Three: Objects of Knowledge I

First daily lesson

3.1.1–6: Self (*ātman*)

- **3.1.1–3:** Self as other than the senses (Chapter 4)
- **3.1.4–6:** Self as other than the body (Chapter 4)

3.1.7–14: The unity of the visual faculty

3.1.15–17: Self as other than the *manas* ("mind")

3.1.18–26: The eternality of the self (Chapter 4)

3.1.27–31: The body

3.1.32–50: Are the sense faculties material? (Chapter 4)

3.1.51–60: Are sensation and the sense faculties single or plural?

3.1.61–72: Objects in general

Second daily lesson

3.2.1–9: The impermanence of cognition

3.2.10–17: The momentariness thesis

3.2.18–41: Cognition as a property of a self

3.2.42–45: Cognition as momentary

3.2.46–55: Cognition as distinct from bodily properties

3.2.56–59: *Manas* ("mind," "internal organ")

3.2.60–72: Embodiment (conjunction of self, mind, and body) determined by karmic merit (Chapter 8)

Chapter Four: Objects of Knowledge II

First daily lesson

4.1.1–2: Purposive action (*pravṛtti*) and vice (*doṣa*) in general

4.1.3–9: The threefold nature of vice

4.1.10–13: Rebirth

4.1.14–18: Is (as Buddhists claim) emptiness or non-existence the foundation of the world?

4.1.19–21: Is God alone the fundamental cause? (Chapter 6)

4.1.22–24: Do things arise by chance?

4.1.25–28: Refutation of universal impermanence

4.1.29–33: Refutation of universal permanence

4.1.34–36: Refutation of universal variety (Chapter 5)

4.1.37–40: Refutation of universal emptiness

4.1.41–43: Refutation of views that reduce all objects to a few kinds

4.1.44–54: Results of action (Chapter 5)

4.1.55–58: Pain and suffering

4.1.59–68: Final beatitude (*apavarga*) (Chapter 8)

Second daily lesson

4.2.1–3: The arising of the knowledge crucial for final beatitude

4.2.4–17: Part and whole

4.2.18–25: The "partless" (the atom) (Chapter 5)

4.2.26–37: Refutations of attacks on the reality of external objects (Chapter 3)

4.2.38–49: Fostering crucial knowledge (Chapter 8)

4.2.50–51: Protecting crucial knowledge (Chapter 8)

Chapter Five: Dialectics

First daily lesson

5.1.1–43: Misleading objections (*jāti*) (Chapter 9)

- **5.1.1–3:** Twenty-four *jāti* types and objections from misleading similarity or dissimilarity
- **5.1.4–20:** Common mistakes about inference corrected by right analysis
- **5.1.21–22:** Misleading conflict with "reasoning to the best explanation" (*arthāpatti*)
- **5.1.23–38:** Further common mistakes about inference corrected
- **5.1.39–43:** Misleading objections to the proper form of an "inference for others"

Second daily lesson

5.2.1–24: Debate clinchers

- **5.2.1–6:** Twenty-two clincher types including five related to the proposition (Chapter 9)
- **5.2.7–10:** Four clincher types concerning meaning
- **5.2.11–13:** Three clincher types of omission of a portion of proper form
- **5.2.14–15:** Repetition
- **5.2.16:** Failure to restate the opponent's thesis
- **5.2.17:** Failure to understand the opponent's thesis
- **5.2.18:** Inability to reply

5.2.19: Interruption
5.2.20: *Tu quoque* ("two wrongs don't make a right")
5.2.21: Failing to censure the censurable
5.2.22: Censuring the uncensurable
5.2.23: Incoherence
5.2.24: Pseudo-provers (fallacies, *hetv-ābhāsa*)

Appendix B

List of Sūtras Translated by Chapter

Chapter 1: Knowledge Sources

1.1.3: The knowledge sources are perception, inference, analogy, and testimony.

1.1.4: Perceptual knowledge arises from a connection of sense faculty and object, does not depend on language, is inerrant, and is definitive.

1.1.5: Next is inference, which depends on previous perception and is threefold: from something prior, from something later, and through experience of a common characteristic.

1.1.6: Analogy produces knowledge through similarity with something familiar.

1.1.7: Testimony is instruction by a trustworthy authority.

1.1.8: Such testimony is of two kinds, because it has two kinds of object: that which is experienced (here in this world), and that which is not experienced (here in this world).

Chapter 2: Doubt and Philosophical Method

1.1.23: Doubt is deliberative awareness in need of details about something particular. It is produced (1) from common properties being cognized, (2) from distinguishing properties being cognized, (3) from controversy, (4) from non-determination by experience, and (5) from non-determination by lack of experience.

1.1.40: *Tarka* is reasoning that proceeds by considering what is consistent with knowledge sources, in order to know the truth about something that is not definitively known.

1.1.41: Certainty (*nirṇaya*) is determination of something through deliberation about alternatives, by investigation of theses and countertheses.

1.1.26: From a system of thought, from a topic, and from a supposition, the stable view that emerges is an accepted position (*siddhānta*).

1.1.27: There are four types of accepted position (*siddhānta*) because of the differences among stable views: (1) accepted in all systems, (2) accepted in a single system, (3) accepted from a topic, and (4) accepted on the basis of a supposition.

1.1.28: A position accepted in all systems is something that is accepted within at least one system while not being opposed in any other system.

1.1.29: A position accepted in a single system is accepted by one school of thought but not others.

1.1.30: When one thing is accepted because it is entailed by something else that has been established, it is a "position accepted from a topic."

1.1.31: When, for the sake of careful examination of the details of a view, there is the suppositional acceptance of something that has not yet been examined closely, this is a position accepted on the basis of supposition.

2.1.16: And knowledge sources may be objects of knowledge, like a measuring scale.

2.1.17: (Objector:) On the view (a) that knowledge sources are themselves established by knowledge sources, the unwanted consequence would be that still other knowledge sources would have to be proved.

2.1.18: (Objector:) Or if we say (b) one *pramāṇa* need not be established by another, then, in the same way, we should accept objects without reasons.

2.1.19: (Answer:) No, *pramāṇas* are established like the light of a lamp.

2.1.20: Sometimes we find that no further source is required while sometimes we find that another source is required. There is no fixed rule.

Chapter 3: In Defense of the Real

4.2.26: (Opponent:) But when we examine things closely through cognition, we do not find true objects, just as we do not find a cloth when we distinguish the threads.

4.2.27: (Answer:) That is not a reason, since it is self-defeating.

4.2.28: (Answer continued:) Objects are experienced as unified, because a whole inheres in its parts.

4.2.29: (Answer continued:) Your argument also fails because objects are established through knowledge sources.

4.2.30: (Answer continued:) And because of the possibility and impossibility of knowledge sources (*pramāṇa*).

4.2.31: (Opponent:) Your conception of things known through knowledge sources is akin to conceptions of objects encountered in dreams.

4.2.32: (Opponent continued:) Or, it's like magic, cities of Gandharvas (castles in the sky), or a mirage.

4.2.33: (Answer:) This is unproven, because you haven't provided a reason to accept it.

4.2.34: And our conception of objects in dreams is like memory and imagination.

4.2.35: The destruction of a false perception results from knowledge of the truth of things, akin to the destruction of conceptions of dream objects upon waking.

4.2.36: Cognition itself is also real, since we apprehend its causes and its existence.

4.2.37: And because of the difference between the real thing and what is supposed, false cognition is to be explained as having a twofold nature.

Chapter 4: Self

1.1.10: Inferential marks for the self are desire, aversion, effort, pleasure, pain, and knowledge.

3.1.1: Because one grasps the same object through sight and touch, there is a self that is distinct from the body and sense organs.

3.1.2: Objection: This is wrong. (There is no self that is distinct from the body and sense organs) because sense organs are restricted to their own proper content.

3.1.3: (Answer:) The very restriction of sense organs to their own proper content is a reason to suppose the existence of a self—thus, the self's existence is not contested.

3.1.4: When a living body is harmed, no sin would be incurred (if there were no self).

3.1.18: Because happiness, fear, and unhappiness are experienced by a new-born appropriately, through connection with what was previously practiced and remembered (a self endures beyond death).

3.2.39: Cognition is a property of the self, since alternatives have been eliminated and undefeated reasons have been given above.

3.2.46: (Opponent:) There is doubt whether cognition is a property of a self, because substances exhibit their own qualities as well as the qualities of other things.

3.2.47: (Response continued:) (Consciousness is not a property of the body) because as long as the body lasts there will be properties like color but not consciousness.

Chapter 5: Substance and Causation

1.1.9: Self, body, sense faculties, objects (of the senses), cognition, mind (*manas*, the "internal organ"), purposive action, vice, rebirth, fruit of action, suffering, and final beatitude are the objects of knowledge.

4.1.38: No, (the anti-realist position is untenable) since it has been proven that existing things have an inherent nature (*sva-bhāva*).

2.1.33: (Objection:) There is doubt about the composite whole, since it remains to be proved.

2.1.34: (Reply:) If the composite whole is not accepted, there would be no knowledge of anything

2.1.35: (Reply continued:) And because holding and pulling are possible, there is a composite whole beyond the mere parts.

2.1.36: If one contends that composite wholes are experienced like an army or a forest, that would be wrong, since atoms are beyond the range of the senses.

4.2.16: Things cannot be divided down to an ultimate dissolution, for there must be atoms. . . .

4.2.25: These opposing considerations do not refute our notion of the atom, for they would lead to an infinite regress and that is impossible.

4.1.49: Because production and destruction are observed.

4.1.50: What is proved, however, by our understanding is the prior non-existence of the effect.

Chapter 6: God

4.1.19: God is the sufficient cause, since we find that human action sometimes does not come to fruition.

4.1.20: No, that is wrong, since in the absence of human action there is no fruition.

4.1.21: That, too, is not a good reason, since fruition is actuated by God.

Chapter 7: Word and Object

2.2.59: Since a word is used to refer to (a) an individual (*vyakti*), (b) a shape or form (*ākṛti*), and (c) a universal or class (*jāti*), there is doubt (sparking inquiry).

2.2.60: (Opponent 1:) It's the individual, since the usage is for an individual in the case of the word "which" as well as with words for group, offering, possession, number, growth, reduction, and color, and in verbal compounds—uninterrupted succession, too.

2.2.61: (Opponent 2:) This is wrong, because there would be no way to ascertain the word's object and meaning.

2.2.62: (Opponent 2 continued:) Even in the absence of what a word denotes, it can have meaning through secondary usage (*upacāra*, "transference"). For example, (a) a *brāhmaṇa*, (b) the "stands," (c) mats, (d) the king, (e) flour, (f) sandalwood paste, (g) the Gaṅgā (Ganges River), (h) cloth, (i) food, and (j) the person, through the relationships of (a) association (walking sticks with *brāhmaṇas*), (b) location (stands locating spectators), (c) purpose (grass collected to make mats), (d) comportment (names of gods used for the king), (e) measure (the measure for the flour measured), (f) container (the container of sandalwood paste specifying the sandalwood paste contained), (g) proximity (land bordering the Gaṅgā), (h) connection (the cloth's color for the cloth), (i) indispensable means (food for life as its means), and (j) importance (the dynasty for the founding person).

2.2.63: (Opponent 3:) It is form or shape (*ākṛti*) that is the primary meaning, because determination of what exists depends upon it.

2.2.64: (Opponent 4:) It is the universal (*jāti*), because a clay cow, though endowed with individuality and shape, cannot be the subject of the consecrating ceremonies of washing, and so on.

2.2.65: (Reply:) Wrong, because the universal is made manifest by the form or shape and the individual.

2.2.66: Nevertheless, the individual, the form or shape, and the universal together constitute the word's object and meaning.

2.2.67: The individual (*vyakti*) is the concrete form that supports particular qualities.

2.2.68: Form or shape (*ākṛti*) is so designated in being the sign of the universal.

2.2.69: The universal (*jāti*) has the character of producing an idea of things being the same.

1.2.12: Equivocation with words is construing a meaning other than that intended, when a speaker's reference to an object is not univocal.

1.2.13: Equivocation with generality is rendering an unintended meaning through excessively generalizing a meaning that is possible.

1.2.14: Equivocation over secondary meaning is denial of the real meaning when a description designates something through imaginative use of its property.

Chapter 8: The Right and the Good

1.1.1: Knowledge sources, objects of knowledge, doubt, motive, example, accepted position, inferential components, suppositional reasoning, certainty, debate for the truth, disputation, destructive debate, pseudo-provers, equivocation, misleading objections, and clinchers: from knowledge of these, there is attainment of the supreme good.

1.1.2: When pain, rebirth, activity, vice, and wrong understanding have been dispelled in reverse order, there is final beatitude (*apavarga*).

3.2.66: As karma causes the construction of a body, it is also responsible for a body's connection with a self.

3.2.67: Accordingly, lack of universality among beings is explained.

4.1.62: Karmic results mentioned do not occur for everyone, because it is impossible for some (for example) to carry out the rites that end with a collection of the sacrificial vessels.

4.2.46: For the purpose of attaining *apavarga*, there should be self-purification by means of yogic restraints (*yama*) and observances (*niyama*) and by psychological instructions and methods taught in yoga.

4.2.47: For the purpose of attaining *apavarga*, there should be repeated study of that science as well as discussion with those who know it.

4.2.48: The one who knows the science of the self should be admitted into the discussion along with pupils, teachers, and colleagues, those well-wishers who are distinguished by their seeking the supreme good.

4.2.49: Alternatively, people who have no countertheses of their own are also to be admitted, to further the purpose of the discussion, if they seek the truth and the supreme good.

4.2.50: To protect truth that has been ascertained, disputation (*jalpa*) and destructive debate (*vitaṇḍā*) may be employed, in the way one would protect seeds and sprouts by covering them with thorns and branches.

4.2.51: Disputation by attacking through those two (*jalpa* and *vitaṇḍā*).

Chapter 9: Debate

1.2.1: Employing the five components of a formal demonstration, taking up theses and countertheses, debate for the truth (*vāda*) is a matter of proving and refuting by means of knowledge sources and suppositional reasoning, without contradicting accepted positions.

1.2.2: Disputation (*jalpa*) includes what has already been explained for *vāda*, but also proving and refuting by means of equivocation, misleading objections, and clinchers.

1.2.3: That becomes destructive debate (*vitaṇḍā*) when there is no effort to establish a counterthesis.

1.1.32: The proposition (*pratijñā*), reason (*hetu*), illustration (*udāharaṇa*), application (*upanaya*), and conclusion (*nigamana*) are the inferential components, *avayava*.

1.1.33: The proposition (*pratijñā*) mentions the property to be proved (*sādhya*).

1.1.34: The reason (*hetu*) establishes a property to be proved from similarity with a supporting illustration.

1.1.35: Likewise from dissimilarity.

1.1.36: The illustration (*udāharaṇa*) is an example of the property to be proved. It is used because of its similarity with other occurrences of the property to be proved.

1.1.37: Or, because of the opposite of that there is the opposite (that is, an instance of something that lacks the property to be proved).

1.1.38: On the basis of the illustration, the application (*upanaya*) resolves the thing to be known as so or not so.

1.1.39: Restatement of the proposition after assertion of the reason is the conclusion (*nigamana*).

1.2.4: The pseudo-provers (*hetv-ābhāsa*) are the deviant, the contradictory, the inconclusive, the unproven prover, and the mistimed.

1.2.5: The deviant is the non-exclusive prover.

1.2.6: Once one has accepted a position as established, the contradictory (*viruddha*) is a pseudo-prover that contradicts it.

1.2.7: The inconclusive is a pseudo-prover that is put forward to generate certainty but allows concern about a topic of controversy to continue.

1.2.8: The unproved is a pseudo-prover that is as nondefinitive as the property to be proved, because it itself remains to be proved.

1.2.18: Objections based on superficial similarities or dissimilarities are "misleading objections," *jāti*.

1.2.19: And distorted understanding and failure to understand, and so on, are clinchers, *nigraha-sthāna*.

1.2.20: There are many kinds of misleading objection, *jāti*, and clincher, *nigraha-sthāna*, because of the many ways they are construed by objectors.

5.2.1: (A) Violating the proposition, (B) changing the proposition, (C) contradicting the proposition, (D) retracting the proposition (E) changing the prover, (F) irrelevance, (G) nonsense, (H) unintelligibility, (I) incoherent speech, (J) the misarranged, (K) incompleteness, (L) superfluity, (M) repetition, (N) failure to register, (O) failure to respond, (P) distraction, (Q) evasion, (R) *tu quoque* (two wrongs don't make a right), (S) overlooking the censurable, (T) censuring the uncensurable, (U) incoherence with accepted views, and (V) advancing a pseudo-prover are clinchers (*nigraha-sthāna*).

Glossary of Sanskrit Terms

1. Proper Names (philosophic schools and some important classical authors and texts)

Advaita Vedānta: influential subschool of the Upanishadic philosophy; becomes a whole school to itself, subscribing to a spiritual monism, "All is Brahman," including—and especially—the seemingly individual self.

Bhartṛhari: (c. 450) grammarian and philosopher of language celebrated for a *sphoṭa*—"comprehension in flash"—theory of sentence comprehension, a platonist theory of universals, and an idealist metaphysics of a "Word Absolute."

Bhāṭṭa: a follower of the Mīmāṃsaka philosopher Kumārila Bhaṭṭa or a view belonging to or deriving from Kumārila.

Cārvāka: philosophic school of materialism, skepticism, and hedonism, famous in epistemology for attacking inference as a knowledge source.

Dharmakīrti: (c. 650) Buddhist logician and epistemologist of the Yogācāra school (here called "Buddhist phenomenalism"), author of *Pramāṇa-vārttika* and other major works of Buddhist philosophy.

Gaṅgā: the Ganges river.

Gaṅgeśa: (c. 1325) systematizer if not the founder of "New Nyāya," *navya nyāya*, author of the influential *Tattva-cintā-maṇi*.

Gautama: (c. 150) author of the sūtras of the *Nyāya-sūtra*, Nyāya's founding text, sometimes called Akṣapāda ("foot-gazer," "lost in thought").

Jaimini: (c. 100 BCE) author of the *Mīmāṃsā-sūtra*.

Jaina philosophy: a tradition commencing with Mahāvīra (c. 450 BCE) with dozens of texts in all periods, probably most famous for an ethics of *ahiṃsā*, "non-injury," and non-absolutism (*anekānta-vāda*) in metaphysics.

Jayanta Bhaṭṭa: (c. 875) early (*prācīna*) Nyāya author of a non-commentarial treatise (the *Nyāya-mañjarī*) reorganizing but ranging over almost all the topics of the *Nyāya-sūtra* while disputing rival theories.

Kaṇāda: (c. 150) author of the *Vaiśeṣika-sūtra*, Vaiśeṣika's founding text.

Kumārila: (c. 650) prominent Mīmāṃsaka philosopher whose metaphysical and epistemological views are both appropriated and disputed by Nyāya philosophers.

Mādhyamika (also Madhyamaka): Buddhist school of skeptical, anti-realist philosophy founded by Nāgārjuna.

Mīmāṃsā: "Exegesis"; a long-running realist school celebrated for its defense of Vedic authority, principles of interpretation, philosophy of language, and epistemology; the *Mīmāṃsā-sūtra* (c. 100 BCE) is the root text; a commentary by Śabara (c. 500) is expanded (and sometimes corrected) by Kumārila Bhaṭṭa (c. 650) and in a second line by Prabhākara (c. 700), the two being the chief proponents of the school, with followers known as Bhāṭṭas and Prābhākaras.

Mīmāṃsaka: an advocate of Mīmāṃsā.

Mīmāṃsā-sūtra: (c. 100 BCE) the founding text of Mīmāṃsā.

Nāgārjuna: (c. 150) prominent Buddhist philosopher understood by Nyāya epistemologists to be a skeptic about "knowledge sources," *pramāṇa*; founder of the Mādhyamika school of Buddhist philosophy.

Naiyāyika: an advocate of Nyāya.

Navya Nyāya: "New Nyāya"; the late Nyāya philosophy of, preeminently, Gaṅgeśa and his followers, pioneered in large part by Udayana.

Nyāya: "Logic"; a school of metaphysical realism and "knowledge sources" in epistemology prominent throughout the classical period, from the *Nyāya-sūtra* (c. 150) on; explicitly combined with Vaiśeṣika in later centuries, beginning with Udayana and sometimes called Nyāya-Vaiśeṣika.

Nyāya-Vaiśeṣika: see NYĀYA.

Nyāya-sūtra (*NyS*): (c. 150) Nyāya's foundational text, attributed to Gautama.

Padārtha-dharma-saṃgraha (*PDS*): ("Compendium of the Properties of the Fundamental Categories") the sole work of Praśastapāda (c. 575) and an important text for New Nyāya for ontological categories and supporting arguments.

Pāṇini: (c. 450 BCE) author of a systematic grammar for Sanskrit, sometimes referred to as Pāṇini's sūtras, which inaugurated the long and rich grammarian tradition of classical India, including "grammarian philosophy."

Prācīna Nyāya: "Old Nyāya"; the philosophy of the *Nyāya-sūtra* and its commentaries and of a few independent treatises; see NYĀYA.

Praśastapāda: (c. 575) author of the *Padārtha-dharma-saṃgraha*, the reformulation and explanation of the *Vaiśeṣika-sūtra* that comes to be the central and defining text of Vaiśeṣika and important for later Nyāya metaphysics.

Śabara: (c. 500) author of the oldest extant commentary on the *Mīmāṃsā-sūtra*.

Sāṃkhya: "Analysis"; an early school of metaphysical dualism analyzing nature (*prakṛti*) to support the project of liberation. A "sister school" to classical Yoga. Advocates the "pre-existence of the effect" before production (*sat-kārya-vāda*).

Śaṅkara: (c. 725) the most prominent philosopher of the Advaita Vedānta school, espousing a radical monism of the sole reality of Brahman, the Absolute.

Udayana: (c. 1000) Nyāya philosopher; prolific author of both commentaries and independent texts and principal unifier of Nyāya epistemology and logic with Vaiśeṣika ontology.

Uddyotakara: (c. 550) author of the core commentary or subcommentary, *Vārttika* (*NyV*), on Vātsyāyana's *Nyāya-sūtra* commentary; adversary of, principally, Buddhist Yogācāra positions.

Upaniṣad: "secret doctrine"; various prose and verse texts appended to the Veda, having mystic themes centered on an understanding of self or consciousness in relation to the Absolute or God, called Brahman; the primary sources for classical Vedānta philosophy, but also recognized as authoritative by Naiyāyikas.

Vācaspatimiśra: (c. 900) major Nyāya author whose *Nyāya-vārttika-tātparya-ṭīkā* subcommentary (*NyVTatp*) is part of the core Old Nyāya literature; author also of texts within four other classical schools, Yoga, Sāṃkhya, Mīmāṃsā, and Advaita Vedānta.

Vaiśeṣika: "Atomism"; a classical philosophy focusing mainly on ontological issues ("What kinds of things are there?") and defending a realist view of material things as composed of atoms as well as a realist ontology of universals or class characteristics; "sister school" to Nyāya from early on, but explicitly and permanently unified with Nyāya by Udayana (c. 1000).

Vātsyāyana: (c. 450) author of the oldest extant commentary, the *Bhāṣya* (*NySBh*), on the *Nyāya-sūtra*.

Veda: "revealed Knowledge"; comprised of four (sometimes three) Vedas, which are collections of hymns to various Indo-European gods and goddesses, as well as instructions on sacrifice and speculations about the origin of the cosmos; the oldest texts in Sanskrit (some hymns possibly as early as 1500 BCE); the most sacred texts of Hinduism.

Vedānta: originally an epithet for Upaniṣads; in the classical period, the philosophy of the *Brahma-sūtra* and of several competing subschools defending Upaniṣadic views.

Yoga: when capitalized, refers to a distinct school of classical "Hindu" philosophy whose main text is the *Yoga-sūtra* of Patañjali, which articulates yoga practices and allied metaphysics; "sister school" to Sāṃkhya.

Yogācāra: Buddhist phenomenalism; the school of the idealists Asaṅga, Vasubandhu, and company, as well as of the great Buddhist logicians Dignāga and Dharmakīrti, who lay out a pragmatist epistemology that is a principal rival of Mīmāṃsā and classical Nyāya.

2. Terms

ābhāsa: false semblance, (mere) appearance, the non-genuine; a *hetv-ābhāsa* is a misleading inferential mark or prover, *hetu*, i.e., a fallacy. A *pramāṇa-ābhāsa* is a misleading cognitive presentation that is not actually produced by a knowledge source, e.g., perceptual illusion as contrasted with genuine perception that reveals a truth about an object.

abhāva: absence, negative fact; an absence invariably has a locus and an absentee; e.g., an absence of a pot on the floor has the floor as its locus and the pot as its absentee.

adharma: religious demerit; unrighteousness.

adṛṣṭa: "Unseen Force," i.e., *karman* or karma.

ākāṅkṣā: syntactic "expectation," a condition governing the intelligibility of a statement, according to Naiyāyikas and others; to cite a classical example, no single word appearing in the accusative case can be understood as a statement (excepting verbal ellipsis)—somewhat like saying "to the cow" standing alone in English—because of a violation of "(syntactic) expectation."

ākāśa: "ether," the medium of sound, an all-pervading unified substance, according to Nyāya-Vaiśeṣika and other classical views.

ākṛti: shape, form; the sign of a universal (*jāti*) according to Nyāya.

anātman: "no self" or "no soul"; an important Buddhist doctrine.

anavasthā: infinite regress, a defeater and conceptual predicament revealed by *tarka*, "suppositional reasoning."

anugama: uniformity, consecutive character; according to Nyāya-Vaiśeṣika, a criterion of a true universal, whose uniformity is taken to underwrite similar or recurrent experience.

anumāna: inference, the inferential process; one of four *pramāṇas*, "knowledge sources," according to Nyāya.

anumiti: inferential knowledge, the result of inference as a *pramāṇa*.

anupalabdhi: "non-cognition"; non-cognition of something in conditions where it should be experienced is grounds for knowing its non-existence, according to Nyāya. I know there is no elephant in my office because I don't see one, and if there were one I would see it.

anuvyavasāya: apperception, "after-cognition," introspection.

anvaya: positive correlations entailed by a natural pervasion, *vyāpti*; see also *VYATIREKA*.

anvaya-vyatireka: positive correlations (things both H and S) and negative correlations (things not-S and not-H) entailed by a natural pervasion, *vyāpti*.

anvaya-vyatirekin: an inference based on both positive and negative correlations; cf., *kevala-anvayin* and *kevala-vyatirekin*.

anvīkṣā: (= *ānvīkṣikī*) "critical reasoning," a term sometimes used by Naiyāyikas and others to refer to philosophy in general and the special concern of Nyāya.

anyathā-khyāti: the view of perceptual error endorsed by Nyāya that finds something presented perceptually as "other than what it is" due to an epistemic deficiency (*doṣa*), such as a departure from the normal workings of the sense organs, etc., and involving a retrieval of previous perceptual information through excitation of a "memory disposition," *saṃskāra*.

apavarga: final liberation or beatitude; the soteriological aim of Nyāya's advocacy of both critical thinking and yoga practice.

āpta: trustworthy authority or testifier, one who knows the truth and wants to communicate it without deception, according to Nyāya.

artha: "object," "purpose," "use."

arthāpatti: "inference to the best explanation," "presumption," "circumstantial implication," an independent *pramāṇa* according to Bhāṭṭa Mīmāṃsakas, a knowledge source viewed as a form of inference by Naiyāyikas; an argument that something would otherwise be impossible or inexplicable; e.g., from the information that fat Devadatta does not eat during the day, we know by *arthāpatti* that he eats at night.

arthavat: "effective," "accurate," "successful," "significant," "fitting." Used to describe knowledge sources by Vātsyāyana in his opening lines of commentary. Taken by subsequent commentators to mean "inerrant" or "factive," a knowledge source's "having an object" (*artha-vat*).

asamavāyi-kāraṇa: "co-inherence" cause, the qualities and relations of the inherent cause that help produce an effect, e.g., the blue color of the threads of a blue piece of cloth is an emergent cause of the blue of the cloth.

āsatti: (proper) "proximity" of words in a spoken statement; proper representation; one of three necessary conditions commonly identified for sentence meaning.

ātman: self, individual self; one of nine basic types of substance, according to Nyāya-Vaiśeṣika.

avayava: (1) "part," material part of a larger composite object, *avayavin*, "part-possessor" or "composite whole," as a potsherd is part of a pot; (2) "(inferential) component," part of a formal "inference for others," e.g., the *proposition*, *reason*, etc., which make up a formal inference.

bādhita: the fallacy or "pseudo-prover" of being defeated in advance; a reason that is refuted in advance by something already known. This comes to replace "the mistimed" as the fifth "pseudo-prover" on standard lists.

brahman: the "Absolute" or "God," the central concern of Vedānta philosophy.

buddhi: "cognition," "experience," "knowledge."

darśana: a perspective on the truth, a philosophy or worldview.

dhāraṇā: meditational practice; one of the limbs of the classical "eight-limbed" yoga of the *Yoga-sūtra*.

dharma: (1) property; (2) virtue, righteousness; (3) correct religious and moral behavior.

dharmin: property-bearer.

dhyāna: mature yogic contemplation, and meditation.

dravya: substance, one of seven metaphysical categories (*padārtha*) of mainstream Nyāya-Vaiśeṣika; nine fundamental types of substance are said to be earth, water, fire, air (four atomic elements), ether (the fifth "material" element, which is non-atomic and the medium of sound), time, space, *manas* (the "mind" or "internal organ"), and self (*ātman*), a non-material substance.

dṛṣṭānta: "example," a case that supports an inductive generalization; a locus known to exhibit both the prover and the property to be proved, or the absence of both.

duḥkha: pain or suffering; the ultimate goal of both theoretical and practical life is, according to Nyāya, to remove suffering; this is most fully done by discovery of and immersion in the deep self.

gavaya: a rare kind of wild buffalo, often used in stock examples of analogy: "A *gavaya* is like a cow."

guṇa: quality; one of seven fundamental categories (*padārtha*) in traditional Nyāya-Vaiśeṣika ontology, e.g., red.

hetu: inferential mark, "prover" (e.g., smokiness or the "smoke" in the inference "since there is smoke on that hill, there is fire there too.")

hetv-ābhāsa: fallacy, pseudo-prover.

indriya-sannikarṣa: connection between an operative sense organ and an object perceived; one of the primary criteria for perceptual knowledge according to the perception sūtra of the *Yoga-sūtra*.

īśvara: God, the "Lord"; the being responsible for the creation or material arrangement of the world but not for atoms or individual selves, which are also eternal.

jalpa: debating for the sake of victory where (in contrast with *vāda*) using tricky arguments is standard.

jāti: (1) universal, natural kind, a property occurring in more than a single instance or locus; (2) misleading objection that distorts a view in order to refute it.

jñāna: cognition or (when veridical) knowledge; an episodic psychological quality that has an intentional object.

karaṇa: "trigger," "proximate instrumental cause," a necessary condition that on being met an effect regularly comes about; e.g., many necessary conditions are required for the production of light in a lamp, but flipping the switch for that lamp would be the *karaṇa*.

kāraṇa: "cause," a necessary and regulative condition for an effect; Nyāya recognizes three major types of cause: "instrumental cause," *nimitta-kāraṇa*; "inherence cause," *samavāyī*; and "co-inherence cause," *asamavāyī-kāraṇa*; see also SĀMAGRĪ.

karman: (1) action, motion; (2) psychological dispositions to act in a certain manner accrued through previous actions; habits, karma; conceived metaphysically as *adrsta*, "Unseen Force," influence affecting future happiness or suffering (as in having good luck or bad), in particular the nature of one's body in one's next reincarnation.

kevala-anvayin: (1) "universally positive," a property with no negative range, nowhere, that is, where it is not; (2) "only positive," an inference whose inductive support consists only of instances of co-presence between the prover (H) and property to be proved (S), with no known instances of co-absence, i.e., things S and H but not things not-S and not-H.

kevala-vyatirekin: "only negative," an inference whose inductive support consists only of instances of co-absence between the prover (H) and property to be proved (S), with no known instances of co-presence, i.e., only things that are not-S and not-H but not things S and H.

kṣaṇa: "point-instant," the smallest increment of time, too small to be perceptible, according to Nyāya; a temporal atom, so to say, according to Yogācāra Buddhists.

lāghavatva: "lightness," parsimony, theoretic simplicity; akin to Okham's razor; a form of *tarka*, "suppositional reasoning." All things being equal, a "lighter" argument or account, which requires fewer theoretical posits, is to be preferred.

manas: the mind or internal organ, the organ operative in the perception of inner psychological properties such as pleasure and pain; filters and regulates sensory information to the perceiving self as well as will and action into the body from the self, according to Nyāya and other classical schools.

mīmāṃsā: (1) science of interpretation; (2) a philosophical school, see MĪMĀṂSĀ.

mithyā-jñāna: false cognition; delusion; for Nyāya, the ultimate basis of suffering, leading to unhealthy behavior, unfortunate patterns of karmic conditioning, and repeated birth.

mokṣa: (*mukti*) "liberation" from rebirth, salvation, the *summum bonum* according to several schools.

muni: a wise person; a sage.

nigamana: the fifth and final part of a formal "inference for another," which concludes that the subject of the inference is indeed qualified by the property to be proved.

nigraha-sthāna: "clinchers"; points of defeat within in a debate, including many informal fallacies.

nimitta-kāraṇa: instrumental or efficient cause, such as a potter, potter's wheel, and so on, when a pot is made.

nirṇaya: reflective knowledge; certified certainty; paradigmatically (but not exclusively) the result of philosophical investigation or *nyāya*.

nirvikalpaka: "indeterminate"; indeterminate perception grasps a qualifier "in the raw," prior to robust conceptual deployment and organization. Given an explicit place within Nyāya's theory of perception in Vācaspatimiśra's commentary on sūtra 1.1.4.

niścaya: warrant, certainty, sufficient epistemic confidence to act unhesitatingly.

nyāya: (1) the philosophic school, see NYĀYA; (2) philosophical examination and argument; (3) maxim or principle.

padārtha: fundamental category, "type of thing to which words refer"; there are seven fundamental categories according to mainstream Nyāya-Vaiśeṣika: (1) substance, (2) quality, (3) motion, (4) universal, (5) particularizer, (6) inherence, and, in the later tradition, (7) absence.

pakṣa: "inferential subject," what one is arguing about when one wants to make a formal inference, and what is presumed to be qualified by an inferential mark; in a stock example, the mountain that has smoke rising above it, about which one infers there is fire present.

pakṣa-dharmatā-bala: the "strength of being a property of the inferential subject." When a property is proved to qualify a specific subject (e.g., that there is smoke flowing out of the windows of *that particular house*), one may fill out details of the case (e.g., not only that the house is on fire but that it is an electrical fire, because we know that *that particular house* had severe electrical problems and that there was no other source of fire present).

paramāṇu: ultimate atom; the smallest possible indivisible object out of which the physical objects of this world are formed.

parāmarśa: reflection or consideration necessary for inference; putting together the evidence of the prover as qualifying the subject and that of the prover's being pervaded by the property to be proved; e.g., seeing a mountain as smoky, while also remembering that where there is smoke there is fire.

parārthānumāna: "inference for others"; a formal proof embedding a valid inference, to be best expressed, according to Nyāya (with a few dissenters), in a five-step argument form understood as a single sentence.

pradhāna: in Sāṃkhya metaphysics, the most fundamental, primordial material "stuff" out of which the manifest world is made.

prakaraṇa: (1) textual and extra-textual "context" of a statement; (2) a section of a philosophic or scientific treatise, often framed as a specific issue or question, e.g., "the self as distinguished from the body."

prakṛti: "nature" in Sāṃkhya philosophy, the uniform basis of all phenomena, of everything material as presented in experience, with all effects as transformations of this primordial stuff, existing latently within it.

pralaya: periodic dissolution of the world, according to many ancient and classical Indian cosmologies.

pramā: knowledge, veridical cognition.

pramāṇa: "knowledge source"; according to Nyāya there are four: perception, inference, analogy, and testimony.

pramāṇa-ābhāsa: misleading pseudo-sources of knowledge; cognitive presentations that look like the functioning of legitimate knowledge sources, but aren't.

prāmāṇya: (1) knowledge, the condition of being generated by a knowledge source, i.e., a true cognition's being generated by a genuine knowledge source, *pramāṇa*; (2) justification, truth-grounded evidence.

prameya: object of knowledge; something knowable.

pratijñā: "proposition"; the first component of a formal "inference for others," the "proposition to be proved."

pratyāhāra: "sensory withdrawal," one of the key practices of the classical eight-limbed yoga of the *Yoga-sūtra*.

pratyakṣa: (1) perception or perceptual knowledge, the veridical result of perception as a knowledge source; (2) the *pramāṇa* itself, the knowledge source that generates instances of perceptual knowledge.

pravṛtti: voluntary or purposive action.

pūrva-pakṣa: a *prima facie* position, the opponent's position (the opponent is the *pūrva-pakṣin*, one who holds the position in question); a portion of a text devoted to exploring views and arguments not accepted by the author who will express his own views in an upcoming and correlated *siddhānta* (q.v.).

ṛṣi: ancient sage; channel of Vedic revelation, according to some Nyāya philosophers.

śabda: (1) "testimony" as a knowledge source; (2) "sound," the quality grasped by the organ of hearing.

sādhana: "prover," synonym for "*hetu*" with respect to a knowledge-producing inference.

sādhya: "property to be proved" in an inference; e.g., fieriness or fire in the inference, "There is fire on the hill, since there is smoke."

samādhi: yogic trance, the ability to shut off mental fluctuations, perfect concentration.

sāmagrī: collection of causal factors sufficient to produce an effect.

sāmānya: universal or common characteristic.

sāmarthya: capacity or ability; causal efficacy.

samavāya: "inherence"; ontic glue, according to Nyāya and other realist schools, relating certain types of things to their loci. A distinct reddish color inheres in a particular apple, and the universal cowness inheres in cows. Also a composite whole such as a chariot is said to inhere in its parts.

samavāyi-kāraṇa: "inherence cause," a substratum in relation to a superstratum, e.g., the clay of a clay pot, an apple in relation to its reddish color.

saṃsāra: "cycle of rebirth," a term for one's entire existence through multiple incarnations governed by karma.

saṃśaya: doubt, uncertainty; the typical inspiration for critical reasoning (*nyāya*).

saṃskāra: memory-impression, mental disposition.

saṃyoga: contact, conjunction; one of the qualities (*guṇa*) recognized in Nyāya.

sapakṣa: in a formal "inference for another," known examples of the property to be proved; in a good inference, a positive example of inductive support, something that possesses both the prover and the property to be proved; e.g. a fiery kitchen hearth, with respect to an inference from smoke to fire.

śāstra: science or craft; a scientific text on a distinct subject (e.g., *yoga-śāstra*).

sat-kārya-vāda: "pre-existence of the effect" in its material cause, a theory of causation advocated by Sāṃkhya. Nyāya's opposed view is sometimes called *asat-kārya-vāda*, "non-existence of the effect" before its production.

savikalpaka: "determinate"; determinate cognition, a cognition with "propositional" content, verbalizable cognition.

siddhānta: "accepted view" or "established thesis" of a school or thinker.

smaraṇa: "remembering"; veridical memory is not considered a *pramāṇa* by Nyāya, as its role is to retrieve information generated by a *pramāṇa*; when correct or veridical, its veridicality is to be accounted for by a veritable *pramāṇa*.

smṛti: (1) memory; (2) second-order of sacred texts in epistemological contrast with a first order, *śruti* (q.v.).

śruti: the Veda, the highest order of "revelation," according to popular Hinduism, to include the Upaniṣads according to Nyāya and other schools.

sūtra: "thread"; an aphorism or summary statement meant to express succinctly a position or argument that is to be explained and fleshed out by commentary whether in written form or orally by a teacher or expert. Famous sūtra texts include the *Yoga-sūtra* on yoga as practice and philosophy, the *Vedānta-sūtra* on Brahman and the teaching of the Upaniṣads, the *Nyāya-sūtra* on *nyāya*, "critical reasoning," and the *Kāma-sūtra* on romantic arts.

sūtra-kāra: sūtra-maker; e.g., Gautama as the author of the *Nyāya-sūtra*.

sva-bhāva: self-nature, independent existence, essence.

sva-lakṣaṇa: particular, individual, the unique, "that which is its own mark" with no generic or universal properties. Buddhist phenomenologists claim that this is the only real object of perception and that all verbalizable aspects of perceptual experience involve inference.

svārthānumāna: "inference for oneself," spontaneous, natural inference, contrasting with formal "inference for another," *parārthānumāna* (q.v.).

tarka: "suppositional reasoning"; according to Nyāya and other classical schools, usually a hypothetical argument revealing a fallacy or defeater (e.g., *virodha*, contradiction) in an opponent's position with the result that one's own position is to be favored so long as it has independent evidence in its favor; though usually destructive, *tarka* is also sometimes positive (e.g., *lāghava*, q.v., "simplicity").

tātparya: "intention," what a speaker or author means to say.

udāharaṇa: "exemplification," the third member of a formal "inference for another," expressing the general rule for inference ("pervasion," *vyāpti*) that is being employed, along with an example.

upacāra: secondary or metaphorical linguistic meaning, "transference"; arises when the primary meaning of a term is obviously inappropriate given the usage. In "The stands are shouting," it is the people in the stands who are referred to by *upacāra*, not the stands themselves.

upādhi: an extra property or condition U that is required for an inference to succeed that would rely on a pervasion relationship of, for example, H by S (H → S): if there is U, then an H does not entail an S and the inference is faulty, unless the *upādhi* is also present: (H and U) → S. The inferential generalization "Wherever there is fire, there is smoke" fails, since it holds only when the fire's fuel is damp or wet. Wet fuel is an *upādhi* for the generalization. This is shown in the counterexample of a hot iron ball where it is thought there is fire but no smoke.

upamāna: "analogy"; analogical acquisition of vocabulary; a *pramāṇa* according to Nyāya and some other classical schools.

upanaya: "application"; the fourth part of a formal "inference for another," which applies the inferential rule given in the third part to the subject of the inference.

vāda: debate to ascertain the truth; the proper vehicle for philosophical development according to Nyāya.

vipakṣa: in a formal "inference for another," known examples of the absence of the property to be proved; in a good inference, a negative example of inductive support, something lacking both the property to be proved and the prover, e.g., a lake with respect to an inference from smoke to fire.

viruddha: "incompatibility," "contradiction"; a fallacy and defeater of an inference where a prover given contradicts accepted positions of the person or group making the argument.

viṣaya: object of experience, topic of conversation.

viśeṣa: (1) distinction, difference, particular; (2) individualizer or particularizer, one of seven irreducible metaphysical categories according to mainstream Nyāya-Vaiśeṣika.

viśeṣaṇa: qualifier; qualities (e.g., blue), universals (e.g., cowhood), motions all count as qualifiers for any particular thing (e.g., a *blue* toy, something as a *cow*, *motion* in a car).

vitaṇḍā: debate for the sake of victory, "destructive debate" without commitment to a thesis of one's own; skeptical argumentation that is denigrated as incoherent by Naiyāyikas.

vyabhicāra: "deviation"; a putative prover occurring in cases where the property to be proved is absent; counter-examples to a proposed *vyāpti*.

vyakti: "particular," "individual." One of the appropriate objects or meanings of a collective noun according to Nyāya.

vyāpāra: "operation," "employment in causal operation," which is said to be required of "triggers" (*karaṇa*) in relation to effects; e.g., the activity of an axe being used to fell a tree is the "causal employment" of the axe with respect to the tree's being cut down.

vyāpti: "pervasion," a relation that grounds inference, a factual relation, according to Nyāya and other classical schools, such that everything exhibiting a prover (H) also exhibits a property to be proved (S), e.g., wherever smokiness, there is fieriness: $(x)(Hx \rightarrow Sx)$.

vyatireka: negative correlations (things not-S and not-H) entailed by a natural pervasion, *vyāpti*, and evidence for one, according to Nyāya; see also ANVAYA-VYATIREKA.

vyavahāra: convention, agreement; common experience and linguistic practice, what people commonly do and say; taken by Naiyāyikas and other classical philosophers as *prima facie* correct.

yathārtha: matching or corresponding to an object; cognition "as something is."

yoga: (1) practices of self-discipline aimed at self-discovery or self-mastery; (2) employment of a methodology, including the methodology of critical reasoning.

yogyatā: semantic fitness, a condition or "excellence" (*guṇa*) governing the intelligibility of a statement and the acquisition of knowledge through testimony, according to Naiyāyikas and others; e.g., "He is wetting the plants with fire," is unintelligible in a non-metaphoric sense, because the semantics of "wetting" precludes fire as an instrument in the action.

Index

Due to their ubiquity, the names "Vātsyāyana" and "Uddyotakara" are not indexed.